JUDGES' HANDBOOK For Criminal Cases

by

Prof. G. Feltoe

First Edition

Legal Resources
Foundation

P.O. Box 918, Harare, Zimbabwe
16 Oxford Road, Avondale, Harare
Telephone: 0772 312 877 (Sales)
E-mail: lpu@lrf.co.zw, lpuprod@lrf.co.zw, lrfsales@lrf.co.zw
Website: www.lrf.co.zw

Printed by Publications Unit of Legal Resources Foundation

First Edition

EAN 9780797450707

Editor:
Professor G. Feltoe

Forward

It is with pleasure that I commend this handbook to judges. The preparation and subsequent production of a comprehensive "Judges Handbook for Criminal Cases" is a most welcome development in our jurisdiction, as this will provide an essential source of information for judges as they carry out their criminal casework duties.

Criminal law is one of the main areas of law, in which our courts have been particularly active and a large body of case law has been built up.

Prof. Geoff Feltoe, drawing from his vast experience as a lecturer in law at the University of Zimbabwe for many years and the vantage point of having researched and authored a number of publications in the area of criminal law, brings together in a single compendium various aspects of procedural, evidential and substantive law that judges encounter when dealing with criminal proceedings.

The handbook, in my view, is not intended for judges to use mechanistically, but intended instead as a quick reference guide on some of the matters that are frequently encountered at various stages of criminal proceedings.

In short, it is and will not be a substitute for thorough preparation required for judges and will usually required adaptation to the circumstances for the particular case. Nevertheless, I hope judges will find the handbook a valuable resource in their day-to-day dealings with criminal cases.

By the Honorable Mr Justice G. G. Chidyausiku

Chief Justice of Zimbabwe
Chief Justice's Chambers
Supreme Court of Zimbabwe
Harare

March 2009

Contents

SECTION 4 – COMMON PROBLEMS OF EVIDENCE

SECTION 10 – APPEALS

SECTION 11 – AUTOMATIC REVIEW AND SCRUTINY

SECTION 12 – MISCELLANEOUS MATTERS

Section 1

Functions and Responsibilities of Judges

Role of judges

Reid-Rowland 16-3 – 16-5

The criminal law regulates behaviour within the society. It seeks to prevent forms of misbehaviour that are detrimental to society. It does this by providing for the imposition of punishment upon all those found guilty of such misbehaviour. Punishment causes suffering and some forms of punishment, such as imprisonment, cause very great suffering. In dealing with criminal cases judges have awesome powers and they thus have a most grave responsibility to exercise these powers in a completely fair and just manner. The fate of fellow human beings lies in their hands. They decide whether a person is innocent or guilty of criminal conduct and thus whether or not that person is to be subjected to punishment. If they make wrong decisions either innocent persons will suffer unfairly or guilty persons will unjustly escape punishment.

Judges must decide all criminal cases on a fair, objective and impartial basis. A judge must first decide whether or not the accused person is guilty after carefully considering all the evidence laid before him or her. If the judge finds the accused person guilty, he or she must then carefully decide upon the appropriate penalty to impose upon the convicted person.

Judges must act scrupulously as impartial adjudicators. They must keep open minds and they must refrain from doing anything that could create the impression that they are biased or partisan in their approach.

In *Musindo* 1997 (1) ZLR 395 (H), the court reiterated the need for judicial officers to treat the prosecutor and unrepresented accused equally and even-handedly. It pointed out that there are many pressures attendant upon the judicial function and many temptations to impatience and cynicism. Those who are charged with the burden of decision cannot always conceal their irritation with the incompetent or unprepared lawyer, with the idle submission or the ignoble stance. But judges owe it to their own self-esteem; to the dignity of their office; to the credibility of the legal system; and most of all, to those who attend their judgment, to comport themselves in such a way as persuades all before them that a fair hearing was afforded and an honest and considered decision was handed down. Audience that is fairly given to both contending parties is most likely to result in a decision that not only commends itself as even-handed but is also just. An appearance of disfavour in the proceedings, conversely, is calculated to result in a decision that fails to command confidence and which is the more likely to be wrong.

The function of judges is more than acting as mere umpires in a game who are there to see that neither side commits fouls. They must direct and control the trial according to recognised rules and procedures and ensure that justice is not only done but is manifestly seen to be done. Judges must strive to ascertain the truth in all cases which come before them. They should not, however, descend into the arena of a trial. In order to find out the truth, judges are entitled and, indeed, are duty bound to question witnesses and accused to clarify points that are unclear in their testimony. They must not, however, take over the examination in chief or cross-examination of witnesses. They must refrain from questioning in a manner and to an extent which gives the impression that they are no longer impartial. They should not engage in prolonged questioning of witnesses. If they do intervene to an excessive extent in a trial they will eliminate or impair their ability to assess the evidence independently and impartially or to adjudicate upon the evidence. For instance, it will be difficult for them to assess the calibre of evidence given by witnesses and to form impressions of their demeanour if they engage in vigorous and extended questioning of those witnesses.

See *Hove* S-64-88 p 5; *Magoge* 1988 (1) ZLR 163 (S); *Wright* S-183-89 pp 6-7. In *Magoge*, the magistrate stepped in and engaged in protracted questioning of State witnesses because their testimony did not wholly support the State case. This, said the Supreme Court, amounted to exhibiting partiality towards the State and created the impression that the magistrate was throwing his weight on the side of the prosecution.

Judges must apply the criminal law without fear or favour as this law applies equally to all persons, immaterial of rank, status or standing within the society. The high and the mighty are to be treated the same as the lowly and humble.

The trial jurisdiction of a judge in criminal matters is more extensive than that of a magistrate, as judges in the High and Supreme Court exercise powers of review and appeal in matters tried in the magistrates courts, and their responsibilities towards achieving justice are just as vital as in the trial court itself. In fact, one would expect a higher burden on a judge whom the entire system sees as the last hope, than on the magistrate who first tried the matter.

Characteristics of good judicial officers

A good judicial officer must be:

- dedicated to the pursuit of justice;
- diligent, disciplined and organised in his or her approach to work;
- fair and completely impartial when hearing cases;
- dignified and neat and tidy in his or her appearance;
- patient and polite but able to command respect and to exercise firm control over the proceedings in the courtroom;
- attentive and observant when listening to evidence;
- logical and able to use commonsense in reasoning out a case and in arriving at a judgment;
- able to make up his or her mind and to reach decisions; and
- have some sense of humour.

A bad judicial officer, on the other hand, will have at least some of the following characteristics:

> He or she will be lazy, badly disciplined, disorganised, sloppy in appearance, impatient and ill-tempered, partisan in favour of the prosecution and against accused, undignified, too weak to exert control over the proceedings, confused and illogical in his or her reasoning processes and indecisive and unable to make up his or her and to arrive at decisions.

Behaviour of judicial officers

If judicial officers behave in a scandalous, disreputable or opprobrious fashion inside or outside the courtroom, the public will have no respect for the system of justice and that system will fall into disrepute and cease to function properly. They must ensure that they conduct themselves both inside and outside the courtroom in a seemly fashion. For example, the public will have little faith in a judge who frequents seedy pubs and is often seen in a badly intoxicated state in public places.

Judicial officers must also refrain from becoming involved in contentious organisations and activities within society. If they did do this it could lead the public to believe that they will be partisan in judging certain types of cases.

See the Hon. Chief Justice Gubbay's article "Attributes, Attitudes and Comportment of Judicial Officers" (1988) *Legal Forum* Vol. 1 No. 1, p 3 and "Judicial Ethics" by the Hon Mr. Justice McNally (1989) *Legal Forum* Vol. 1 No. 5, p 1.

Judges must conscientiously perform their duty to administer justice. They must conduct criminal trials fairly and impartially. Their own personal behaviour must be beyond reproach because, if it is not, the system of justice will be brought into disrepute.

Bias and Recusal

For the public to have confidence in the administration of justice, it is essential that the courts are seen to be fair and impartial. A judge should therefore not try a case if X or the complainant is his or her friend, his or her enemy or his or her relative. Although the judge may be confident that he or she can exclude from his or her mind his or her relationship with the party concerned and judge the case solely on the basis of the evidence, he or she should recuse himself because the public may well believe that his or her decision was influenced by his or her relationship to X or the complainant. Thus, if he or she ends up convicting and severely sentencing a person whom he or she is known to have quarrelled with in the past, it might well be thought that his or her decision was influenced by his or her hostility to X. So too, he or she should not try a case involving his or her spouse's mother or the spouse of one of his or her long-standing and trusted court officials.

The judicial officer must not conduct a criminal trial in a manner that will create the impression that he or she is biased against the accused. In *Jesse* v *Pratt & Anor* 2001 (1) ZLR 48 (H), it was held that the conduct of the magistrate towards the applicant throughout the trial was such that a fair trial of the applicant was impossible in her court. Apart from a number of irregularities, there were numerous indications of biased and irrational conduct on the part of the magistrate, all of which showed that the applicant would have reasonable grounds to suppose that he or shemight be disadvantaged in the trial by reason of bias or prejudice actuating her.

Where a reasonable suspicion of bias could be created, he or she should transfer the case to one of his or her brother or sister judges at the court.

The question arises as to how a judge should respond to an application that he or she should recuse himself or herself.

In *Mutizwa* HB-4-06, the accused asked the magistrate to recuse herself, as he had heard, through prison talk, that she had a reputation for imposing harsh sentences. The magistrate dismissed the application. The court held that an impartial judicial officer is a fundamental prerequisite for the fair trial and a judicial office should not hesitate to recuse himself if there are reasonable grounds on the part of a litigant for apprehending that the judicial officer, for whatever reasons, was not or will not be impartial. The duty of recusal arises where it appears that the judicial officer has an interest in the case or where there is some other reasonable ground for believing that there is a likelihood of bias on the part of the judicial officer: that is, that he or she may not adjudicate impartially. The matter must be regarded from the point of view of the reasonable litigant and the test is an objective one. The fact that in reality the judicial officer was impartial or is likely to be impartial is not the test. It is the reasonable perception of the parties as to his or her impartiality that is important. The issue of actual bias does not arise. *In casu* the accused had not established an appearance or apprehension of bias; the basis for the application is that the magistrate is known for imposing severe sentences. The accused sought recusal so that he could be tried by a magistrate who was perceived to impose lenient sentences. This "fishing" for judicial officers is not what this principle is intended to achieve. Severe sentences are not indicative of bias, nor are lenient sentences indicative of fairness or lack of bias. It is the competence of the sentence that matters, and the judicial officer has wide discretion on the question of punishment.

If a judge has to recuse himself or herself during the course of the trial, the case cannot be taken over from that stage by another judge. The case will have to start *de novo* before a different judge. If, however, a judge recuses himself or herself after he or she has convicted X, the case can be referred to a different judge for sentence: *Moyo & Ors* HB-211-87.

If the prosecutor wrongly discloses the previous convictions to the judge during the course of the trial, the judge is obliged to recuse himself or herself.

In *Shaw* HH-122-88, the High Court ruled that a magistrate had not been obliged to recuse himself in a case of fraud even though he had prior knowledge of the general nature of the allegations against X. X had expressly requested that the magistrate should try the case. X had pleaded guilty and the case was dealt with on the basis of agreed facts.

In *Muzuza & Ors* S-105-89, the Supreme Court severely censured a defence lawyer who had made serious allegations of partiality and bias on the part of a magistrate in an effort to get him to recuse himself. He had simply repeated his client's assertions without having made any effort to check whether there were any facts to substantiate these allegations.

Descending into arena

Judges who are presiding over criminal cases must not descend into the arena in the sense that they must not intervene during the course of trials in such a manner or to such an extent as to lead to an inference of lack of impartiality and open-mindedness. They are entitled to ask questions of witnesses in order to clarify the evidence, but they must refrain from bombarding them with questions to such an extent that they are disconcerted. If judges take over the role of cross-examining witnesses they will not be able objectively to adjudicate on the evidence.

However, judges are obliged to ensure that undefended accused receive fair trials. Especially where undefended accused are unfamiliar with court proceedings, judges must appraise the accused persons of their rights and, where necessary, ask questions of witnesses to discover the truth.

In *Kaseke* 1996 (1) ZLR 51 (S), the Supreme Court pointed out that while judicial officers are frequently cautioned not to descend into the arena, this does not mean that they must simply adopt the position of an umpire in a game, to see that neither side commits a foul. They are there to direct and control the trial according to recognised rules and procedures and to ensure that justice is not only done but seen to be done. They have the right, if not the duty, to examine witnesses or the accused in order to clarify some point in the interests of justice, but must refrain from doing so in a way which may, on the one hand, either disconcert the witness or unjustly affect the quality of his or her replies and, on the other hand, preclude an objective determination and adjudication of the issues that they are being called on to determine.

Management of Case Flow

Case Flow Management can be used by judges as a tool for ensuring that speedy, smooth and inexpensive justice is achieved through early disposition of cases.

Section 2

Pre Trial Matters

Constitutional provisions

Every person is entitled to the protection of the law: s 18(1).

Every person has a right to personal liberty, but a person can lawfully be deprived of liberty upon reasonable suspicion that he or she has committed or is about to commit a criminal offence: s 13(1) & (2).

Any person arrested on reasonable suspicion that he or she has committed or is about to commit a criminal offence must be brought without undue delay before a court and if the arrested person is not tried within a reasonable time, then, without prejudice to any further proceedings that may be brought against him or her, he or she must be released either unconditionally or upon reasonable conditions, including in particular such conditions as are reasonably necessary to ensure that he or she appears at a later date for trial or for proceedings preliminary to trial: s 13(4).

Any person who is unlawfully arrested or detained is entitled to compensation from that other person or from the person who arrested or detained him or her or the authority on whose behalf or in the course of whose employment that other person is acting: s 13(5).

Any person who is arrested or detained must be informed as soon as reasonably practicable and in detail of the reasons for his or her arrest and detention. Such person is also entitled to engage a legal practitioner to represent him or her and to hold communications with this legal practitioner. The arrested person must be permitted to see his or her lawyer *without delay*: s 13(3).

A person charged with a criminal offence must be afforded a fair hearing within a reasonable time by an independent and impartial court established by law: s 18(2).

Arrest warrants

Reid-Rowland 5-4

A warrant of arrest is a document issued by a judicial officer or a justice of the peace authorising the police to arrest a person in connection with the offence specified in the warrant.

An arrest warrant will be issued in terms of s 33 CPEA. The application for such a warrant may only be made on written application by the Attorney-General or the local public prosecutor or a police officer who is an inspector or higher in rank or is a member in charge of a police station who is a section officer or higher in rank.

In the written application, the applicant must:

- specify the person to be arrested and the offence alleged to have been committed by that person; and
- declare that on the basis of the information available to him or her that he or she has reasonable grounds for suspecting that this person has committed the specified offence.

The judge may also issue an arrest warrant on the basis of information given on oath before him or her by another person that he or she has information which leads him or her to have reasonable grounds for suspecting that a specified offence has been committed by the person.

Where the application is a written one, the question arises whether the judge hearing the application must satisfy himself that the applicant does actually have reasonable grounds for suspecting that an offence has been committed. In other words, does the judge have to probe the facts upon which the application is based to satisfy himself or herself that there are reasonable grounds for suspicion? All that the section requires is that the applicant declares that on the basis of the information available to him, the applicant has reasonable grounds for suspecting that the specified offence has been committed. It does not say that the applicant has to give details of the facts upon which he or she formed his or her suspicion. At face value, the section does not require the judge to delve into the facts as the applicant is not obliged to set out the facts in his or her application. In the South African case of *Prinsloo & Anor* v *Newman* 1975 (1) SA 481 (A), the South African Appellate Division decided that as the applicant in a written application is not obliged to set out the facts upon which he or she relies for his or her conclusion that there are reasonable grounds of suspicion, the magistrate is not called upon to consider the correctness of the conclusion of the applicant. This does not mean that the magistrate does not exercise a discretion in considering whether or not to issue a warrant. He or she must satisfy himself that the alleged offence is an offence at law, and that it is of such a nature and gravity as to justify the issuing of a warrant.

There is no case in Zimbabwe that has decided this issue. However, it could be argued that the whole purpose of court applications for arrest warrants is to allow the court to exercise a supervisory role in respect of such applications and that, impliedly, therefore the court must satisfy itself that there are reasonable grounds for the issuing of a warrant and it can only do this if it probes the facts. After all, section 13 of the Constitution requires that a person only be deprived of his or her liberty upon reasonable suspicion of his or her having committed or being about to commit a crime: see *Muzonda* v *Minister of Home Affairs & Anor* S-17-93. Thus, if the court issued a warrant where there were no reasonable grounds for suspicion it would be authorising an unlawful arrest. On the other hand, if the section does not require the applicant to state the facts upon which his or her suspicion is based, the court would not have before it the facts and this makes it impossible for the court to exercise this sort of supervisory role as the legislation stands at present. By contrast s 50(1), CPEA dealing with search warrants explicitly requires the judge to delve into whether there are reasonable grounds for believing that any such article is in the person's possession or upon any premises.

A magistrate may only issue a warrant for arrest if the offence was committed in his or her area of jurisdiction or the person to be arrested is suspected to be or is in his or her area of jurisdiction when the warrant is issued.

The warrant may be issued on any day of the week and it remains in operation until it is cancelled by the person who issued it or until the person is arrested on the basis of the warrant.

In terms of s 33(1) CPEA where a person has been arrested without warrant, an application can be made by the police to a judge for the further detention of that person. This warrant is supposed to be made in the same manner as the ordinary warrant for arrest. Judges should grant warrants for further detention on a very sparing basis as in the past the police have sought further detention warrants simply in order to have a longer period of time to interrogate accused persons without bringing them before the courts. An accused has a right to be brought before a court as soon as possible so that he or she can apply for bail and so that he or she has a chance to complain about any mistreatment he or she has received while in police custody.

Where the person is arrested on the basis of an arrest warrant, he or shemust be brought as soon as possible to a police station or a charge office unless the warrant specifically authorises that he or she be taken to some other place: s 34(3) CPEA.

Thereafter, he or she must be brought as soon as possible before a judicial officer upon the charge mentioned in the warrant: s 34(3) CPEA.

Arrest without warrant

In cases of arrest without warrant, a person can only be *lawfully* arrested in connection with a criminal offence if the person arresting him or her has a reasonable suspicion that the person has committed or is about to commit a criminal offence. Where an arrest warrant has been obtained, however, by one police officer, it can be lawfully executed by another officer, even though the second officer may not himself know the basis upon which the warrant was issued and thus cannot say that he or she reasonably suspected that the person he or she was arresting had committed an offence. This applies whether the arrest was on the basis of a warrant of arrest or was done without warrant.

The circumstances in which a person may lawfully be arrested without warrant are set out in s 25 CPEA. They include cases where the person arrested has committed or has attempted to commit a crime in the presence of the peace officer arresting him or her and where the peace officer has reasonable grounds for suspecting that the person has committed any of the offences contained in the First Schedule. The offences in the First Schedule are common law offences, except for certain offences which are excluded such as bigamy, and statutory offences where the maximum punishment is imprisonment for more than six months without the option of a fine.

If the person making an arrest without warrant does not have a reasonable suspicion that a crime has or is about to be committed, the arrest is illegal and the lawyer representing the arrested person can apply to the High Court for the immediate release of that person. See s 13(2)(e) of the Constitution of Zimbabwe. The arresting officer and the Ministry of Home Affairs should be cited as the respondents.

Reasonable suspicion is not the same as proof beyond reasonable doubt. What is required is that the person making the arrest must have information on the basis of which a reasonable person would hold a suspicion that the person to be arrested had committed or was about to commit the criminal offence: *Purcell-Gilpin* 1971 (1) RLR 241; *Miller* 1973 (2) RLR 387; *Moll* v *Commissioner of Police & Ors* 1973 (1) ZLR 234 (H); *Allan* v *Minister of Home Affairs* 1985 (1) ZLR 339 (H); *Bull* v *Attorney-General & Anor* 1986 (1) ZLR 117 (S); *Gwenyure* v *Minister of Home Affairs* HH-702-87; *Attorney-General* v *Blumears* 1991 (1) ZLR 118 (S); *Feldman* v *Minister of Home Affairs* S-210-92; *Gous* v *Minister of Home Affairs & Ors* HH-171-92; *Muzabazi* v *Jambawu & Ors* HH-234-92.

Even if there was reasonable suspicion, the police have the discretion whether or not to arrest. If, in the circumstances, the arrest was not justified, the arrest will still be unlawful and the arrested person will be entitled to claim delictual damages. The exercise of this discretion to arrest may be interfered with when exercised grossly unreasonably. In *Muzonda* v *Minister of Home Affairs & Anor* 1993 (1) ZLR 92 (S), it was held that, although the police officer was authorised to arrest the appellant, he had a discretion as to whether to do so or not; the power of arrest is not intended always, or even ordinarily, to be exercised. Further, the principles applicable to administrative law applied: that the court would have to find that the exercise of the discretion was so outrageous in its defiance of logic or of accepted moral standards that no sensible person who had applied his or her mind to the question could have arrived at it. Some of the considerations to be taken into account in determining whether an arrest is open to challenge are the possibility of escape, the prevention of further crime and the obstruction of police enquiries. On none of these grounds could the exercise of the discretion be justified. In *Paradza* v *Minister of Justice & Ors* S-46-03, the Supreme Court held that there had been an abuse of discretion which was unconstitutional on the basis that it violated ss 13 and 18 of the constitution – right to liberty and to protection of the law. See also *Botha* v *Zvada & Anor* 1997 (1) ZLR 415 (S); *Nyatanga* v *Mlambo NO & Ors* HH-85-03.

The onus is upon the person making the arrest to prove that the arrest was lawfully justified: *Stambolie* v *Commissioner of Police* 1989 (3) ZLR 287 (S).

Where a person is arrested without warrant he or she must be taken as soon as possible to a police station or a charge office and if he or she is not released, he or she may not be detained for more than forty-eight hours (or not more than ninety six hours if there is a holiday or a Sunday within the forty-eight hour period). However, the detention can be extended beyond this period if a judge, magistrate or justice of the peace issues a warrant for further detention: s 32(2) CPEA.

In the case of *Nyamhoko & Ors* v *OC ZRP Manicaland Province & Ors* HH-37-06, the applicants were arrested by the police on allegations of committing offences under the Public Order and Security Act. They were maltreated while in custody and denied access to their legal practitioners. State counsel who tried to intercede were threatened by the police and had to flee the district. The applicants sought a declaratur that their detention, which had been for more than 48 hours, was unlawful, as well as an order for the return of property taken from them. No warrant for further detention was shown to the court. The court held that where an applicant has been held beyond the 48-hour period, it is competent to declare the whole detention period illegal. Even assuming in favour of the respondents that somewhere in their offices warrants for further detention lay unattended, the facts before the court required that the detention be declared illegal.

The provision for obtaining a warrant for further detention is open to abuse as the police can obtain this warrant without even having to appear personally before a magistrate and without taking the prisoner before the magistrate by applying to a justice of the peace who is a police officer, or obtaining authorization for further detention from a magistrate. On occasions it has apparently been used as a device for keeping the prisoner *incommunicado* for extended periods without access to his or her lawyer or relatives and without access to the courts to apply for bail. If the police are using these provisions in an abusive fashion, an urgent application can be made to the High Court for a court order to oblige the police to take the arrested person before a court so that the case can be properly remanded and an application for bail can be made. Although the provisions are not entirely clear on this point, it was surely not envisaged that the 96 hour upper limit for bringing a person arrested without warrant before a court can be completely circumvented by relying upon the provisions relating to further detention. The police officer who has denied access and the Ministry of Home Affairs can be cited as respondents in this action.

Where a person whose arrest is attempted resists the attempt and cannot be arrested without the use of force, the person attempting to carry out the arrest has the right to use such force as it reasonably justifiable in the circumstances to aver any resistance put up to the arrest. The court must place itself in the shoes of the accused when looking into whether or not the force applied to effect the arrest was reasonable: *Ncube & Ors* HB-61-03.

Maximum periods of custody

Arrest with warrant

Where the person is arrested on the basis of an arrest warrant, he or she must be brought as soon as possible to a police station or a charge office unless the warrant specifically authorises that he or she be taken to some other place: s 34(3) CPEA.

Thereafter he or she must be brought as soon as possible before a judicial officer upon the charge mentioned in the warrant: s 34(3) CPEA.

Arrest without warrant

Where a person is arrested without warrant he or she must be taken as soon as possible to a police station or a charge office and if he or she is not released, he or she may not be detained for more than forty-eight hours (or not more than ninety six hours if there is a holiday or a Sunday within the forty-eight hour period). However, the detention can be extended beyond this period if a judge, magistrate or justice of the peace issues a warrant for further detention: s 32(2) CPEA.

The provision for obtaining a warrant for further detention is open to abuse as the police can obtain this warrant without even having to appear personally before a magistrate or judge and without taking the prisoner before the magistrate by applying to a justice of the peace who is a police officer, or obtaining authorization for further detention from a judge or magistrate. On occasions it has apparently been used as a device for keeping the prisoner *incommunicado* for extended periods without access to his or her lawyer or relatives and without access to the courts to apply for bail. If the police are using these provisions in an abusive fashion, an urgent application can be made to the High Court for a court order to oblige the police to take the arrested person before a court so that the case can be properly remanded and an application for bail can be made. Although the provisions are not entirely clear on this point, it was surely not envisaged that the 96 hour upper limit for bringing a person arrested without warrant before a court can be completely circumvented by relying upon the provisions relating to further detention. The police officer who has denied access and the Ministry of Home Affairs can be cited as respondents in this action.

Special provisions for offences in Ninth Schedule

There are special provisions for prolonged detention of persons who are charged with offences in the Ninth Schedule of CPEA. There apply both to persons arrested with warrant and those arrested without warrant.

There are special provisions in connection with charges under the Ninth Schedule. If the charge is for an offence in paragraph 10 of the Ninth Schedule and the judicial officer is satisfied that there is a reasonable suspicion that he or she has committed the offence, he or she *must* order the continued detention of that person for a period of 21 days: s 34(4)(a) CPEA (with warrant) and s 32(3a) CPEA (without warrant).

If the charge is for any offence in the Ninth Schedule, the Attorney-General may produce a certificate that the offence in question involves significant national interest of Zimbabwe and further detention for a period up to 21 days is necessary because of the complexity of the case, and/or the difficulty of obtaining evidence in relation to the offence, and/or the likelihood of X concealing or destroying evidence relating to the offence. Where such a certificate is produced and the judicial officer is satisfied that there is a reasonable suspicion that X committed the offence, he or she *must* order the continued detention of X for a period of 21 days or the lesser period specified in the Attorney-General's certificate: s 34(4)(b) CPEA (with warrant) and s 32(3a) and (3b) (without warrant). However, with arrest without warrant there are certain requirements in addition to the Attorney-General's certificate. The arresting officer must be an officer of or above the rank of assistant inspector at the time of the arrest and where the arrest was disclosed through an anonymous complaint, a copy of the recorded complaint must be laid before the judicial officer.

No court may admit to bail any person detained for 21 days under the provisions above: s 34(5) CPEA and s 32(3c) CPEA.

Where X is detained for 21 days under these provisions, the arresting officer must make periodic reports at intervals of not more than 48 hours to the Attorney-General on the progress of the investigations. If the Attorney-General believes on the basis of such a report that X's detention is not longer justified, he or she may order the immediate and unconditional release of the person: s 34(5) and 32(3c) CPEA.

Within 48 hours of the expiry of the 21 day detention period the detaining authority may obtain an order or warrant for further detention of such person pending the outcome of their criminal investigations. However, X will still have the right to apply for bail: s 34(6) and s 32(3d) CPEA.

Search warrants

Reid-Rowland 7-9

A search warrant is a document issued by a judicial officer or a justice of the peace authorising the police to carry out a search and to seize certain items. Such a warrant is issued in terms of s 50 CPEA.

Before issuing such a warrant on the application of the police, the judge should satisfy himself that the police have reasonable grounds for applying for such a warrant. Searches of premises and persons constitute an invasion of privacy and are only justifiable where there are good grounds for carrying out the searches. Section 17 of the Constitution forbids the searching of a person or his or her property or the entry onto his or her premises by others unless this is done for the enforcement of the law in circumstances where there are reasonable grounds to believe that the search or entry is necessary for the prevention or detection of a criminal offence or for the seizure of property which will provide evidence in relation to a criminal offence.

The application for a search warrant must therefore, be supported by an affidavit from a police officer setting out the reasons why a search warrant is being sought. A search warrant must only be issued where, on the basis of the information from the police, the judge is satisfied that there are reasonable grounds to believe that the search will result in the discovery of certain articles which are believed on reasonable grounds to be concerned in the commission of a crime. The police may believe that the items have already been used to commit a crime or that they will be so used or that they will provide evidence of the commission of a crime.

The premises or persons who may be searched must be precisely described. In respect of search of premises, it must be stated whether the search is to be carried out during the day or night.

The items to be searched for and to be seized if found must again be specifically and precisely stated. The police may not be issued with a warrant which allows them to "go on a fishing expedition" in the hope that they may find some illegal items during the search.

In the case of *Elliott* v *Commissioner of ZRP* 1986 (1) ZLR 228 (H), the High Court held that a search warrant which had been issued was invalid because it was far too general and vague. No offence was identified and no attempt was made to identify the particular documents which were to be searched for and seized and to relate these documents to a particular offence.

When a warrant is issued the judge will fill in the standard form in which the relevant particulars will be entered. (See sample form in Appendix.)
Under the Serious Offences (Confiscation of Profits) Act [*Chapter 9:17*] there are special provisions relating to the issue of search warrants to search for "tainted property" as defined in that legislation. See s 26 of that Act.

The Police have power under s 49 CPEA to search for and seize articles which are, or are on reasonable grounds believed to be, concerned in the commission of a crime; or which the Police reasonably believe may afford evidence of the commission of a crime; or which are intended to be used in the commission of a crime or which the Police reasonably believe are intended to be so used.

Remands

Reid-Rowland 5-21

Generally

A remand will usually be requested by the State when it is not ready to bring a case to trial because police investigations are still taking place or the police may be experiencing difficulties in locating vital State witnesses. The State will ask that X be remanded either in custody or out of custody. If X is remanded out of custody, he or she may be remanded on bail or without bail being required. The judge may not order a remand in excess of fourteen days without X's consent: proviso to s 165 CPEA. (See Appendix for sample Remand Form.)

Other reasons why remands may be requested by the State include these:

- the prosecutor is awaiting the Attorney-General's authority to prosecute or his or her instructions as to which court the case should be tried in;
- the prosecutor needs time to arrange the court roll so that the case can be fitted in for trial;
- the prosecutor has returned the docket to the police so that certain points can be clarified or further investigations can be carried out on certain points and the police have not yet responded to these points.

X himself or herself may also request a remand. He or she may do so in order that he or shecan have time to organise legal representation or in order to contact defence witnesses.

In terms of s 13(2)(e) of the Constitution, deprivation of a person's liberty on the grounds of the commission of a criminal offence is only permissible if there is a reasonable suspicion that he or she committed that crime. In terms of s 18(2) of the Constitution, a person charged with a criminal offence is entitled to have his or her case tried within a reasonable period of time. This applies whether or not he or she is held in custody.

Section 160(2) CPEA provides that if an accused person is not brought to trial after the expiry of six months from the date of his or her committal for trial, his or her case shall be "dismissed". Such "dismissal" does not amount to an acquittal, nor does it relate to prescription. It relates to the committal and the effects or consequences or implications thereof. The subsection is meant to protect accused persons from being unreasonably kept under committal for trial for longer than six months when the trial has failed to take place during that period, as well as to ensure that the Attorney-General ensures that trials of accused persons committed for trial are expeditiously conducted – *Mukuze & Anor* v *A-G (2)* HH-17-05.

Reasonable suspicion

Where at the initial or subsequent remand the State is seeking the remand in custody of X, the court must only grant this application provided that there is a reasonable suspicion that X committed the crime with which he or she is being charged. In the case of *Attorney-General* v *Blumears & Anor* 1991 (1) ZLR 118 (S), the following principles were laid down by the Supreme Court:

> " The State must allege facts that constitute a crime and justify a reasonable suspicion that the accused committed the crime. The accused may submit that the State has not alleged such facts or may lead cogent evidence which obliges the magistrate to reject those facts. The remand procedure is an important protective process to ensure the finding of a reasonable suspicion by someone independent of the police and prosecution. The hearsay rule and the rules relating to cross-examination of witnesses do not apply. Statements can be made from the bar by legal counsel. Although the onus is on the State, it does not have to show guilt beyond reasonable doubt or on a balance of probabilities. The court cannot reject State allegations simply because they seem to be of doubtful validity."

In *Lupepe* v *A-G & Anor* HB-130-93, the court said that before putting anyone on remand, the police must satisfy themselves that the information they are acting on is sufficient to raise a reasonable suspicion and that there are enough grounds to place him or her on remand. The State must disclose to the court grounds which when tested objectively give rise to a reasonable suspicion against X. The failure of an unrepresented accused to oppose the initial remand did not assist the State. The applicant had been detained and remanded on the basis of the fact that that information had been received implicating him or her in a gold robbery and murder. The State at no stage said what the source of that information was; the co-accused did not implicate applicant and he or she was not found in possession of anything which could implicate him. He or she was entitled to apply to the High Court for an order for his or her release.

In *Smyth* v *Ushewokunze & Anor* 1997 (2) ZLR 544 (S), it was held that, in order to justify the applicant's deprivation of freedom on the grounds of reasonable suspicion that he or she had committed an offence, it was not necessary to establish his or her guilt beyond a reasonable doubt or even on the balance of probabilities. The test was the same as that for arrest without a warrant. There had to be sufficient information to warrant a prudent person in suspecting that the applicant was legally responsible for the alleged offence.

The prosecutor must be as open and forthright as possible when advising the remand court of the facts relied on. It can be very difficult deciding what to reveal and what to conceal in sensitive investigations which X might interfere with, but he or she should never conceal facts simply to hinder the defence and must ensure that he or she alleges enough to implicate X.

Even if X does not complain that there is no case against him or her and therefore that there is no basis for remanding him, the court must still satisfy itself that there are reasonable grounds for the remand. The remand court should obtain information from the prosecutor justifying the existence of a reasonable suspicion on the initial remand, and the prosecutor must assure and satisfy the court that there is still a reasonable suspicion against him or her at all subsequent remands. This applies especially when X is not legally represented.

Maltreatment in custody

If a person brought to court for remand complains that he or she has been tortured or assaulted by police officers or prison officers whilst in custody, the judge must investigate this matter. The judge should make written notes about the complaint and may also ask the prisoner to show him or her the injuries that he or she claims have been inflicted. Again the judge must make notes on what injuries he or she has observed on the prisoner. Where allegations are made of serious mistreatment and particularly the judge has observed physical signs of such mistreatment, the judge should order that the prisoner be medically examined. If the medical report points to physical mistreatment in custody, the judge should then order the authorities to conduct an expeditious inquiry and make a report to him or her about the results of this inquiry.

In *Makawa & Anor* 1991 (1) ZLR 142 (S), the court commented that it was aware "that allegations of police maltreatment are commonly made by accused persons and that such allegations are often spurious. But the frequency with which they are made ought not to justify ignoring them. It is a matter of gravity to the State that policemen have abused their positions in this manner. It is even more serious to allege that the reason for such abuse was to force the victim to say or do something he or she would not otherwise have said or done. Where an accused person stands in jeopardy of a criminal conviction, should the statement made because of the alleged maltreatment be believed, it is incumbent on the judicial officer to investigate to the fullest possible extent the veracity of the allegations.

The civil court will award substantial damages where a person has been tortured whilst in police custody. In *Karimazondo & Anor* v *Minister of Home Affairs* 2001 (2) ZLR 363 (H), a police officer and his wife were arrested on allegations of murder. The wife was tortured while in custody and suffered long-lasting physical and psychological effects, full details of which were disclosed in medical reports. The court held that the circumstances of the case were exceedingly grave and warranted a substantial award of damages. The actions of the police were in flagrant and reckless disregard of the rights of the persons concerned. The fact of the detention in itself created a hardship. The brutality and callousness with which the assaults were perpetrated on the woman instilled in any right thinking person a sense of horror and shock. The unlawful and inhumane treatment to which P1 was subjected to was totally unnecessary, vindictive and malicious. The court made an award which in money terms expressed its disapproval of the seriousness, brutality and humiliating effect of such treatment. The decline in the value of money in recent years was also taken into account.

In the case of *Reza & Anor* HH-02-04, the court strongly condemned the practice of torture by police officers. The two police officers had tortured a criminal suspect by beating him on the soles of his feet. The officers were convicted of assault with intent to do grievous bodily harm. The court stated that the torture inflicted by the police officers called for severe censure in terms of punishment

Unreasonable delay in bringing for trial

Section 18(2) of the Constitution provides that everyone charged with a criminal offence is entitled to a fair hearing within a reasonable time

Section 160(2) CPEA provides that if X is not brought to trial after the expiry of six months from the date of his or her committal for trial, his or her case shall be “dismissed”. This provision is meant to protect accused persons from being unreasonably kept under committal for trial for longer than six months when the trial has failed to take place during that period, as well as to ensure that the Attorney-General ensures that trials of accused persons committed for trial are expeditiously conducted. In *Mukuze & Anor* v *A-G (2)* HH-17-05, the court decided that the six-month period mentioned in s 160 could be interrupted: (a) if X is through circumstances beyond the control of the Attorney General not available to stand trial; or (b) if the Attorney-General has in terms of s 108 ordered a further examination to be taken.

It is the responsibility of the judge hearing applications for initial and further remands to ensure that the Constitutional provisions are observed. In terms of s 18(9) every person is entitled to a fair trial within a reasonable time.

It is the duty of the remand court to decline to grant requests from the State for further remands when unreasonably long periods of time have elapsed since X was first charged. It must ensure that the State proceeds to trial within a reasonable time: *Bull* v *Minister of Home Affairs* 1986 (1) ZLR 202 (S). The responsibility of the court to prevent unreasonable delays is a continuing one. At each further remand the progress of the investigations should be checked. If, at the last remand the State has asked for further time so that the police can locate a missing witness or carry out some further investigations and the State is now applying for a further remand on the basis of the same reason advanced previously, the court should obviously check that the police have been vigorously attempting to deal with these matters.

Even where X is out of custody pending trial, the State is nonetheless obliged to ensure that the case is brought for trial within a reasonable time. Where X is in custody it is obviously even more important that the case be brought for trial within a reasonable time. The responsibility of the court to prevent unreasonable delays is a continuing one. At each further remand the progress of the investigations should be checked. If, at the last remand the State has asked for further time so that the police can locate a missing witness or carry out some further investigations and the State is now applying for a further remand on the basis of the same reason advanced previously, the court should obviously check that the police have been vigorously attempting to deal with these matters.

Not only at the first remand but at each subsequent remand the remanding judge must note in the record why X is being remanded.

The court has the primary responsibility for the protection of the right of the unrepresented accused to a speedy trial because an unrepresented accused who is unfamiliar with the criminal process will be likely to be unaware of his or her rights to be tried within a reasonable period. The court before whom the unrepresented accused is brought must take the initiative to ensure that the constitutional right of X to a speedy trial is not violated. It should not wait for X to raise a complaint of a violation of his or her constitutional right and to ask the court to deny any further remands. The court should probe the reasons for any apparently undue delays and, where no satisfactory explanations are forthcoming, it should take appropriate action. At very least, the it would be expected that the court would inform X of his or her rights. But the informing of such an accused of his or her rights should not be seen as been a sufficient safeguarding of X's rights. Even after being given such information, he or she may still be ignorant about what remedies he or she has and how he or she should go about raising this issue. The undefended accused may still lack the ability to assert those rights. He or she may be inarticulate, nervous and overawed when he or she appears in court. If he or she is in custody, he or she may be worried about the consequences of raising complaints about undue delays in bringing the case to trial.

The court has the power to require explanations for the delays from the prosecutor which X has not. See *Tao* HH-182-96; *Msindo* HH-63-97; *Chakwinya* 1997 (1) ZLR 109 (H).

The remand court, therefore, should not go on granting requests for further remands when an unreasonably long period of time has elapsed since X was first charged. It should seek to ensure that the State proceeds to trial within a reasonable period of time. *Bull* v *Minister of Home Affairs* 1986 (1) ZLR 202 (S).

Accused in custody

If X is in custody he or she can apply for the release from custody on the ground that an unreasonably long period has elapsed in bringing the case for trial. Section 13(3) of the Constitution specifically lays down that if a person who is being held in custody is not brought for trial within a reasonable period of time, he or she must be released from custody conditionally or unconditionally but may still be brought to trial later. The onus is on the defence to establish that the accused person is entitled to be released because of unreasonable delay: In re *Hativagone & Anor* S-67-04.

X may also ask that, in addition to the release of his or her client, the State should either proceed to trial within a short space of time or that the charges against his or her client be withdrawn.

In *Fikilini* v *Attorney-General* 1990 (1) ZLR 105 (S), it was laid down that in determining whether a person's detention pending trial had become unlawful because of failure to bring him or her to trial within a reasonable time the court should take account of:

- whether in all the circumstances the length of his or her detention has been unreasonably long. The nature of the charge and the investigation process required to investigate that charge should be examined. Is the charge a complex one which demands lengthy and painstaking investigation or is it simple and straightforward and could have been disposed of speedily if the police had been efficient? Does the case require the gathering of evidence in other countries? Are there some vital witnesses which the State is still trying to locate?
- the reasons which the State has advanced for the delay. The State should obviously be required to advance reasons for the delays which have occurred in bringing the matter to trial. A proper reason, such as difficulties in locating a vital witness will justify an appropriate delay. But if it turns out that the State is improperly delaying bringing the case to trial in order, for instance, to hamper the defence, this will weigh heavily against the State.
- whether the accused asserted his or her right to have the case brought to trial within a reasonable time. If he or she has asserted his or her right this is evidence that he or she is being deprived of this right; but if he or she has not

done so this may be indicative that his or her right is not being breached. (But the undefended accused may fail to assert this right because he or she does not know that he or she has this right.)

- the prejudice which may be occasioned to X by the delay. Will the preparation of the defence be impaired by the delay? Will it cause oppressive pre-trial incarceration? Will it lead to disproportionate anxiety and mental suffering?

Accused out of custody

If X is out of custody, the defence lawyer can ask that a trial date within the near future be set, failing which the charge should be withdrawn.

As mentioned above s 160(2) CPEA provides that if X is not brought to trial after the expiry of six months from the date of his or her committal for trial, his or her case shall be "dismissed". In *Mukuze & Anor* v *A-G (2)* HH-17-05, the court decided the "dismissal" of the case does not amount to an acquittal, nor does it relate to prescription. It relates to the committal and the effects or consequences or implications thereof. The subsection is meant to protect accused persons from being unreasonably kept under committal for trial for longer than six months when the trial has failed to take place during that period, as well as to ensure that the Attorney-General ensures that trials of accused persons committed for trial are expeditiously conducted. The court also decided that the six-month period mentioned in s 160 could be interrupted: (a) if X is through circumstances beyond the control of the Attorney-General not available to stand trial; or (b) if the Attorney-General has in terms of s 108 ordered a further examination to be taken.

In re *Hativagone & Anor* S-67-04, the appellants were arrested on criminal charges in 1998 and placed on remand. They denied the charges. In 1999 the charges were withdrawn before plea. Four years later, the accused were summoned to appear to answer the charges. The Attorney-General had deferred the prosecution of the applicants until the trial of the accomplice who was to be the principal witness against them was complete. This person had been prosecuted, but the proceedings were set aside and had to be restarted. The applicants brought an application for a permanent stay of proceedings, arguing that their right under s 18(2) of the Constitution to a fair trial within a reasonable time had been violated. The court held that in order for the application to succeed, it was necessary to consider

- the length of delay and whether it was presumptively prejudicial;
- the reasons for the delay;
- whether the applicants had asserted their right to a speedy trial; and
- the prejudice to the applicants.

In considering the length of the delay, the fact that the charge had been withdrawn before plea did not assist the State, as the withdrawal was not unconditional. The overall delay was presumptively prejudicial. However, the reasons given for the delay were reasonable in the circumstances and to a large extent the Attorney-General was not to blame for the delay. The applicants had failed to discharge the onus on them to show that they had asserted their right to a speedy trial. Although the applicants were prejudiced by the fact

Grounds	Factors
Likelihood that if X is released he or she will endanger the safety of the public or a particular person or will commit a First Schedule offence.	In deciding whether this ground has been established, the court must, where applicable, take into account these factors: ➢ the degree of violence towards others implicit in the charge; ➢ any threat of violence which X may have made to any person; ➢ the resentment X is alleged to harbour against any person; ➢ any disposition of X to commit First Schedule offences, as evident from X's past conduct; ➢ any evidence that X previously committed a First Schedule offence whilst out on bail; ➢ any other factor which in the opinion of the court should be taken into account.
Likelihood if X is released he or she will attempt to intimidate witnesses or conceal or destroy evidence.	In deciding whether this ground has been established the court must take into account these factors: ➢ X's ties to the place of trial; ➢ whether X has assets and where they are located; ➢ X's means of travel and possession of or access to travel documents; ➢ the nature and gravity of the offence or the nature and gravity of the likely penalty therefor; ➢ the strength of the case for the prosecution and the corresponding incentive of the accused to flee; ➢ the efficacy of the amount or nature of the bail and enforceability of any bail conditions; ➢ any other factor which in the opinion of the court should be taken into account.

Grounds	Factors
Likelihood that X will attempt to influence or intimidate witnesses or to conceal or destroy evidence.	In considering whether this ground has been established, the court must take into account — ➢ whether X is familiar with any witness or the evidence; ➢ whether any witness has made a statement; ➢ whether the investigation is completed; ➢ X's relationship with any witness and the extent to which the witness may be influenced by the accused; ➢ the efficacy of the amount or nature of the bail and enforceability of any bail conditions; ➢ the ease with which any evidence can be concealed or destroyed; ➢ any other factor which in the opinion of the court should be taken into account.
Likelihood that if X is released he or she will undermine or jeopardise the objectives or proper functioning of the criminal justice system, including the bail system	In considering whether this ground has been established, the court must take into account — ➢ whether X supplied false information at arrest or during bail proceedings; ➢ whether X is in custody on another charge or is released on licence in terms of the Prisons Act; ➢ any previous failure by X to comply with bail conditions; ➢ any other factor which in the opinion of the court should be taken into account.
Where in exceptional circumstances there is a likelihood that X's release will disturb the public order or undermine public peace or security	In considering whether this ground has been established, the court, where applicable, must take into account— ➢ whether the nature of the offence and the circumstances under which the offence was committed is likely to induce a sense of shock or outrage in the community where the offence was committed; ➢ whether the shock or outrage of the community where the offence was committed might lead to public disorder if X is released; ➢ whether the safety of X might be jeopardised by his or her release; ➢ whether the sense of peace and security among members of the public will be undermined or jeopardised by X's release; ➢ whether X's release will undermine or jeopardise the public confidence in the criminal justice system; ➢ any other factor which in the opinion of the court should be taken into account.

that potential defence witnesses were not available, having either died or emigrated, nonetheless, because the Attorney-General's explanation was reasonable and because the applicants had failed to assert their rights, the application must fail.
In *Watson* S-17-06, the applicant, while driving his or her vehicle, had negligently caused the death of a pedestrian. He or she was initially placed on remand on a charge of culpable homicide, but later placed off remand. Eleven years later, he or she was summoned to appear on the same charge. It was held there was an inordinate delay by the State in bringing the applicant to trial. The explanation for the delay was neither adequate nor reasonable. The delay was, by any standards, unreasonably long and could not be supported by any court of law. The applicant's rights under s 18(2) of the Constitution to a fair hearing within a reasonable time had been infringed. Anyone arrested or detained on a criminal charge should be promptly brought before a competent court of law, which will then exercise its judicial power over him, and such trial should be held within a reasonable time. This is to ensure that the accused does not suffer unduly prolonged uncertainty and that evidence is not lost in the process. The inordinate delay caused irretrievable prejudice to the applicant and a permanent stay of proceedings would be granted.

Similarly, in In re *Masendeke* 1992 (2) ZLR 5 (S), there had been seven years' delay in a case involving a policeman who was on two simple charges of taking bribes. The magistrate referred the case to the Supreme Court under s 24(2) of the Constitution. There was no justification for such a protracted delay and it was not suggested that the accused was to blame for the delay. The Supreme Court ordered a permanent stay of proceedings.

In *Tau* 1997 (1) ZLR 93 (H), it was suggested that if X has been on remand for a period approaching a year, the court should question the State very closely indeed if it applies for a further remand.

See also *Ruzario* 1990 (1) ZLR 359 (S) and *Kundishora* 1990 (2) ZLR 30 (S).

Where X alleges that there has been an undue delay in bringing his or her case for trial the onus is on him or her or her to prove that there has been such an undue delay: *Fikilini* v *Attorney-General* 1990 (1) ZLR 105 (S) and that he or she has asserted his or her right to a speedy trial. In re *Hativagone & Anor* S-67-04.

Where the defence alleges that there has been an undue delay in bringing his or her case for trial, the onus is on it to prove that there has been such an undue delay: *Fikilini* v *Attorney-General* 1990 (1) ZLR 105 (S) and that he or she or she has asserted his or her right to a speedy trial: In re *Hativagone & Anor* S-67-04.

See also *Ruzario* 1990 (1) ZLR 359 (S) and *Kundishora* 1990 (2) ZLR 30 (S).

Child offenders

It is most undesirable that child offenders should be remanded in prison custody along with adult prisoners up to the time they are tried. If they have to be remanded in custody, all efforts must be made to place them in an institution such as a juvenile reformatory until they are tried. Judges should ensure that young offenders are brought for trial as soon as possible.

In terms of the Constitution, every person has a right to a fair trial within a reasonable period of time and not to be deprived of his or her liberty unless there is a reasonable suspicion that he or she has committed a criminal offence. Judges presiding at remand hearings have a duty to ensure that these rights are respected by the State. A person should not be remanded in custody unless the Judge is satisfied that there are facts indicating that there is a reasonable suspicion that the person has committed a crime. The Judge should not continue to remand a case if there have been unreasonable delays in bringing it to trial.

Postponement of cases

Reid-Rowland 15-4

All applications for postponement of cases before they have commenced must be made in open court. (The same applies to the postponement or adjournment of cases after they have commenced.) The prosecutor or X or his or her legal representative must explain to the court why a postponement or further remand is being sought. The court must be satisfied that the reason provided is a genuine one and that the postponement is necessary. The reasons for the postponement must be recorded. Where there is doubt about the genuineness of the reason for the requested postponement, the matter can be stood down and, if necessary, the matter can be referred to the Senior Public Prosecutor or to the senior prosecutor at the station.

This procedure ensures that there is a written record of who applied for the postponement and why. This will be important in the event of questions later being raised as to undue delay in the completion of the trial and who was responsible for the delay. Disputes can arise months later between the defence and prosecution as to who was to blame for the delay in finalising the case. These disputes can be easily resolved by checking the record of the case. This will ensure that accuseds do not escape proper punishment where they are in fact responsible for the delay and not the State as alleged.

In *Martin* v *A-G & Ors* S-53-93, the State applied to remand applicant on a charge under the Prevention of Corruption Act. The defence argued that the facts alleged did not disclose an offence, therefore that a remand was in violation of the Constitution, and asked for the matter to be referred to the Supreme Court. The magistrate considered the matter and held that the essential elements of the offence were alleged, and refused to refer the matter because it was frivolous and vexatious. Applicant applied to the Supreme Court under s 24(1) of the Constitution.

The appeal court decided that:

- The magistrate should not have decided the point of law and then decided that the application was vexatious or frivolous. He or she was obliged to refer the decision on the law to the Supreme Court unless it was clearly groundless and so devoid of any merit that no reasonable person could argue it, or clearly *mala fide* and put forward in the knowledge that it could not succeed.
- Every individual can rely on s 13(2)(e) of the Constitution to challenge a remand on the grounds that there is no reasonable suspicion that he or she has committed an offence (or is about to do so). He or she can adduce evidence at the remand.
- A remand even out of custody is a deprivation of personal liberty. An order to surrender his or her passport is a deprivation of the constitutional right under s 22(1) to leave and re-enter Zimbabwe. Refusing to refer the matter to the Supreme Court is a denial of his or her constitutional right under s 18(1) to the protection of the law.
- A man claiming to be deprived of such constitutional rights is entitled to apply to the Supreme Court for redress under s 24(1), subject to s 24(3), for an order declaring that the Declaration of Rights has been breached by the magistrate, and declaring that the remand was unconstitutional.
- In this case, the State had not alleged sufficient facts and the application was allowed with costs.

Courtesy to witnesses

Out of courtesy and consideration for the witnesses they should be told why the trial cannot proceed and an apology should be given to them for the time that they have wasted in coming to court in vain.

Witnesses often suffer great inconvenience in having to come to court, especially where they reside at a place far away from where the proceedings are taking place. It is an even greater burden if they have to come back again on one or more subsequent occasions and steps must be taken to ensure that such inconvenience does not occur by trying to avoid unnecessary postponements. If postponements cannot be avoided, then the witnesses are at least entitled to receive an explanation and apology. The best person to do this is the judge rather than it being done by the prosecutor in the corridors. By bringing the witnesses before the judge, the witnesses are at least given the impression that they have been "heard" by the court and the judge is able to convey the message that their attendance on this occasion is appreciated.

Witnesses in attendance should be brought into court and warned by the court to come back on the new trial date. The names of the witnesses so warned and the new trial date must be recorded. This device saves the police having to serve fresh subpoenas on these witnesses.

If the reason why there has to be a postponement is that X has failed to attend for his or her trial, no new trial date will be fixed as there will be uncertainty as to when X will be located and when he or she can be brought to court. The witnesses should then be told that the case has had to be postponed because of the absence of X. The witnesses must be told that they will have to come back to give evidence at a date which will be fixed in the future and that they will receive subpoenas telling them when to come back.

However, if calling of the judge will take some time, it will be better if the prosecutor informs the witnesses as soon as he or she knows that a matter will have to be postponed.

If it is known that the case will have to be postponed at the start of the court day, then witnesses should not be kept waiting around until the end of the day and then dismissed; they should be dismissed as early as possible with an appropriate explanation and apology.

The prosecutor dealing with the case which has been postponed should personally ensure that the new trial date is inserted in the set down book for the appropriate court. Postponed cases should be given priority over all other cases set down for that date. The more often the case has been postponed, the greater the priority it must be accorded. Whenever possible, cases should not be remanded to a date a long time hence. Indeed, wherever possible, cases should be rolled-over to the next day if there is a realistic prospect that they can be heard then. Witnesses who have travelled long distances can then be accommodated overnight, heard the next day and then be allowed to return to their homes.

Witnesses should never be dismissed without being heard simply because a "vital" witness is not available. The "vital" witness can be heard at a later date.

All applications for postponements of cases must be made in court. There must be valid reasons for granting postponements. When granting a postponement the magistrate must record who applied for the postponement and on what basis.

Bail Pending Trial

Reid-Rowland Chapter 6

General policy

In our law persons are presumed innocent until their guilt has been proven. When a person applies for bail he or she has not yet been tried and the allegations against him or her have not yet been proven. Pre-trial incarceration cuts across the presumption of innocence as a person is being incarcerated before trial despite the fact that he or she may be found not guilty when he or she is tried. Wherever the interests of justice will not be prejudiced by pre-trial release, the courts should lean in favour of liberty and grant release on bail with or without additional conditions. This is particularly so if the offence with which X is being tried is not likely to attract a prison sentence. Pre-trial incarceration of petty offenders means that they end up being punished to a disproportionate extent. If they are found guilty and fined, they will already have spent time in custody; if they receive short prison sentences, they may already have spent longer in prison waiting for their trial than the period of the prison sentence imposed. For petty offences, therefore, there must be very cogent reasons for refusal of bail.

The right to liberty is one of the most fundamental human rights and should not be lightly interfered with. The court should lean in favour of protecting liberty unless the State establishes the necessity to deprive X of his or her liberty pending the trial.

In *Biti* HH-23-02, it was stated that the court should always grant bail where possible and should lean in favour of the liberty of the applicant provided that the interests of justice will not be prejudiced. The approach is one of striking a balance between the interest of society (i.e. the applicant should stand trial and there should be no interference with the administration of justice) and the liberty of an accused (who, pending the outcome of his or her trial, is presumed to be innocent).

In *Ndhlovu* 2001 (2) ZLR 261 (H), the court stated that in bail applications, the court has to strike a balance between the interests of society (which are that the accused should stand trial and that there should be no interference with the administration of justice) and the liberty of the accused (who is presumed to be innocent). Grounds for refusal of bail should be reasonably substantiated. The court should always grant bail where possible and should lean in favour of the liberty of the subject, provided the interests of justice will not be prejudiced.

The right to liberty is one of the most fundamental human rights and should not be lightly interfered with. The court should lean in favour of protecting liberty unless the State establishes the necessity to deprive X of his or her liberty pending the trial.

Onus of proof

Section 117(1) CPEA establishes a general entitlement to bail unless the court finds that it is in the interests of justice that the accused be detained in custody pending trial. The provision reads as follows:

> (1) Subject to this section and section 32, a person who is in custody in respect of an offence shall be entitled to be released on bail at any time after he or she has appeared in court on a charge and before sentence is imposed, unless the court finds that it is in the interests of justice that he or she should be detained in custody.

It would seem that by granting an entitlement to bail unless the interests of justice require that bail not be granted, the legislature has placed the onus on the State to establish that there are clear grounds justifying the refusal of bail. In the South African case of *Maki & Ors* (1) 1994 (2) SACR 630 (E), the court stated that the onus is on the State to show, on a balance of probabilities, that the applicant's further detention is necessary for the proper administration of justice.

Hlatshwayo J purportedly altered the law regarding the onus in bail applications in *Kuruneri* HH-111-04. In that case, it was held that there is no statutory authority for placing an onus upon an applicant for bail, and that prior rulings to that effect were based on South African cases. These are based on a statute which is materially different from the Zimbabwean legislation. In arriving at the decision, the learned Judge held that Section 13(4) of the Constitution requires that any person who is arrested or detained should be tried within a reasonable time, failing which he or she should be released from custody. In other words, the discretionary power of a magistrate to deny bail may not be exercised in violation of the accused's constitutional right to be brought to trial within a reasonable time or be freed from custody. What is in dispute is whether there is an onus on the accused person to show on a balance of probabilities why it is in the interest of justice that he or she should be freed on bail. Decisions of the superior courts of Zimbabwe have followed decisions of the South African courts, but the South African provisions are not worded the same as the Zimbabwean ones. The notion of the accused having an onus to discharge to enable him or her or her to be admitted to bail is not part of our law as legislated. The constitutional presumption of innocence in bail application operates fully and at the general level. It is because of the presumption of innocence that the courts are expected, and indeed required, to lean in favour of the liberty of the accused. If the State's fears that the accused will abscone or interfere with witnesses and the applicant's assurances to the contrary are equally balanced, then the presumption of innocence would require the court to lean in favour of the liberty of the accused person and grant bail.

There are a number of earlier Zimbabwean cases in which the Supreme Court it is laid down that after the State has led sufficient evidence to show that there is a real likelihood that the administration of justice will be prejudiced if X is admitted to bail, the onus lies on the person applying for bail to show on a balance of probabilities that his or her admission to bail would not prejudice the interests of justice: *Chiadzwa* 1988 (2) ZLR 19 (S); *Hussey* 1991 (2) ZLR 187 (S). Part IX CPEA was amended in 2006, however, and the current provisions (particularly s 117(1), quoted above) are more in line with the views expressed in *Kuruneri*'s case than in those earlier cases.

In *Ncube* S-126-01, the court said that in considering a bail application, a judicial officer must bear in mind the presumption of innocence, and should grant bail where possible. The onus (the quantum of which varies from case to case) is on the accused to show why he or she should be granted bail. He or she can discharge this onus by calling witnesses to show that the allegations against him or her are unfounded. Failure by the court to allow him or her to call such evidence is a serious misdirection, one which would allow the Supreme Court to interfere with a decision of a judge of the High Court to refuse bail.

Procedure in bail case

In *Ncube & Anor* HB-126-02, the judge pointed out that bail applications are *sui generis*: there is no prescribed format or procedure. It is the duty of the presiding officer, with due allowance for the circumstances of each case, to determine the way in which each party must submit its evidence. In a majority of cases *ex parte* statements are made by both the defence and by the public prosecutor who intimates what the police objections are. There are no formalities; no evidence is led, no affidavits are placed before the court and the record is so meagre that there may be little or nothing to place before the superior courts if the matter is taken on appeal.

In bail applications both sides may make submissions from the Bar or lead evidence. Evidence should be led in support of any fact which is in dispute.

In the South African case of *Maki & Ors* (1) 1994 (2) SACR 630 (E), the court said that the procedure for hearing and adjudicating on bail applications should be flexible and adaptable. The laying down of rigid rules as to what evidence is admissible in a given situation should be avoided, except that both oral evidence and affidavits should be admissible and, in appropriate cases, other material such as *ex parte* statements.

Restrictions on granting bail

Judges

There are no restrictions on the granting of bail by judges. A judge may grant bail in respect of any offence at any time after he or she has appeared in court on a charge and before sentence is imposed. [s 116(a)]

Magistrates

Judges should be familiar with the restrictions placed on magistrates in granting bail. The power of magistrates to grant bail or alter bail conditions is now severely restricted. In terms of s 116(1)(b) CPEA, where X has been charged with any of the offences specified in the Third Schedule, magistrates may only grant bail if the Attorney-General has consented to X's admission to bail. Section 117(6) contains further restrictions on the granting of bail by magistrates.

The specified offences in Part 1 of the Third Schedule are:

- murder where it was committed in certain specified circumstances such as where it was premeditated;
- rape or aggravated indecent assault where it was committed in certain specified circumstances such as multiple rape of a victim;
- robbery where it was committed in certain specified circumstances such as where firearms were used;
- assault or indecent assault of a child under 16 involving the infliction of grievous bodily harm;
- kidnapping or unlawful detention involving the infliction of grievous bodily harm;
- contravening the following sections of CLCA: 20 (treason); 21 (concealing treason); 22 (subverting constitutional government); 23 (insurgency, banditry, sabotage or terrorism); 24 (recruiting or training insurgents, bandits, saboteurs or terrorists); 25 (training as insurgent, bandit, saboteur or terrorist); 26 (supplying weapons to insurgents, bandits, saboteurs or terrorists); 27 (possessing weapons for insurgency, banditry, sabotage or terrorism); or 29 (harbouring, concealing or failing to report insurgent, bandit, saboteur or terrorist);
- An offence in Part II of the Third Schedule where the accused has previously been convicted of any offence specified in the Third Schedule or has allegedly committed such offence whilst on bail in respect of an offence in the Third Schedule.

The offences specified in Part II to the Third Schedule are:

- treason;
- murder in circumstances other than those specified in Part I;
- attempted murder involving the infliction of grievous bodily harm;
- malicious damage to property involving arson or conspiracy, incitement or attempt to commit this offence;
- theft of a motor vehicle or conspiracy, incitement or attempt to commit this offence;
- any offence relating to dealing in or smuggling of ammunition, firearms, explosives or armaments or the possession of an automatic or semi-automatic

firearm, explosives or armaments or conspiracy, incitement or attempt to commit this offence;

- any offence where the Attorney-General has notified the magistrate of his or her intention to indict the case direct to the High Court.

For any offences other than those specified, the magistrate may grant bail in his or her discretion without the consent of the Attorney-General. However, in terms of s 116(5) CPEA, bail must be refused if X has been extradited from another country to Zimbabwe and if the Zimbabwean Minister of Home Affairs has given an undertaking to the government of that other country that X will not be admitted to bail while in Zimbabwe. A certificate from the Minister, which states that he or she has given that undertaking, must be produced. If the Minister has given the undertaking that X will only be admitted to bail on certain conditions, then the court may grant bail on those conditions. The court may impose further conditions which are not inconsistent with the conditions specified by the Minister.

The Attorney-General's Office issued a circular (No. 2 of 1992) in which the matter of bail in the magistrates courts was dealt with. See Appendix 8 for the text of this circular. However, portions of this circular are no longer applicable, as the power of magistrates to grant bail has been restored for a number of offences mentioned, such as housebreaking. Portions of this circular are also no longer relevant as, for instance, the power of magistrates.

When and how applied for

An accused can make an oral application for bail at any time to a judge before whom he or she is appearing. A written application for bail must be in the form of a petition and must be accompanied by a copy of the document authorising the detention of the applicant or an affidavit that a copy is denied. All such applications must be disposed of without undue delay: s 117(3) CPEA. See Appendix 5 for sample bail application form.

Section 117A contains these provisions relating to bail applications:

In bail proceedings the court may receive:

- evidence on oath, including hearsay evidence;
- affidavits and written reports which may be tendered by the prosecutor, the accused or his or her legal representative;
- written statements made by the prosecutor, the accused or his or her legal representative;
- statements not on oath made by the accused.

It may also require the prosecutor or the accused to adduce evidence.

In bail proceedings, the accused is compelled to inform the court whether:

- the accused has previously been convicted of any offence; and
- there are any charges pending against him or her and whether he or she has been released on bail in respect of those charges.

If the legal representative submits this information on behalf of the accused, the accused will be required by the court to declare whether he or she confirms this information.

For the purposes of bail proceedings, an accused may not have access to any information, record or document relating to the offence in question, which is contained in, or forms part of, a police docket, including any information, record or document which is held by any police officer charged with the investigation in question, unless the Attorney-General otherwise directs.

Grounds for refusal

The fundamental principle governing the court's approach to bail applications is to uphold the interests of justice. The court must take into account the factors set out in s 117 of CPEA and try to strike a balance between the protection of the liberty of the individual and the administration of justice. In our law persons are presumed innocent until their guilt has been proved. When a person applies for bail he or she has not yet been tried and the allegations against him or her have not yet been proved. Therefore, pre-trial incarceration cuts across the presumption of innocence as a person is being incarcerated before trial despite the fact that he or she may be found not guilty when he or she is tried. Whenever the interests of justice will not be prejudiced by pre-trial release the courts should lean in favour of liberty and grant release on bail with or without additional conditions. This is particularly so if the offence with which X is being tried is not likely to attract a prison sentence. Pre-trial incarceration of petty offenders means that they end up being punished to a disproportionate extent. If they are found guilty and fined, they have already spent time in custody; if they receive short prison sentences, they may already have spent longer in prison waiting for their trial than the prison sentence imposed for their crime. For petty offences, therefore, there must be very cogent reasons for the refusal of bail.

Section 117 provides detailed guidelines to courts on how to go about deciding whether it is or is not in the interests of justice to grant bail.

It provides that it would be in the interests of justice to refuse bail if one or more of the certain grounds are present and sets out the factors that the court should take into account in deciding whether these grounds are present. The table below sets out the specified grounds and the factors that are to be taken into account in respect of each of these grounds.

Well founded grounds for State opposition to bail

It was made quite clear in *Hussey* 1991 (2) ZLR 187 (S) that where the State seeks to rely on one or more of these grounds when opposing bail, it is insufficient for the State merely to make bald assertions that the particular grounds applied. Its assertions must be well-grounded. It must produce cogent reasons why the particular ground in question applies and these reasons must be supported by proper information. In *Malumjwa* HB-34-03, it was held that in bail applications the court has to strike a balance between the interest of society (that the applicant should stand trial and there should be no interference with the administration of justice) and the liberty of an accused person (who pending the outcome of his or her trial is presumed to be innocent). The likelihood of a lengthy prison term being imposed (i.e. the seriousness of the offence) is a factor to be taken into account in assessing the risk of absconding. Where is has been shown that the accused has interfered with evidence, the court is justified in denying him or herbail. The court should, however, not refuse bail on the bare assertion of the State; there must be enough reason for such a conclusion. In other words, grounds for refusal of bail should be reasonably substantiated.

Likelihood of absconding

An accused who has decided not to stand trial may either flee the country if he or she has the capacity to do so or try to go to a place inside the country where he or she believes the authorities will be unable to find him. The problems of bringing to justice a person who has fled the country are obviously greater than if he or she hides himself within Zimbabwe.

If there are good grounds for believing that X will take flight and become a fugitive from justice if he or she is granted bail then bail must be refused: *Hussey* 1991 (2) ZLR 187 (S). If, before or after his or her arrest, X escaped or tried to escape from custody, this would clearly show his or her predisposition to abscond and not to stand trial: *Chiadzwa* 1988 (2) ZLR 19 (S). In *Jongwe* 2002 (2) ZLR 209 (S), it was held that when assessing the risk of an applicant for bail absconding before trial, the court will be guided by the character of the charges and the penalties which in all probability would be imposed if convicted; the strength of the State case; the accused's ability to flee to a foreign country and the absence of extradition facilities; the past response to being released on bail; and the assurance given that it is intended to stand trial. The most critical factors are the nature of the charges and the severity of the punishment likely to be imposed upon conviction and also the apparent strengths and weaknesses of the State case.

In deciding whether flight is likely and in the absence of such concrete evidence of a predisposition to abscond, account must be taken of a number of factors which common experience have shown influence a person either to stand trial or to take flight.

These factors are the gravity of the charge and the likely sentence for that crime, the capacity of and opportunities for X to flee and whether he or she has contacts abroad who will offer him or hersanctuary or whether X has substantial assets abroad. Other factors which are relevant are the property holdings of X and his or her status in society. It may be that he or she would lose so much if he or she absconded that flight is unlikely.

There is need for the court to assess the strength of State case. Where allegations in police papers raise a *prima facie* case, there is need for accused to rebut allegations and show that he or she should be granted bail. In *Makamba* S-30-04, the appellant was refused bail in the High Court on various charges under the exchange control legislation. Among other grounds of appeal, it was argued that the judge *a quo* should not have relied on the mere allegations made by the investigating officer. The strength of the State case had not been assessed by the judge *a quo*, though it should have been. However, the allegations made in the affidavit of the investigating officer were fairly detailed and raised at least a *prima facie* case against the appellant. In such circumstances an applicant would be expected, in attempting to discharge the onus upon him, either to deny the allegations; or to place before the court such information as would tend to establish his or her innocence; or to show that even if he or she were to be convicted the likely penalties were not such as to present a temptation for him or her or her to abscond; or to show that the interests of justice would not be prejudiced by his or her release on bail

The case of *Chiadzwa* 1988 (2) ZLR 19 (S) examines the combination of factors which make international flight likely. Where a person is facing a serious charge which will lead to lengthy incarceration on conviction and the evidence against him or her is very strong and conviction probable, and that person has the capacity to leave the country and has someone outside the country who will support him or her, there will be a substantial risk of external flight. In these circumstances the person may be quite prepared to abandon substantial assets in Zimbabwe to avoid the prospect of spending years in prison. With less serious charges, in respect of which the evidence is weak, it would be unlikely that a wealthy person will flee the country leaving behind substantial assets, especially if that person has no external assets and few acquaintances outside the country who could assist him or her to re-establish himself. See also *Aitken & Anor* v *Attorney-General* 1992 (1) ZLR 249 (S) and *Aitken* (2) 1992 (2) ZLR 463 (S).

In considering whether flight is likely the courts take into account whether a person has a fixed abode and whether he or she has a job. In these days of high unemployment favourable consideration should be given to employment in the informal sector. With the drastic shortages of accommodation in urban areas, the fact that a person does not have permanent accommodation should not necessarily be held against him. The attachment of regular reporting conditions will usually ensure that a person who only has temporary accommodation can be located when necessary.

If the State opposes bail on the ground that X is of no fixed abode and will therefore probably not attend court when his or her case is to be tried, but X asserts that he or she lives at a particular address, then the State should indicate in specific terms the basis for its belief that X does not live at that place: *Gwatiringa* HH-128-88.

In *Mambo* 1992 (1) ZLR 245 (H), X had been refused bail on the grounds that he was very likely to abscond. On appeal, it was held that bail should be granted as, on the probabilities, it was unlikely that X would abscond. He was aware for some time that he was under investigation for the alleged fraud in question and had not absconded; he had travelled to South Africa and when he was informed that the Zimbabwean police were looking for him, he had returned to the country and surrendered himself to the police. The fact that X is facing a very serious charge and that the sums involved in the alleged fraud are considerable is not a sufficient basis for refusing bail.

In *Biti* HH-23-02, the court decided that where evidence is given that there is a strong case for the prosecution, that a heavy sentence is likely, increasing the risk of the accused absconding, and that other perpetrators of the crime are still at large, the onus then falls on the accused to show that the interests of justice will not be prejudiced, namely, that it is likely that he or she will stand his or her trial and not otherwise interfere with the administration of justice or commit an offence.

In *Jongwe* S-62-02, Chidyausiku CJ indicated that when assessing the risk of an applicant for bail absconding before trial, the court will be guided by

- the character of the charges and the penalties which in all probability would be imposed if convicted;
- the strength of the State case;
- the accused's ability to flee to a foreign country and the absence of extradition facilities;
- the past response to being released on bail; and
- the assurance given that it is intended to stand trial.

He pointed out that the most critical factors are the nature of the charges and the severity of the punishment likely to be imposed upon conviction and also the apparent strengths and weaknesses of the State case.

In Ndhlovu 2001 (2) ZLR 261 (H), the court said that in deciding whether there is a risk of X absconding, the court should consider such factors as the seriousness of the offence, the likely sentence and the incentive to abscond, X's mobility and access to cross-border travel, and the strength of the prosecution case. It may be desirable for X to disclose his or her defence and not merely make a bald statement that he or she is not guilty of the offence. Such a defence is of great, and often of decisive, importance in the exercise of the court's discretion. X's personal circumstances, such as financial position and business interests, are of little value in assessing the risk of absconding. They may, in some cases, be used to facilitate absconding. The fact that X surrendered to the police should normally be a factor in his or her favour, though if he or she surrendered under a false name with the intention of deceiving the police, it would not count in his or her favour.

Often the attaching of conditions to the granting of bail, such as reporting to a designated police station at particular hours, may be enough to minimise any danger of X absconding.

Likelihood of commission of further offences

The public must be protected against further criminal activities of a person pending trial. This is especially so in respect of dangerous criminals who may commit grave crimes whilst out on bail. However, the majority of persons facing trial are unlikely to commit further crimes if released prior to trial. The impending trial will usually act as a restraint as it will be realised that they will face serious penalties if they engage in further criminal conduct before their trial.

If the State maintains that further criminal conduct is likely, it must point to some facts that suggest there is such a danger and that this cannot be averted by the imposition of stringent bail conditions. It is permissible for the State to produce a list of X's previous convictions: *Fourie* 1973 (1) SA 100 (D).

If he or she has a string of previous convictions there is a substantial chance that he or she might commit further crimes whilst on bail. In the case of *Attorney-General* v *Phiri* 1987 (2) ZLR 33 (H), the evidence of the propensity to commit further crimes whilst at liberty was particularly strong. In addition to a bad criminal record, there was evidence that X had committed further similar crimes to the crimes for which he was yet to be tried. Such previous conduct whilst on bail showed a disregard for the law and a contempt for the administration of justice. Bail was understandably refused.

However, in the case of *Demba* HH-133-89, the High Court said that if after a person has been granted bail for one offence, he or she is then suspected of having committed another similar crime some time before the current offence, this does not necessarily mean that he or she will be more likely to commit yet another offence whilst at liberty such that he or she should now be refused bail. See also *Patel* 1970 (3) SA 565 (W).

Likelihood of tampering with evidence

The argument that there is a likelihood of interference with evidence will obviously be strong if the State can show that there have already been attempts to do this. This was the situation in *Maharaj* 1976 (3) SA 205 (D) where X had already tried to persuade a State witness to disappear; in *Chiadzwa* 1988 (2) ZLR 19 (S) where there was evidence suggesting X had attempted to bribe a police officer and had composed a plan whilst in prison to discredit witnesses against him; and in *Maratera* S-93-91 where there was evidence that there had been an interference with the course of justice. See also *Bennett* 1976 (3) SA 652 (C).

What if there is no such clear evidence of a preparedness to interfere with the evidence? In the South African case of *Hlongwa* 1979 (4) SA 112 the court stated that it may, in appropriate circumstances, rely on the investigating officer's assertion that X was likely to tamper with evidence if he or she were to be released even if this assertion is unsupported by any direct evidence. On the other hand, in the case of *Hussey* 1991 (2) ZLR 187 (S) the

Supreme Court seems to have laid down that more is required than simply bald assertions by the State that X was likely to interfere with witnesses who may be called by the State. The assertion must be well grounded and the State is obliged to place cogent reasons before the court, supported by information to justify the assertion.

If X lives or works with the State witnesses there will be a greater likelihood of interference with witnesses.

State not opposing bail

Even if the prosecution does not oppose the granting of bail, the court still has "the duty to weigh up the personal interests of the accused against the interests of justice" and decide whether it is in the interests of justice to grant bail. [s 117(5) CPEA] The court can require the prosecutor to put on record the reasons for not opposing bail. [s 117A(4) CPEA]

Whether opposition by State to bail is decisive factor

In *Ndhlovu* 2001 (2) ZLR 261 (H), the court stated that the attitude of the Attorney-General is a relevant but not a decisive factor. His or her opinion commands respect because of his or her experience and the responsibility of his or her office, unless it is evident that he or she is no better informed than the court. However, his or her assertion cannot be substituted for the court's discretion.

The attitude of the police or prosecutor is not a decisive factor in the grant or refusal of bail. It was held to merely be a relevant consideration in *Mahata* v *Chigumira NO & Anor* HH-24-04. Accordingly, bail cannot merely be refused on the grounds that the state is opposed to it.

Invalid reasons for refusing

The seriousness of the offence is not in itself a reason to refuse bail: *Kanoda & Ors* HH-200-90; *Hussey* 1991 (2) ZLR 187 (S). The fact that the charge is a serious one and is prevalent, and would attract a lengthy prison term if X is found guilty, is only a factor to be considered together with other factors in deciding whether X should be kept in custody until his or her trial: *Hussey* 1991 (2) ZLR 187 (S).

It is not proper to refuse bail merely because a date has been set for trial, except in exceptional cases as, for instance, where the date of trial is a few days away and the release of X on bail would create transport or accommodation problems for him or her. *Chiadzwa* 1988 (2) ZLR 19 (S).

Fears for the safety of the accused because of the unlawful actions of a mob outside the court room, threatening to kill the accused, are not a ground to refuse to grant bail, particularly once the accused is removed from the area: *Bhebhe & Ors* HB-25-02.

Jointly charged accused

Where two or more persons have been jointly charged in one case, for the purposes of considering whether bail should be granted each case must be considered there is still an obligation to consider each individual case separately as well as treating the person as part of a group: *Mutambara & Ors* v *Minister of Home Affairs* 1989 (3) ZLR 96 (H).

Amount of bail

If bail is to be granted an excessive amount of bail must not be demanded: s 120 CPEA. If bail is set beyond the capacity of X to raise the amount, he or she will end up in custody and the granting of bail will have been a futile gesture; in effect a person is denied bail if bail is set well beyond his or her means to pay. In respect of persons with little or no financial means, bail can be set at a low level or a person can be released on his or her own recognizances, with or without further conditions, or he or she can be released subject to sureties being found, provided that there is a reasonable prospect of his or her finding such sureties. The magistrate must therefore investigate X's means and whether X has relations or other persons who would be prepared to pay the bail or stand surety for him or her.

Deposit of property or recognizance in respect of property

Instead of or in addition to cash bail, the court can order X to deposit property belonging to him or her enter into a recognizance in respect of property belonging to him or her. Thus, in *Aitken (2)* S-168-92 the court ordered that, in addition to cash bail, X enter into a recognizance in a certain amount against the security of a house registered in his or her name: s 131 and s 118 (1) CPEA.

Sureties

Bail may be taken from X or X and one or more sureties: s 118(1) CPEA. When bail is taken from sureties, it must be properly explained to them that if X defaults on his or her bail condition, they may have to pay the amount of money pledged in surety.

Conditions

Conditions may be added —

- requiring X to surrender all his or her travel documents;
- specifying that he or she report to the police or other authority at a specified place and at specified times;
- forbidding him or her from going to particular places;
- prohibiting him or her from communicating with prosecution witnesses;
- imposing other conditions as to his or her conduct, such as that he or she

places himself or herself under the care and supervision of a particular organisation: s 118(3) CPEA.

In imposing conditions, a magistrate must carefully consider the surrounding circumstances in order to give a reasonable ruling: In *Prior* HH-163-02, The appellant was charged with failing to vacate her farm, in respect of which an acquisition order had been made under s 8 of the Land Acquisition Act [*Chapter 20:10*]. She was granted bail, one of the conditions of which being that she should not return to the farm other than to collect her possessions. She appealed in respect of that condition. The court held that it was not reasonable to order that she should not return to her home. She was contesting the acquisition, and until that issue had been determined, she was entitled to exercise her rights of ownership. The section provided for eviction only after conviction; the bail condition effectively amounted to eviction before conviction. The condition would be altered to require her to reside at her home.

Once conditions are imposed, it is not permissible for the State to seek further conditions to those already imposed in the absence of further violations while on bail. In *Tsvangirai & Ors* 2003 (1) ZLR 618 (H), the accused were on trial on charges of treason. They had been granted bail, and had not breached any of the conditions. The State applied to have further conditions added. It alleged that the accused had indulged in activities which occurred after the grant of bail and which were unlawful and bordered on treason. No charges were being brought in respect of those alleged activities. It was held that the grant of bail is a consequence of the arrest and remand of an accused person on a specific charge. The nature of the offence charged and other relevant considerations are factors to be taken into account in determining the grant or refusal of bail and, where such bail is granted, the conditions to be attached to the recognizance. Any conditions attached to a recognizance must have some bearing to the offence of which the accused is charged, in particular the need to secure his or her attendance; to ensure that he or she does not interfere with the evidence and to ensure that he or she does not commit further offences whilst awaiting trial. The conditions added to the recognizance cannot refer to some other allegation that the accused person may possibly face in future and in respect of which he or she has not been charged. What the State wanted was to prevent the accused from conducting themselves unlawfully. It could not do so through conditions added to bail.

In another linked application, the court expressed the view that conditions should be imposed where these can dispense with State fears adequately. In *Tsvangirai* 2003 (1) ZLR 650 (H), the applicant, along with 2 others, was on trial on charges of treason. They had been granted bail, and had not breached any of the conditions. The State unsuccessfully applied to have further conditions added. That application was dismissed on the grounds that bail conditions cannot refer to some other allegation that the accused person may possibly face in future and in respect of which he has not been charged. The applicant was then arrested on a further charge of treason, based on statements he or she was alleged to have made, urging a mass stay-away as a means of removing the government from power. The State conceded that it had no reason to fear that the applicant would not stand trial or interfere with the evidence, but expressed apprehension that, if granted bail, the applicant was likely to commit or influence his or her supporters to commit similar crimes; that the applicant has a propensity to commit such crimes when out of custody. The court held that the fact that the applicant was facing other charges previously preferred against him and for which he had not been convicted was not by itself a reason for denying him bail. However, the State's fears that hemight commit similar crimes were not totally unfounded, but could be catered for by the imposition of appropriate conditions, something the court was empowered to do. Bail was granted on that basis.

Equal treatment of accused

In *Lotriet & Anor* 2001 (2) ZLR 225 (H), the applicants were granted bail by a magistrate but the Attorney-General's appeal against the grant of bail was upheld by the High Court, so they remained in custody. In a further application to the High Court it was revealed that an accomplice had been granted bail. The court granted their application on the basis of two fundamental principles: the right of the individual to liberty and the need for justice to be seen to be administered evenly. The judge commented that it was "vital that in the administration of justice there does not appear any form of discrimination, particularly in a matter where the liberty of a person is involved".

Cancellation and forfeiture of bail

If X breaches any of the conditions of his or her bail the judicial officer who admitted him or heror her to bail or the judicial officer before whom X is brought may declare the bail to be forfeited: s 133(a) CPEA.

Where X has failed to appear in court for trial (his or her name having been called three times both inside and outside the courtroom), the prosecutor may apply for a warrant of apprehension and for the forfeiture of X's bail and any recognizances that have been entered into: s 119 CPEA.

The court will usually refrain from ordering forfeiture of bail until X is arrested and brought before the court and asked to explain his or her default. The correct procedure is merely to issue a warrant for the apprehension of X. The court should only order forfeiture when, after hearing X's explanation, it is satisfied that the default was wilful or deliberate: *Sibanda* (1) 1980 ZLR 413 (GD). X's lawyer can appear at this hearing to explain why his or her client failed to appear in court for trial and to try to persuade the court not to order forfeiture of bail but instead to extend the previous bail and to set a new trial date. However, if the default of X was wilful the court *is obliged to order forfeiture of bail*: *Knight NO* v *van Tonder & Ors* 1962 R & N 405 (SR).

It is impermissible for the court to order both forfeiture of bail and the imposition of a fine for failure to appear in court. This amounts to punishing X twice for the same offence: *Sibanda (1)* 1980 ZLR 413 (GD).

Alteration of bail conditions

In *Musariri* HB-41-95, X had suggested that certain bail conditions which the State accepted, including undertaking to remain at his or her house except for necessary visits to the court or to doctors. Four weeks later, he sought a variation of the conditions saying that he was being subjected to virtual house arrest. Variation was refused.

Bail during trial

Bail generally comes to an end, unless expressly stipulated, once X pleads at the commencement of the trial. The court can, however, extend the bail for the period of the trial or grant fresh bail on new conditions.

Further applications for bail

A person may make more than one application for bail. The further application can be made either to the magistrate who heard the first application for bail or to another magistrate. Any further application for bail must, however, be based on facts which were not placed before the magistrate who heard the previous application: s 116(1)(c) proviso (ii) CPEA.

The passage of time since the last application for bail can be a new fact arising after the last application. See *Murambiwa* S-62-92 and *Aitken (2)* 1992 (2) ZLR 463 (S). The fact that the police have had sufficient time since the last application to investigate the case but have not been able to strengthen their case will be a factor which must be considered in the further application for bail. See *Murambiwa* and *Aitken (2)*. In *Stouyannides* 1992 (2) ZLR 126 (S), the court pointed out that where a considerable period of time has elapsed, the Attorney-General acts at his or her peril if he or she fails to put before the court specific facts strengthening the case over the period of time which has elapsed. This was confirmed *Barros & Ors* 2002 (2) ZLR 17 (H) where the judge held that a postponement of a trial is a change in circumstances entitling a court to reconsider the question of bail. Whether bail should in fact be granted will depend on the circumstances of the case in question, the length of the postponement and the nature of the charges.

If X previously had no money for bail but now has raised some, his or her lawyer can inform the court of this and request that bail now be granted.

Appeal against decision on bail by magistrate

Where X applies to a magistrate for bail, and the magistrate refuses his or her application, he or she is entitled to appeal against the refusal to a judge of the High Court: s 121(1)(b) CPEA as read with s 121(2)(b). If the magistrate grants his or her application, on the other hand, the Attorney-General or his or her representative has seven days within which to appeal against the decision to a judge of the High Court: s 121(1)(a) CPEA as read with s 121(2)(b). And the decision is suspended for seven days if, immediately after the decision, the Attorney-General or his or her representative announces that he or she wishes to appeal against it; and if he or she lodges his or her appeal within that seven-day period then the decision is suspended until the appeal has been decided: s 121(3) CPEA

Where a person applies for bail in the magistrates court and the application is refused he or she is only entitled to a single appeal against this decision to the High Court. Section 121(8) of the Criminal Procedure and Evidence Act had removed the right of the person concerned who had appealed to a judge of the High Court against the bail decision of a magistrate to take the judge's decision, subject to leave, on appeal to a judge of the Supreme Court.

In *Chiyangwa* v *AG & Ors* S-1-04 it was held that there is only one appeal against the grant or refusal of bail by a judge or magistrate, no matter which party appeals. If a magistrate refuses bail and a judge of the High Court grants bail on appeal by the accused, that is the end of the matter. The Attorney-General has no right of appeal to the Supreme Court. See also *A-G* v *Lotriet & Ors* 2001 (2) ZLR 168 (H).

However, an exception arises in respect of currency offences, as in the case of *Attorney-General* v *Fundira* S-33-04. In that case, the respondent, who was charged with currency offences, had been granted bail in the High Court. The Attorney-General immediately announced his or her intention of appealing and applied for leave to appeal. The judge refused leave, and within two days the Attorney-General applied to the Supreme Court for leave to appeal. The respondent argued that as the Attorney-General had not noted an appeal within 7 days, there was no appeal before the court and the respondent should be released. It was held no appeal lies to the Supreme Court from an order of a High Court judge sitting as an appeal judge in a bail application. However, there is an exception in respect of persons charged with currency offences: applications for bail in respect of those offences can commence in the magistrate's court, then proceed to the High Court and thereafter to the Supreme Court. No party is relieved of the requirement to obtain leave to appeal in a bail application, where the appeal is against the decision of a judge of the High Court. The Attorney-General's application, within 7 days, for leave to appeal constituted compliance with s 121 of the Criminal Procedure and Evidence Act. It cannot have been the intention of the legislature to require the Attorney-General to file the notice of appeal at a time when it was legally not possible to file such a notice of appeal, by reason of awaiting the outcome of his or her application for leave to appeal.

Where bail has been granted by a magistrate, and the state appeals, the High Court cannot substitute its own discretion for that of the magistrate in the absence of misdirection or irregularity: *A-G* v *Ruturi* HH-26-03. When there is an appeal against a decision to admit a person to bail, that decision should not be set aside unless there are compelling reasons to do so.

Bail pending appeal and review

This is dealt with under "Appeals and Reviews" in this Handbook.

Use of evidence in bail cases

In the South African case of *Adams en Andere* 1993 (1) SACR 611 (C), the court said that the evidence in a bail application is admissible against X in his or her subsequent trial.

For a number of criminal offences magistrates may now only grant bail if the Attorney-General has given his or her consent.

In respect of the criminal offences for which magistrates may grant bail without the consent of the Attorney-General magistrates must balance the interests of unconvicted persons against the interests of justice. They should, however, lean in favour of liberty where there is little or no danger of prejudicing the interests of justice by releasing the persons before they are tried.

Confirmation of Statements made by Accused to Police

Reid-Rowland 20-9 – 20-12

Purpose of confirmation proceedings

In terms of s 113 CPEA, an accused person may be brought before a magistrate for the purpose of having a statement made by him or her confirmed. It is not mandatory that there be confirmation of the statement. Statements include confessions. Also encompassed are statements made to the police while X is pointing out things or making indications and statements made on the way to the location where indications are to be made. This is the case despite the fact that the indications themselves are admissible in terms of s 258(2) CPEA: *Ndlovu* 1988 (2) ZLR 465 (S); *Jana* S-172-88.

The confirmation procedure was introduced to cut down on the number of trials within trials consequent upon challenges in court by accused to the admissibility of their confessions. The purpose of the confirmation proceedings is to give X the chance to object to the manner in which a statement was extracted from him.

The intention is that an accused person should be brought before a magistrate as soon as possible so that if he or she alleges ill-treatment, the magistrate can make a note of any visible injuries and order a medical examination where appropriate.

Once a statement has been properly confirmed, it becomes far more difficult to challenge the admissibility of that statement. This is because the onus is then placed on the defence to prove, on a balance of probabilities, that despite its confirmation the statement was not made by X or that it was not made freely and voluntarily and without undue influence: s 256(2) CPEA.

On the other hand, if the police have not had the statement confirmed or the magistrate refuses to confirm it because X has alleged that it was not made freely and voluntarily, the onus will then rest on the State to prove beyond reasonable doubt that the statement was made freely and voluntarily and without undue influence.

Role of magistrate

The role of the magistrate at such a hearing is essentially an investigatory one: *Attorney-General* v *Slatter & Ors* 1984 (1) ZLR 306 (S). There must be a thorough enquiry into all salient matters: *Munukwa & Ors* 1982 (1) ZLR 30. This includes looking into whether X's wish to have access to his or her legal representative is being improperly frustrated: *Attorney-General* v *Slatter & Ors* 1984 (1) ZLR 306 (S). The magistrate asked to confirm the statement must take the utmost care to ensure, through the official court interpreter, that the English translation of statements made in the vernacular in fact represents what X actually said, and the magistrate should record that he or she has satisfied himself about this fact: *Ndhlovu* 1981 ZLR 618 (S).

If he or she accepts that the statement was made by X and that it was made freely and voluntarily and without undue influence, the magistrate then confirms it and if X challenges that statement at his or her trial the onus is upon him or her to prove its inadmissibility.

At the confirmation proceedings, the magistrate must investigate carefully whether X did make the statement and made it on a free and voluntary basis and without undue influence.

Statements not made freely and voluntarily

A confession or a statement made by X is admissible in terms of s 256 (1) CPEA if it is "freely and voluntarily made by X without his or her having been unduly influenced thereto".

The statement will not have been made freely and voluntarily and without undue influence if X made the statement because he or she:

- was tortured, beaten up or physically maltreated in some other way, such as by being deprived of sleep or food and drink for long periods in order to force him or herto confess;
- was threatened with death or with torture or physical brutality unless he or she made the statement;
- was told that dire consequences would occur to members of his or her family unless he or she made the statement;
- was offered some benefit or advantage if he or she confessed to the crime,

such as that he or she would be released from custody as soon as he or she confessed or that if he or she confessed he or she would receive only a light sentence such as a fine;

- had been kept in solitary confinement for a long period and no one had been allowed to visit him or her and he or she confessed simply because he or she could no longer bear this isolation;
- he or she had been denied access to his or her lawyer after requesting access to him or her and had been pressured into making a statement in the absence of his or her lawyer;
- had been subjected to such intensive, hostile and prolonged questioning that his or her freedom of volition had been overborne as a result of this psychological pressure.

See *Ananias* 1963 RN 938 (SR); *Hlupe* 1964 RLR 333 (GD); *Murambiwa* 1952 SR 271 (SR); *Michael & Anor* 1962 R&N 374; *Dube* 1965 RLR 177 (RA); *Hackwell* 1965 RLR 1 (RA); *Edward* 1966 (2) SA 359 (R); *Mfungelwa* 1967 RLR 308; *Schaube-Kuffler* 1969 (1) RLR 78 (A); *Attorney-General* v *Slatter & Ors* 1984 (1) ZLR 306 (S); *Mthombeni* S-80-90; *Nkomo & Anor* 1989 (2) ZLR 117 (S); *Jana* S-172-88; *Ndlovu* 1988 (2) ZLR 465 (S).

The reason why such evidence is not admissible is that the contents of a statement made in these circumstances will be highly unreliable.

In *Woods & Ors* 1993 (2) ZLR 258 (S), the court ruled that the wilful denial of proper access to a legal practitioner may render inadmissible any statements made before a person has consulted with his or her lawyer. If accused are denied access to their lawyers confirmation proceedings are vitiated.

Procedure for confirmation

The procedure at confirmation proceedings is as follows:

- The prosecutor produces the statement by handing it to the magistrate and informing the magistrate of when, where and to whom it was made.
- The statement is then read over to X and he or she is informed of when, where and to whom he or she made the statement. The magistrate will then ask X whether he or she admits making the statement and making it freely and voluntarily and without being subject to undue influence.
- The magistrate must explain to X that if he or she admits that he or she freely made the statement, or refuses to answer the question whether he or she freely made it, the statement will be confirmed and then can be admitted in evidence at his or her trial on mere production.

- If X then admits that he or she freely made the statement or refuses to say whether he or she so made the statement, the magistrate will proceed to confirm it.
- If X denies he or she made it or alleges it was not freely made, the magistrate will then ask him or her to give sufficient facts to back up his or her denial or his or her allegation of duress or undue influence and, where it is reasonably possible for him or her to do so, to identify those who applied the undue pressure on him or her. The magistrate must also tell X that if he or she fails to mention any facts salient to his or her allegations concerning the making of the statement, adverse inferences may be drawn from this failure when the admissibility of his or her statement is being dealt with at his or her trial.
- If X alleges that he or she has been subjected to physical ill-treatment to extract a confession, the magistrate must note and record any signs of injuries which X says were the result of physical mistreatment by the police. The magistrate also has power to order an immediate medical examination of X. This power should usually be invoked in these circumstances in order that any evidence of ill-treatment can be detected by a medical expert.
- The magistrate also has the power to order such other investigations as he or she considers to be necessary or desirable in the circumstances.
- If X says anything in his or her replies to questions which imply that there has been some inducement to make the statement which is the subject of the confirmation proceedings, the magistrate must attempt to clarify the position and must not confirm the statement until he or she has done so: *Slatter & Ors* 1983 ZLR 144 (H).
- The magistrate should also be on the lookout for suspicious factors which may point in the direction of undue pressure having been applied, such as that an appreciable amount of time has elapsed between the recording and signing of a confession and the bringing of X to have his or her statement confirmed. If X has alleged he or she was tortured to extract a confession and confirmation has been sought a long time after the statement was made, this may suggest that this time lapse was to allow signs of injury to disappear.
- If X indicates that parts of his or her statement were not freely and voluntarily made, the magistrate should decline to confirm the whole statement. It is not proper to confirm some parts and to decline to confirm the parts which X has said were not freely and voluntarily made: *Munukwa & Ors* 1982 (1) ZLR 30 (S).
- During these proceedings, the magistrate must ensure that the police investigating officer and his or her colleagues remain outside the courtroom and that they are far away enough from the courtroom so they cannot hear what is being said inside the courtroom.

- The proceedings must be held *in camera* and the investigating officer must not be present in court.
- The procedure does not entail getting the investigating officer to take the oath and getting him or her to tell the court that he or she wants the statement confirmed and testifying that accused gave statement freely and voluntarily.
- The statement is merely handed over to the magistrate in court and proceedings are held *in camera* and the recording detail is not called to give evidence.
- If the statement was made in the vernacular and then translated into English, the official court interpreter could be asked to check the accuracy of the translation.
- After the confirmation proceedings X — if he or she is not granted bail — should be remanded to a prison rather than returned to the custody of the police: *Munukwa & Ors* 1982 (1) ZLR 30 (S).

If these procedures are not strictly adhered to the confirmation proceedings will be invalid. In *Slatter & Ors* 1983 (2) ZLR 144 (H), it was laid down that denying X access to his or her lawyer violates the constitutional rights of X and constitutes undue influence upon him. If X is denied access to his or her lawyer before or during the confirmation proceedings, the confirmation proceedings will be rendered invalid and the onus would revert to the State to prove that the statements were made freely and voluntarily. This would even apply where relatives of a person in police custody had instructed the lawyer without X being aware of this and the lawyer is prevented from seeing the person concerned subsequently.

In many cases the defence lawyer will only be brought in at a stage when his or her client has already made an incriminatory statement to the police and the statement has already been confirmed before a magistrate. It may still, however, be possible to challenge the admissibility of the incriminatory statement at the trial. If the defence can establish that the confirmation proceedings were improperly conducted, the proceedings will be ruled to be invalid and the statement will be treated as if it had not been confirmed. Where the defence challenges the validity of the confirmation proceedings, as opposed to challenging the admissibility of the confirmed statement, the State bears the onus of proving beyond a reasonable doubt that the proceedings were properly conducted.

Even if the confirmation proceedings were properly conducted, the admissibility of the statement can still be challenged either on the basis that the original statement was not made freely and voluntarily without undue influence or on the basis that the statement was not made at all by X and the statement is not true. The onus lies on the defence to prove, on a balance of probability, the inadmissibility of a confirmed statement. In determining the admissibility of a statement the court may draw adverse inferences from X's failure to mention facts at the confirmation proceedings which in the circumstances he or she could reasonably have been expected to have mentioned: s 115 CPEA. Any failure of X to tell the magistrate about the undue pressure applied to him or her to force him or her to make the statement would therefore have to be explained. The reason for X's failure may have been that he or she was threatened with further violence by the police when he or she was returned to their custody if he or she did not tell the magistrate that he or she had made the statement freely and voluntarily.

Statements by juveniles

The magistrate should check to see whether the juveniles had access to their parents or guardians before they made the statements. See *Kondile & Anor* 1995 (1) SACR 394 (SEC).

Partial admission by accused

If X indicates that parts of his or her statement were not freely and voluntarily made, the magistrate should decline to confirm the statement. It is not proper to confirm some parts and decline to confirm the parts which X has said were not freely and voluntarily made: *Munukwa & Ors* 1982 (1) ZLR 30 (S).

A statement must only be confirmed if the magistrate is satisfied that it was made by X and was made freely and voluntarily. If X denies that he or she made it or refuses to say whether he or she made it or asserts that the statement or portions thereof was not made freely and voluntarily it must not be confirmed. In this latter event, X must be asked why he or she is saying these things and the magistrate may order that there be further investigations into these allegations.

Legal Aid

Section 10 of the Legal Aid Act [*Chapter 7:16*] provides for the provision of legal aid in certain criminal cases. Where a magistrate believes that it is in the interests of justice that an accused person be provided with legal aid and that person may have insufficient financial means to engage his or her own lawyer, he or she can recommend to the Director of the Legal Aid Directorate that the person should be provided with legal aid. He or she will decide whether to provide legal aid to such person after assessing that person's financial means.

If X makes application for free legal assistance to be provided to him, the magistrate will have to decide whether it is desirable in the interests of justice that X be legally represented at his or her trial. In deciding this matter, the criteria set out in the case of *Dube & Anor* 1988 (2) ZLR 385 (S) must be satisfied. These criteria are listed below in the section dealing with the trial stage under the heading of "Legal representation".

Mental unfitness of accused in custody

Reid-Rowland 12-5

Where an accused is mentally unfit to stand trial he or she must be dealt with under the Mental Health Act [*Chapter 15:06*]. The important sections are ss 26 and 27.

In terms of s 27(1) of the Mental Health Act if it appears that a person being held in custody pending trial is mentally disordered or defective, the Attorney-General or the person in charge of the place of detention (which may be a police station or a prison) must report this without delay to a magistrate of the province in which the place of detention is situated.

The procedures to be followed in this sort of case are set out in subsections (2), (3), (4) and (5) of s 27.

In the Chief Magistrate's Circular No. 9 of 1984 it is suggested that in this sort of case the magistrate should request the prosecutor, as soon as possible, to obtain copies from the police docket of the witness statements as to X's conduct at the time of the crime, and where necessary, any further information about his or her mental condition from relatives and associates. The case should be remanded. The circular says that on receipt of the information if it appears that X may be mentally disordered, arrangements should be made through the police or prisons for the requisite medical examination to be undertaken as required by the Mental Health Act.

Section 27 actually requires that, within twenty-four hours of receipt of a report, the magistrate must direct that the medical examination take place.

Two medical practitioners (or if only one is available the second examination can be done by a psychiatric nurse practitioner) must state in writing their opinion as to the mental condition of the prisoner. (See the Mental Health Regulations RGN 792 of 1977.) Based on this opinion the magistrate must then decide what to do with the person concerned. If such person is considered to be unfit to stand trial because he or she is mentally disordered or defective he or she will be committed to a mental institution until he or she has recovered. After recovery he or she can then be put on trial: s 30 of the Mental Health Act.

There are special provisions relating to petty cases. A petty case is one in which the judicial officer considers that the charge will not merit imprisonment without the option of a fine or a fine of over level 3.

If after consideration of medical certificate and any other inquiry that he or she thinks fit to make, a magistrate or other judicial officer is satisfied that X is mentally disordered and would not be able to understand the nature of any criminal proceedings or properly to conduct his or her defence, he or she must order that:

- X submit himself or herself to examination or treatment at a specified institution; or
- X's spouse, guardian or close relative to apply for a civil detention order;

and may give such directions for X's release from custody or continued detention or transfer to any institution or other place as he or she considers necessary to ensure that X receives appropriate treatment.

Often persons who are mentally unfit to stand trial may also have been mentally disordered or defective when they committed the crime. It is therefore useful and saves time if the doctors consider whether X is likely to have been mentally disordered or defective at the time that the offence was committed. This may save having to have a further medical investigation after X has recovered. If the doctors say that this person was mentally disordered or defective at the time of the offence it would seem that there is little point in putting him or heron trial after his or her recovery. If he or she were to be tried, a special verdict would be returned under the Mental Health Act. He or she would then have to be sent to a mental institution despite the fact that he or she has already been in a mental institution and he or she has recovered from his or her mental condition.

As regards the procedure for dealing with accused persons who display signs of being mentally disordered after the trial commences, see later under "Trials Mental unfitness of accused to stand trial".

See Appendix for samples of various Mental Health Act forms.

Section 3

Trial

Crimes committed extra- territorially

Section 5 of CLCA provides that a court can try any crime either in terms of CLCA or any other enactment if the crime or an essential element of the crime was committed:

- wholly inside Zimbabwe;
- partly outside Zimbabwe if the conduct that completed the crime took place inside Zimbabwe;
- wholly or partly outside Zimbabwe if the crime is a crime against the public security in Zimbabwe or against the safety of the State of Zimbabwe or the crime has produced or was intended to produce a harmful effect in Zimbabwe or the accused realized there was a real risk that it might produce such an effect.

Section 5(2) provides that any other enactment providing for extra-territorial effect will continue to apply. For instance, there are various offences under the Exchange Control Act [*Chapter 22:05*] which can be committed extraterritorially.

For the position under the common law, see *Mharapara* 1985 (2) ZLR 211 (S) and *Kapurira* S-110-92.

Accused illegally brought into jurisdiction

This a complex issue. If this issue arises in a case in the magistrates court, the magistrate should refer to case of *Beahan* 1991 (2) ZLR 98 (S) where this matter is dealt with. If X has been kidnapped from the foreign State, thereby violating the sovereignty of that State, jurisdiction will not be assured. But the court will have jurisdiction if X is surrendered by the foreign State in contravention of the municipal law of the State of refuge.

Bias of judicial officer

Every accused person has the right to a fair trial by an impartial judicial officer. If the judicial officer is biased or there is a reasonable suspicion that he or she will be biased, the defence lawyer has a duty to raise this matter and to request that the magistrate recuse himself or herself. The tests for bias on the part of a judicial officer are objective: whether, as a matter of fact, there is a real possibility of bias, or whether there is a reasonable belief that a real likelihood of bias exists. In either case the party seeking recusal must show a reasonable fear, based on objective grounds, that the trial will not be impartial: *Standard Chartered Finance Zimbabwe Ltd* v *Georgias & Anor* 1998 (2) ZLR 547 (H).

Before making an application for a judicial officer's recusal, the legal practitioner must satisfy himself or herself that there are well-founded grounds for applying for the recusal of the judicial officer concerned. The legal practitioner must not simply base the application on what he or she has been told by his or her client without checking this information. Thus in the case of *Muzana & Ors* S-105-89, the Supreme Court severely censured a defence lawyer who had made serious allegations of partiality and bias on the part of a magistrate in an effort to get him or herto recuse himself. He or she had simply repeated his or her client's assertions without having made any effort to check whether there were any facts to substantiate these allegations. In the case of *S C Shaw (Pvt) Ltd* v *Minister of Lands* S-32-05 the lawyer representing a client who was challenging the validity of compulsory acquisition of land alleged that the acceptance of offers of land by judges prior to the determination of the validity of the acquisition of the land, together with improper pressures brought to bear on judges by members of the government and cabinet, was not compatible with constitutional concept of a fair trial before an independent tribunal. No evidence was submitted in support of this allegation. It was held that courts in Zimbabwe have a responsibility to protect their dignity. Where legal practitioners, who are officers of the court, and as such, are expected to know better, make irresponsible submissions scandalizing the court mere admonition is inadequate and action should be taken to punish such legal practitioners for contempt of court.

An application for the recusal of a judicial officer must be made respectfully and tactfully. The judicial officer should where possible be informed of the application and the grounds for it before it is made. This can be done by going to see the judicial officer in his or her chambers, together with the prosecutor, and telling him or her why it is felt he or she should recuse himself or herself. This will enable the judicial officer to consider the question in private and to avoid the possible embarrassment of an application being made in open court.

For the public to have confidence in the administration of justice, it is essential that the courts are seen to be fair and impartial. A judicial officer should therefore not try a case if X or the complainant is his or her friend or enemy or is his or her relative So too he or she should not try a case involving his or her wife's or her husband's mother or the spouse of one of his or her long standing and trusted court officials.

If the prosecutor wrongly discloses the previous convictions to the magistrate during the course of the trial, the judicial officer is obliged to recuse himself or herself. If he or she does not do so, the defence lawyer should request that he or she recuse himself or herself.

The conduct of a judicial officer during the course of the trial can lead to a reasonable apprehension of bias. Judicial officers who are presiding over criminal cases must not descend into the arena in the sense that they must not intervene during the course of trials in such a manner or to such an extent as to lead to an inference of lack of impartiality and open-mindedness. They are entitled to ask questions of witnesses in order to clarify the evidence, but they must refrain from bombarding them with questions to such an extent that they are disconcerted. If magistrates take over the role of examining or cross-examining witnesses they will not be able objectively to adjudicate on the evidence. They should not engage in questioning in way that gives the appearance that they are displaying bias in favour of prosecution. In *Jesse* v *Pratt & Anor* 2001 (1) ZLR 48 (H), it was held that the conduct of the magistrate towards the applicant throughout the trial was such that a fair trial of the applicant was impossible in her court. Apart from a number of irregularities, there were numerous indications of biased and irrational conduct on the part of the magistrate, all of which showed that the applicant would have reasonable grounds to suppose that he might be disadvantaged in the trial by reason of bias or prejudice actuating her.

In *Masedza* 1998 (1) ZLR 36 (H), the applicants were being prosecuted for a criminal offence in the magistrates court. During an adjournment of the proceedings, the applicants became aware of certain facts and, based on these facts, they applied for the recusal of the presiding magistrate. The magistrate refused the application. The trial was postponed to enable the magistrate's decision to be taken on review. The applicants applied to the High Court for an order stopping the criminal proceedings in the magistrates court, pending a review of the decision in relation to the application for recusal. The High Court held that if in the present case the application for recusal had been well founded, the court would have been prepared to grant an order stopping the trial pending review, as no purpose would have been served by putting accused through motions of a trial that would have been abortive. If there had been a reasonable apprehension of bias then justice will have failed and it might not be attained by other means. However, it found that the grounds upon which recusal was requested did not give rise to a reasonable apprehension of bias and thus the application for stopping the criminal proceedings failed.

If a magistrate has to recuse himself during the course of the trial, the case cannot be taken over from that stage by another magistrate. The case will have to start *de novo* before a different magistrate. If, however, a magistrate recuses himself after he or she has convicted X, the case can be referred to a different magistrate for sentence: *Moyo & Ors* HB-211-87.

Securing attendance of accused

Reid-Rowland Chapter 5

If an accused person is in custody, he or she will simply be brought to court on the date which has been set down for his or her trial.

If X is out of custody, his or her attendance at his or her trial can be brought about in a number of ways.

- he or she can be summonsed to appear (s 140 CPEA);
- he or she can be warned by a magistrate to appear on a particular date, time and place to answer the charge (s 142 CPEA);
- if a peace officer to on reasonable grounds that a magistrates court on conviction will not impose a fine more than level 3, he or she can give written notice to the person to appear in court at the date, time and place specified by the police to answer the charge and he or she will then be released: s 141 CPEA;
- he or she may, instead of paying a deposit fine assessed by the police in terms of s 132(1) CPEA, appear in court at the date, time and place specified by the police in the deposit fine form to answer the charge.

A person who fails to appear in court after receiving a deposit fine form can be treated in the same way as a person who fails to obey a summons.

If he or she fails to comply with a summons which has been properly served upon him, the prosecutor can request that a warrant for arrest be issued against him or herand when he or she is brought to court he or she can be fined up to level 3 or can be imprisoned for up to one month or both such penalties can be imposed: s 140(4) CPEA. This fine, however, must be imposed when he or she is brought before the magistrate. It cannot be imposed some time afterwards: *Ncube* HH-174-83; *Knight NO* v *van Tonder* 1962 R&N 405 (SR).

In *Dietrichson* v *Resident Provincial Magistrate Hwange & Anor* HB-35-95, the applicant was remanded by a magistrate to stand trial at Binga on a certain date; he or she protested that he or she could not attend on that day, in vain. He or she asked a lawyer to deal with the case; his or her lawyer arranged with the Senior Public Prosecutor for the case to be reconsidered, then set down for another day if necessary, excusing applicant on the remand date. The SPP did not advise the court so a warrant of arrest was issued and applicant came before the court and was fined $200.

He or she took the decision on review, alleging gross irregularity in rejecting his or her explanation, and no jurisdiction to impose that fine. The magistrate claimed he or she acted under s 71(3) MCA, but this was only applicable when a person defies an order given in terms of that Act, whereas the remand was an order given under CPEA. The section should also only be used for disobedience or neglect to obey an order when actually appearing before the court. The fine was set aside.

The magistrate actively opposed the review application and was ordered to pay the costs personally. The Minister (second respondent) did not oppose the application, merely the claim for costs. His or her Ministry employed the magistrate but could have no control over him or her in the exercise of his or her judicial functions: there should be no award of costs against him.

If the person who failed to appear is out on bail, when he or she is brought before the magistrate after being arrested, the magistrate will order the forfeiture of his or her bail if the default was wilful or deliberate. (See under "Bail" above.)

It is impermissible both to fine and to order forfeiture of bail as this would amount to punishing a person twice for one offence: *Sibanda* (1*)* 1980 ZLR 413 (GD).

On how the magistrate should deal with a situation where X is present but refuses to participate in his or her trial see *Mupatsi* HH-40-98. Here a case had been remanded on a number of occasions. When the case came next to court, the State wanted the trial to commence. X asked for a further postponement of the case because he or she said he or she had not prepared his or her defence as he or she had been unaware that the trial was going to commence on that day. The prosecutor maintained that it had been made clear to X at the previous remand hearing that the trial would commence on the next occasion X came to court. The magistrate refused to allow a postponement, taking the view that X's request for time to prepare was not genuine but that he or she was simply trying to obstruct the proceedings because he or she had no defence to offer. She ordered the trial to commence. X refused to participate in the proceedings. He or she refused to give a defence outline. During the proceedings, he or she would walk out of the dock and go to sit outside the courtroom. The State witnesses were nonetheless called to gave evidence in the absence of X and thus without any cross-examination from X.

On review, the court found that the proceedings were entirely irregular and had to be set aside. In terms of the s 18(3) of the Constitution, a person charged with a criminal offence has a right to be present at his or her trial unless he or she behaves in such a way that the proceedings cannot continue unless he or she is excluded. Although X had behaved in a contumelious way, he or she had not behaved in such a way as to warrant ejecting him or her from the court. In any event, he or she had not been ejected. For the magistrate to have permitted the charade of a trial in X's self imposed absence was improper and undignified and made a mockery of the judicial process. What the magistrate should have done was to have ordered X to be arrested and brought him or her before the court and if appropriate, to have punished him or her for contempt of court. Only if he or she had then disrupted proceedings, the magistrate would, after due warning, have been justified in having him or her removed from court and continuing with the trial in his or her absence.

Trial in absence of accused

Section 18(3) of the Constitution requires that criminal trials be held in the presence of X unless he or she consents or so conducts himself as to render the continuation of the proceedings in his or her presence impracticable.

The CPEA provides for two exceptional circumstances in which the court may proceed with the trial in the absence of X. These two exceptions are dealt with in Chapter 10 of the *Prosecutors Handbook* and in Reid-Rowland's Criminal Procedure in Zimbabwe at 16-25 – 16-27.

The first exception is provided for in s 194(1) CPEA. This applies where X so conducts himself as to make the continuation of the proceedings in his or her presence impracticable. This provision must be very sparingly invoked, especially where X is not legally represented. X must have continued to disrupt the proceedings by acting in a particularly outrageous fashion, despite being ordered to desist from such misbehaviour, before the court can resort to ordering his or her removal and exercise the discretion to continue with the trial in his or her absence. Often the outrageous behaviour will suggest mental disorder on the part of X, in which case his or her mental fitness to stand trial at all will be cast in doubt. In these circumstances, the judge must deal with the matter by ordering a psychiatric examination of X in terms of the Mental Health Act.

The second exception is provided for in s 357(1) & (2) CPEA which allows proceedings to be conducted in X's absence if:

- he or she fails to appear on the trial day after having been properly summoned to appear;
- the offence with which he or she has been charged is a petty one for which the punishment is a fine, with imprisonment being imposable only as an alternative to the fine; and
- the court is satisfied that the ends of justice will be met if the trial is heard in the absence of X.

As regards the first of these requirements, the judge would have to see the return of service to ensure that the summons had been properly served.

Section 357(2) CPEA was relied upon in *Kamanga* HH-134-91. X had failed to appear in court after receiving a warning to appear in connection with a traffic ticket. The High Court said that in such a case the trial could go ahead without X. The court must, however, hear the evidence before convicting. It must be established that there is a *prima facie* case. The court does not have to speculate on the possible defences to the charge as X's failure to appear will give rise to the inference that he or she has no defence to offer.

In the case of *Mupatsi* 1998 (1) ZLR 224 (H), the court pointed out that there are very few provisions of the law which permit a trial, or any part of it, to be conducted in the accused's absence. One is the reception of evidence on commission in the absence of the accused in certain circumstances and with his or her consent. The second is the payment by a person admitting guilt of a deposit fine in lieu of an appearance in court. Again, this is predicated on the accused's consent and scarcely qualifies as a trial in his or her absence. The third is the adjudication of minor offences, for which a fine only is prescribed, in the absence of the accused and with his or her consent. In this case, X, on arraignment, said he or she was not ready for trial and requested a two week postponement. This was refused on the grounds that there had been previous postponements and the accused had been told that the next appearance would be for trial. X denied that he or she had been told that this was to be his or her trial date, and left the dock. The magistrate ordered the trial to continue, although for most of it X was outside the court room. The magistrate convicted the accused. The High Court held that to conduct the trial in the absence of X was in these circumstances a fatal irregularity. By permitting the trial to proceed in the way it did, the magistrate allowed the proceedings to degenerate into low farce. The correct course would have been for the magistrate to have X arrested and brought before the court and then to have considered whether a sanction for contempt of court was appropriate. Only if X then conducted himself in a way practically disruptive of the proceedings would the magistrate have been justified, after due warning, in causing his or her removal from court and the continuation of the trial. The matter was remitted for trial *de novo*.

In *Weinberg* 1993 (2) ZLR 448 (H), the court ruled that, in a criminal case X may appear through a lawyer instead of personally in terms of s 357(1) CPEA only if the penalty prescribed is a fine or in default of payment imprisonment. Whenever the law permits imprisonment without the option of a fine for that offence, the section cannot be used. A conviction of a foreigner in hisabsence for contravening the Road Traffic Act was incompetent.

If the court proceeds with the trial where X has failed to obey the summons, it would then be inappropriate to issue a warrant for the arrest of X in terms of s 140(4) CPEA as the purpose of this section is to bring X before the court to explain his or her default.

The constitutionality of the provision allowing for the trial to proceed when X has failed to obey a summons is, however, open to doubt. This exception is not provided for in the constitution. See 1992 Vol. 4 No. 3 *Legal Forum* 29.

Mental unfitness of accused to stand trial

Reid-Rowland 15-2

In terms of s 192 CPEA, if at any time after the commencement of a criminal trial it is alleged or it appears that X is not of sound mind, the case must be dealt with under the Mental Health Act [*Chapter 15:06*]. If at any stage during the proceedings the behaviour of X is such as to suggest that he or she may be mentally disordered or defective, the judge must order a medical examination of X to determine whether he or she is fit to stand trial.

Section 27 of the Mental Health Act sets out what is to be done in such a case. The judge should adjourn the proceedings for up to fourteen days and direct that X be medically examined by two doctors, or by a doctor and by a psychiatric nurse practitioner if only one doctor is available.

After the judge has heard this medical evidence and any other evidence he or she thinks fit, or she will make his or her finding. If he or she considers that X would be unable to understand the nature of the proceedings or to conduct his or her defence properly because of some mental disorder or defect, he or she will issue an order directing that X be removed to a mental institution for treatment.

When X has recovered, he or she can then be made to stand trial.

There are special provisions relating to petty cases. A petty case is one in which the judicial officer considers that the charge will not merit imprisonment without the option of a fine or a fine over level 3.

Where a person is appearing before a magistrate on a petty charge the magistrate may stop the proceedings and order that —

- X submit himself to examination or treatment at a specified institution; or
- that person's guardian, spouse or close relative make application for his or her examination and possible treatment in an institution; or
- two medical practitioners shall certify what the mental state of A is, provided that if only one medical practitioner is available, he or she may direct a psychiatric nurse practitioner to examine A and provide the second opinion required.

As regards accused persons who are deaf or dumb or both deaf and dumb, such persons may be perfectly competent mentally but, in order to stand trial, interpreters who can communicate properly with them in sign language would have to be brought in so that they can fully understand the proceedings.

In terms of s 193 CPEA, if the court is satisfied on the evidence that it is necessary for the deaf or dumb or deaf and dumb accused to be kept in custody to protect the public or X himself or herself, the court may order that he or she be kept in custody in an ordinary prison. There would have to be compelling reasons for such a drastic step to be taken. If the reason for such an order is evidence of mental disturbance then the case should be dealt with in terms of the Mental Health Act.

Juvenile accused

Reid-Rowland 13-2 – 13-3

It is provided in s 142(5) CPEA that unless the magistrate otherwise directs, when the police arrest a person under the age of 18 in order to bring him or her to court on a criminal charge or warn him or her to appear before the court to answer a charge, they must also warn the parents or guardian, if they can be located, to attend court when the juvenile appears. It is obviously important that with juvenile offenders (especially those between seven and fourteen) the court should, wherever possible, hear from the parents or guardian as to the domestic circumstances of X and other salient matters.

A child under the age of seven may not be tried for a criminal offence as such a child is irrebuttably presumed to be incapable of committing a crime; he or she is deemed to be *doli incapax*, that is, incapable of forming the required criminal intention.

A child between the ages of seven and fourteen can be prosecuted provided that the Attorney-General has given his or her consent to the prosecution: *Eva* 1967 (1) RLR 113 (GD). However, such a child is rebuttably presumed to be devoid of the capacity to commit a crime and the State must prove that the child in question was sufficiently mature to understand and that he or she did understand the wrongfulness of his or her conduct. If the State rebuts this presumption it must then prove that the essential elements of the crime were present. In the case of *F* 1988 (1) ZLR 327 (H), the magistrate convicted a ten-year-old boy of indecent assault on an eight-year-old girl. The magistrate failed to examine whether the child had the requisite capacity. X was prosecuted despite the fact that a probation officer had stated that both X and the complainant were too young to appreciate either the wrongfulness of what they were doing or to understand criminal proceedings. The conviction was set aside, after the review judge severely criticised both the prosecutor and the trial magistrate.

Joint trials

Reid-Rowland 15-3

Where persons are implicated in the same offence they may be tried together: s 158 CPEA. Thus where a number of persons commit a crime they can be tried together; accomplices can be tried with the principal offender; and accessories after the fact can be tried with the principal offender.

In *Ismail* S-52-94, it was pointed out that s 190 CPEA gives a judicial officer the discretion, at any time during the course of a trial, to separate the trials of two or more persons appearing before him or heron a joint charge. The discretion must be exercised judicially and an appeal court will interfere only if it is shown that its exercise resulted in a miscarriage of justice. A further requirement of s 190 is that the exercise of the trial court's discretion should be pre-conditioned on an application for separation being made by either the prosecutor or X. A court does not fall into error if, without invocation, it does not *mero motu* separate the trials of accused persons jointly charged.

There is no rule of law that separate trials should be ordered where an essential part of one accused person's defence amounts to an attack on a co-accused, but the matter is one which the judicial officer should take into account in determining an application for separation.

In *Donaldson & Anor* S-5-95, two persons were charged in separate indictments for separate crimes with contravening the same section of an Act. They were represented by the same lawyer and each admitted committing the crime at the same date and place and were tried jointly. On appeal, it was held that the proceedings were a nullity. There was no provision in the Criminal Procedure and Evidence Act allowing for the joint trial of persons separately charged with different offences, even if there were some common features. The Act allows for the joint trial of any number of participants in the same offence, although committed at different times. It also allows for the joint trial of persons who have committed separate offences, provided that the accused are jointly charged and that the prosecutor informs the court that, in his or her opinion, evidence at the trial of one accused would be admissible as evidence at the trial of the other. Neither requirement was met in this case. It was held, further, that even if there had been no objection by the appellants' legal practitioner to the joint trial, this would not have given the trial court jurisdiction, for criminal jurisdiction cannot be conferred by consent. That being so, it would not avail the State to show that there had been no prejudice to the appellants.

See also *Kondoni* 1982 (1) ZLR 76 (S) at 79C-D, and *Machona & Ors* 1982 (1) ZLR 87 (S) at 92E.

The holding of joint or mass trials of persons whose alleged offences are unconnected is totally irregular. However, joint trials are permissible for persons charged with different offences where the requirements of s 159 CPEA are satisfied. This section allows for joint trials where different accused, not acting together, commit different crimes at the same place and at about the same time and the prosecutor informs the court that there is admissible evidence which will be common to the different charges. Thus if a number of persons, not acting in concert, have all stolen maize from the complainant at around the same time, it would be appropriate to allow the joint trial of X to save the complainant from being called on numerous occasions to state that the property was stolen from him.

In *Shuma & Anor* 1994 (4) SA 583 (E), the court said that in deciding whether or not to order a separation of trials under s 190 CPEA, the court must exercise its discretion judicially in the promotion of the interests of justice after weighing up the prejudice likely to be caused to the applicant by a refusal to separate, against the prejudice likely to be suffered by the other accused person or the State if the trials are separated. The "interests of justice" is a wide concept, and in the context it encompasses the interests of the individual accused as well as the wider interests of society. It must be emphasised that prejudice to X is the primary consideration, but the mere fact that a joint trial lawfully deprives an accused of his or her right to call his or her co-accused as a witness does not per se constitute prejudice entitling him or her to a separation of trials. The mere possibility of prejudice is not sufficient; there must be a probability or a substantial possibility of prejudice.

Holding cases *in camera*

Reid-Rowland 15-7

In order for justice to be seen to be done criminal proceedings are normally held in public. The public are entitled to attend criminal trials and the press is entitled to report on criminal proceedings so that the public can assure themselves that the processes of justice are fair and that persons found guilty of criminal offences are appropriately punished. It is only dictatorial regimes which make indiscriminate use of secret trials.

In Zimbabwe criminal proceedings are only held *in camera* in exceptional circumstances for valid and justifiable reasons. Indeed, the Constitution lays down that, subject to certain specified exceptions, all court proceedings must be held in public and the outcome of trials shall be publicly announced.

Section 3(1) of the Courts and Adjudicating Authorities (Publicity Restriction) Act [*Chapter 7:04*] sets out the exact powers of the courts to order the exclusion of persons (except parties to the proceedings and their legal representatives) from the proceedings or to place restrictions on the disclosure of information pertaining to the proceedings. The grounds upon which these powers may be exercised are set out in s 3(2). Essentially, the court can use these powers if it considers this to be necessary or expedient on the grounds of defence, public safety, public order, the economic interests of the State, public morality, in the interests of the welfare of persons under the age of eighteen years, to protect witnesses who believe on reasonable grounds that harm will befall them or their families if it is known that they have given evidence, or to protect the lives of persons related to or connected with any person concerned in the proceedings. These powers can be exercised on the judge's own initiative or on application from one of the parties to the proceedings.

Additionally, the responsible Minister has extensive powers to prohibit publicity and disclosure of information regarding different aspects of criminal trials where it is not in the public interest that there be such publicity or disclosure.

Right of accused to be legal represented at own expense

Although an accused person has a constitutional right to be legally represented at his or her own expense by a legal practitioner of his or her own choice, there are some instances where the court can order the trial to proceed without the accused having legal representation. In the case of *Nyathi* HB-90-03 the court stated that the trial court has a discretion, in appropriate cases, to order that the trial should proceed. Before exercising this discretion, the court must clarify whether the absence of the accused person's legal practitioner is the fault of the accused or of the legal representative. The right to legal representation imposes an obligation to permit, not to ensure, legal representation. The accused had sufficient time to secure services of another legal practitioner or request a postponement to secure one. He or she was dilatory in securing legal representation. He or she should have requested for a postponement in order to do so.

Not every refusal of an adjournment or postponement of a trial to give the defence time to call a witness who is not available at court constitutes a gross irregularity. The question is whether in refusing the adjournment all the material facts were taken into consideration. In this case, the accused abandoned his or her intention to call his or her witness after two postponements failed to secure the attendance of the witness.

Provision of legal representation by State

Reid-Rowland 15-3

Previously, this matter was governed by the Legal Assistance and Representation Act [*Chapter 9:13*]. Section 3 provided that, if it appeared to a judge that it is desirable in the interests of justice that a person who is standing trial should have legal assistance in the preparation and conduct of his or her defence and the means of that person are insufficient to enable him or herto obtain legal assistance, the judge may certify that the person ought to have such legal assistance.

Under s 5, this person would then have a legal practitioner assigned to him or herif it is practicable to procure the services of a legal practitioner and the State will pay the remuneration of the legal practitioner according to a fixed tariff.

Hitherto, these provisions have almost never been invoked in criminal cases in the magistrates courts. However, over the last few years, the Supreme Court has made a series of pronouncements in which it has pointed out that in certain types of cases it may be impossible for accused to receive a fair trial if they are not legally represented. The

Supreme Court has said that if it is clear to the presiding magistrate that X does not have the financial means to engage his or her own lawyer, the magistrate should certify that it is in the interests of justice that a lawyer paid for by the State be assigned to him. The magistrate should so certify even if X himself or herself has not made an application for free legal representation.

The cases which the Supreme Court has identified as potentially falling into the category of cases where a fair trial may not be possible in the absence of legal representation are complex cases involving such things as problematical points of statutory interpretation or of evidence or of sentencing or where long prison sentences are likely.

In *Dube & Anor* 1988 (2) ZLR 385 (S) at 392, the Supreme Court explained in more detail what it had in mind. Complex cases are cases such as:

- cases where the ascertainment of the facts includes difficult questions of law, which arise when issues like "possession", "consent" or "knowledge" are involved;
- difficult cases such as the South African case where X was alleged to have committed a crime seven years previously, the State case relied solely on fingerprint evidence and the defence of alibi was difficult to establish after such a long time;
- cases where there is a need to prove "special reasons" or "special circumstances" if a minimum sentence is to be avoided;
- cases where long sentences are likely to follow conviction.

The Legal Representation and Assistance Act has been replaced by the Legal Aid Act [*Chapter 7:16*].

Section 10 of the Legal Aid Act provides for the provision of legal aid in certain criminal cases. Where a judge believes that it is in the interests of justice that an accused person be provided with legal aid and that person may have insufficient financial means to engage his or her own lawyer, the judge can recommend to the Director of the Legal Aid Directorate that the person should be provided with legal aid. He or she will decide whether to provide legal aid to such person after assessing that person's financial means.

Non-attendance of witnesses

Reid-Rowland 8-4

If a witness has been served with a *subpoena* to appear in the court named at the particular date and time and he or she fails to appear, he or she can be punished under s 237(3) CPEA. (The word *subpoena* in fact means "under punishment").

Acting under this section, the prosecutor will hand the magistrate the return of service or he or she may prove service by evidence on oath. He or she will then apply for a warrant of arrest. On the arrest of the witness, the court can inquire summarily into the reasons for his or her non-appearance and may fine him or her or imprison him or her if he or she has no valid reason for his or her default.

A witness can also be served with a particular type of *subpoena*, namely a *subpoena duces tecum* which requires the witness to produce a specified document or thing. If the witness disobeys this *subpoena* he or she can be dealt with under s 233 CPEA.

Also, the court may warn a witness to attend. Failure to obey the warning may be treated as contempt of court.

Start of trial

At the time the judge enters the court, the orderly will call for silence in the courtroom and all people will be expected to stand. The legal practitioners will bow to the judge before he or she is seated.

At the start of the trial, X will be required to be in the dock. However, if a company is being prosecuted, a representative of the company who is not being charged personally as well does not have to sit in the dock.

When witnesses give testimony, the remaining witnesses who have not yet testified will be expected to wait outside the courtroom at a place where it is not possible for them to hear the testimony of the witnesses currently testifying.

Application for separation of trials of co-accused

In *Kachipare* 1998 (2) ZLR 271 (S), X and Y were jointly charged with the murder of a newly born child. On appeal, it was argued that the trial judge should have ordered a separation of trials. Held, that because neither the prosecutor nor counsel for the appellant applied for a separation of trials, the judge could not order a separation *mero motu*. The power to order a separation is pre-conditioned by the making of an application.

Persons brought before wrong court

This is provided for in s 164 CPEA. If, in the magistrates court, a case is brought before a court and it appears that the case is not properly triable in this court, X is not to be acquitted. If X requests that the case be transferred, the magistrate may transfer the case. If X does not request transfer of the case, the magistrate may proceed with the trial as if the magistrate originally had jurisdiction. To try X however, X still had the right to plead to the jurisdiction of the court.

The Charge

Correct formulation

Reid-Rowland 10-5

The trial starts off with the reading of the charge. Before the charge is put to X, the judge should ensure that the charge is clearly and correctly formulated and is properly laid, either under common law or under statute.

The offence must be properly described and adequately particularised. Where the charge is a statutory one, the judge must ensure that the correct section of the Act or Statutory Instrument has been cited, and that the particulars correspond with the provision itself: *Chamurandi* HH-182-86; *Vhere* HH-211-86; *Zvinyenge & Ors* 1987 (2) ZLR 42 (S).

It was pointed out in *Siphambili* 1995 (2) ZLR 337 (S) that if the indictment is deficient in particularity that deficiency would not necessarily be fatal. The test was whether it would prejudice the accused. Unless time is of the essence of the charge, it is sufficient if the day or period alleged in the charge falls within a period of three months before or after the commission of the offence: s 173 CPEA. The court decided that any embarrassment which might have resulted from the inaccuracy in the charge should have been raised before plea, as a request for further particulars or as an exception. If the defence does not object before plea to the lack of particularity in a charge which discloses an offence, then the defence cannot rely on the defectiveness of the charge at the end of the trial: s 170 CPEA.

It was made clear in *Sabawu & Anor* 1999 (2) ZLR 314 (H) that it is the prosecutor's right to determine which charges to prefer and to ensure that the accused is charged with the correct offence.

Although this is not mandatory, where X is unrepresented and the statutory offence with which he or she is charged is made subject to exemptions or is not committed if there is a lawful excuse, it is desirable that the charge be formulated so as to make it clear that the offence is not committed if it falls under an exemption or there is a lawful excuse. This makes it clear to X that, although he or she may have done the act prohibited, he or she will escape conviction if he or she has a lawful excuse or falls under an exemption: *Janyure* 1988 (2) ZLR 470 (S) at 474.

The charge of theft on the basis of a general deficiency is authorised by the provisions of s 148 CPEA. The object of the section is to make things easier for the State when it does not know what has happened to the money. All it knows is that there is less money in the account than there should be, and that X was in charge of the account: *Mboma* S-28-92.

Amendment by the court

In the case of *Shand* 1994 (2) ZLR 99 (S), it was pointed out that in terms of s 202(1) CPEA, a court may, in certain circumstances, amend a charge. This provision only allows the court to make corrections to the existing charge and it does not allow the court to substitute a totally different charge. In any event, in the present case, there was a possibility of prejudicing the appellant if the Appeal Court allowed the substitution of a new charge.

Alteration of charge by court

The general rule is that the prosecutor is the *dominus litis* and has the prerogative to prefer charges against the accused. *Sabawu & Anor* 1999 (2) ZLR 314 (H).

However, this rule is not absolute. In the case of *Thebe* HB-16-06, the judge pointed out that while the prosecutor is *dominus litis*, this rule is not absolute. The trial court, as a trier of facts whose main object is to do justice between man and man, therefore has inherent powers to ensure that suitable charges are preferred against those who appear before it. It is, therefore, within its power to prevent the State from proceeding on a lesser charge where justice clearly requires a more serious one.

It is not in the interests of justice that a person should be charged with a lesser offence when the admitted facts show that he or she is guilty of a more serious charge. In such an event, the trial court should at least query why X is being charged only with the less serious charge. Thus if the State allegations clearly suggest that X has committed the crime of assault with intent to do grievous bodily harm but the State has brought only a charge of common assault against X, the magistrate should question the prosecutor on why the lesser charge has been preferred. Similarly, the magistrate should query why a person has only been charged with contravening s 45(1) of the Road Traffic Act [*Chapter 13:11*] if the evidence discloses a contravention of s 46(1) of this Act: *Chidodo & Anor* 1988 (1) ZLR 299 (H).

Alternate charges

Reid-Rowland10-14– 10-13

As a matter of practice, the most serious charge is usually set out first. This, however, is not a legal requirement. There can be a number of alternate charges. All charges and alternate charges must be read out to X before he or she is asked to plead, rather than each charge being read out and him or her being asked to plead to each in turn.

Exception to charge

Reid-Rowland 10-14

The procedure when there is an exception to the charge is set out in s 171 CPEA. It will usually be X's lawyer who will except to the charge on behalf of his or her client. If the exception is made before plea, the court must deal with this matter first before requiring X to plead: s 171(1) CPEA. This applies both to an exception that the charge does not disclose an offence, and that the charge does not disclose reasonably sufficient particulars to inform X of the nature of the charge against him or her as required by s 146 CPEA.

If the exception is dismissed X will then be asked to plead.

If X pleads and excepts together, the court has the discretion whether to dispose of the plea or the exception first: s 171(2) CPEA.

Charge lacking in particularity

It was pointed out in *Siphambili* 1995 (2) ZLR 337 (S) that if the indictment is deficient in particularity that deficiency would not necessarily be fatal. The test was whether it would prejudice the accused. Unless time is of the essence of the charge, it is sufficient if the day or period alleged in the charge falls within a period of three months before or after the commission of the offence. The court decided that any embarrassment which might have resulted from the inaccuracy in the charge should have been raised before plea, as a request for further particulars or as an exception. If the defence does not object before plea to the lack of particularity in a charge which discloses an offence, it cannot rely on the defectiveness of the charge at the end of the trial.

Splitting of charges

Reid-Rowland 10-29 – 10-30

Principles

It is unfair that X be charged with two or more separate crimes in circumstances where he or she should have been charged with one crime only because the conduct really only constitutes one criminal offence.

In *Zacharia* 2002 (1) ZLR 48 (H), it was held that there are two tests for whether there has been an improper splitting of charges, the "single intent" or "continuous transaction" test and the "same evidence" or "dominant intent" test. The latter is related to the intention of the accused person as he or she performs several acts which are logically and intrinsically connected to the one offence which he or she then commits. The concern whether the criminal conduct is in reality a single conviction is aimed at avoiding prejudice to the accused where the duplication of convictions arises. If no prejudice is occasioned to the accused, then the question whether or not there has been a duplication of convictions becomes one of little or no consequence. The prejudice to the accused may be avoided by treating all the separate counts as one for the purposes of sentence.

Simply because criminal acts form part of one related transaction does not mean that separate crimes have not been committed and that there has been an improper splitting of charges. There will, however, have been an improper splitting of charges if either:

- a person commits two acts, each of which standing alone would be criminal but does so with a single intent and both acts are necessary to carry out that intention; or
- where the same evidence which is essential to prove one criminal act is also essential to prove another criminal act.

In both these instances, X should be convicted of only one crime: *Peterson & Ors* 1970 RLR 49; *Chinemo* 1985 (1) ZLR 32 (H).

Where the charging of more than one offence would constitute improper splitting, the State should charge the offence which represents the dominant intention of X in engaging in that conduct: *Jambani* 1982 (2) ZLR 213 (H).

Cases in which court found that there was splitting

In *Mhandu* 1985 (1) ZLR 228 (S), it was held to be an improper splitting to charge X with three separate offences of "statutory rape" where he had had sexual intercourse with an under-age girl on three separate occasions during one month.

In *Matimba* 1989 (3) ZLR 173 (S), the Supreme Court ruled that it constituted an improper splitting to charge breaches of the various duties under s 61 of the Road Traffic Act, 1976 (failing to stop, failing to attend to injured persons, and so on) as separate offences.

In *Tugwete* HH-672-87, it was pointed out that where a person drives a motor vehicle without footbrakes and a handbrake he or she commits a single offence not two offences.

Cases in which court found there was no splitting

In *Peterson & Ors* 1970 RLR 49, Xs stole a car and later abandoned it but burnt it to prevent the discovery of any finger prints in the car. Xs were correctly convicted of both theft and malicious injury to property because, although the offences were related and formed part of one continuous transaction, there was not a single intent and the evidence of theft was not essential to prove malicious injury to property. (The related nature of these crimes could, nonetheless, be taken into account for the purposes of sentence.)

In *Maniko & Anor* HH-44-91, the reviewing judge decided that in neither of two cases had there been improper splitting. In the first, a person had properly been convicted of two counts of assault where he or she had assaulted one person and had then assaulted another who had tried to intervene. In the second, an accused had properly been convicted of two counts of stock theft where X had stolen cattle from two people at the same place but an hour apart.

Other Case Examples:

Frank 1968 (1) RLR 257 (A) (assault and malicious injury to property);
Attorney-General v *Jakubec* 1979 RLR 267 (A) (excessive blood alcohol and negligent driving);
Lamont 1977 (1) RLR 112 (A) (incitement and substantive offence incited);
P & Ors 1976 (1) RLR 142 (GD) (possession of arms of war and act of terrorism);
Tebie & Anor 1965 RLR 198 (GD) (robbery and theft);
Simon 1980 ZLR 162 (GD) (robbery and impersonation of policeman).

Withdrawal of charge before plea

Reid-Rowland 16-10

If the State withdraws the charge before plea, no verdict is entered and the State is at liberty to bring X back to court at a later date. The State may decide to withdraw the charge before plea for a variety of reasons such as illness of a vital witness or delay in securing important evidence.

The defence lawyer may try to insist that the plea be put to X before the charge is withdrawn. If, however, the prosecutor has made a firm decision that withdrawal will be before plea, the court has no right to order that the charge be put and that a plea be taken before the withdrawal of the charge. The decision as to whether the withdrawal will be before or after the plea lies solely with the State.

The Plea

Reid-Rowland 16-14 – 16-25

Types of plea

At the start of the trial X is asked what his or her plea is to the charge. It should be noted that even where X is legally represented X must personally plead to the charge; his or her lawyer cannot enter a plea on his or her behalf.

If he or she pleads guilty, after checking that X is genuinely and correctly admitting the charge, he or she can then be found guilty and sentenced.

In murder cases the court will always enter a plea, even if the accused pleads guilty. The State will then be required to lead evidence to establish the guilt of the accused. See *Nangani* 1982 (1) ZLR 150 (S) at 154 B and s 271(1) CPEA.

If X pleads not guilty, the case then goes for trial.

If X refuses to plead at all or refuses to answer directly and unequivocally to the charge, a plea of not guilty should be entered.

The plea may be a limited one. For example, if he or she is charged with assault with intent to commit grievous bodily harm, he or she may have been advised by his or her lawyer to plead not guilty to this charge but guilty to the lesser charge of common assault. A plea of not guilty to the actual charge must be entered. X may also plead guilty in a qualified way. If charged with assault with intent to do grievous bodily harm, he or she may plead guilty but may say that he or she committed the crime because he or she was very drunk or had been badly provoked by the complainant. A plea of not guilty must be entered in this instance and the matter should proceed to trial to determine whether X in fact had the requisite intention to inflict grievous bodily harm upon the victim despite the presence of intoxication or provocation.

Guilty pleas from undefended accused

Reid-Rowland 16-17

Petty Crimes

With crimes not meriting imprisonment or a fine over level 3 (petty crimes) the court can convict on a guilty plea and impose a sentence other than imprisonment or a fine in excess of level 3: s 271(2)(a) CPEA.

This provision is only appropriate for trivial cases. It cannot be used in any case where imprisonment may be imposed even if the period of imprisonment is then wholly suspended: *Honde & Ors* HB-27-91. There is seldom, if ever, any justification for proceeding under this section if the charge against X is assault with intent to cause grievous bodily harm: *Kendai* HH-269-82.

More Serious Crimes

Testing the plea

With crimes meriting imprisonment or a whipping or a fine over level 3 (more serious crimes) there are stringent safeguards which have to be applied before a guilty plea is accepted by the court from an unrepresented accused. Before convicting a person who is not legally represented on a guilty plea the court must satisfy itself that X fully understands and admits the charge and all its essential elements: *Mteiswa* 1976 (1) RLR 314 (GD).

In order to so satisfy itself, the court must first carefully explain the charge and its essential elements and inform X of the acts or omissions upon which the charge is based or, if these are not clear from the charge sheet, it must require the prosecutor to state upon what acts or omissions the charge is based: s 271(2)(b) CPEA; *Choma* 1990 (2) ZLR 33 (H). During this inquiry, the court may call upon the prosecutor to present evidence on any aspect of the charge.

In *Chirodzero* HH-14-88, the court stressed the need for extreme care to be exercised in this situation. It emphasised that magistrates must constantly bear in mind the dangers inherent in convicting persons upon guilty pleas. The provision provides for an extraordinary procedure for disposing of criminal trials after a truncated form of trial. Magistrates must do all in their power to ensure that this truncated procedure does not result in injustice. They must be satisfied that the admission of guilt is genuine, unqualified and unequivocal before acting on it. They must be satisfied that X is admitting the facts alleged and the charge and all its essential elements. They must also be satisfied that X is guilty in fact and in law.

Each element of the offence must be examined in turn and the replies of X in respect of each element should be recorded. The procedure should not be short-circuited by rolling the elements of the offence together. They must be taken individually.

The court should be careful not to regard every fact as having been proved just because it is admitted. If, for instance, X admits to being in possession of a prohibited item, the court should establish just what it is he or she has admitted to, as possession is a difficult legal concept. The court must ascertain whether there was, indeed, possession in the legal sense.

When exploring whether X is admitting to each essential element, the court should not restrict itself to eliciting bald "yes" or "no" answers and then be satisfied with such bald answers. The questioning of X must be done in such a way as to elicit full information. To decide whether the "breaking" element of housebreaking is being admitted the judge might ask, "Did you break into the premises and enter them as alleged?" to which X may simply reply "yes". This does not, however, elicit proper details so it is far better to ask whether he or she entered the premises and, if he or she did, to ask how he or she effected entry.

The question, "Why did you do this?" should always be put to see whether there is some defence which may be open to X. If X does have any defence, the defence will most likely come out in response to this question. If no defence emerges, the response to this question will be likely nonetheless to reveal the motive and this may have a bearing on sentence.

With crimes like theft and malicious damage to property the judge should always investigate whether X committed the crime under any sort of claim of right. See, for instance, *Kawocha* S-22-92, where a defence of claim of right was not sufficiently investigated on a charge of stock theft.

If a statute provides that an offence is only committed if the act was done without "lawful excuse" or "reasonable excuse" or some other defence, the judge must carefully investigate that X does not only admit that he or she did the prohibited act, but that he or she did it without any lawful or reasonable excuse as envisaged by the statutory provision.

Difficult, technical elements of the offence must be properly explained. These include elements such as "consent", "knowledge" and the "grievous bodily harm" element in the offence of assault with intent to do grievous bodily harm and phrases such as "without lawful authority or reasonable excuse, the proof whereof shall lie on X". Unless the court explains such terms to X, it will not be possible to ascertain whether X admits that he or she did the thing which is required for that element to be satisfied. The court must satisfy itself that X properly understands what he or she is admitting and is competent to make the admission: *Dube & Anor* 1988 (2) ZLR 385 (S); *Sibanda* 1989 (2) ZLR 329 (S); *Deka & Anor* S-199-88; *Kaja* S-129-89; *Njiva* S-120-89.

In *Hove* S-20-92, the appellant was convicted of contravening s 3(a) of the Criminal Law Amendment Act [*Chapter 9:05*] in that he or she had had sexual relations with a girl under the age of 16. The appellant, who was not legally represented, had maintained that he believed that the complainant was over 16. In terms of the statutory provision it is only a defence if X proves on a balance of probabilities that he *bona fide* believed, and had reasonable cause to believe, that the complainant was above the age of 16. The Supreme Court held that where an accused is not legally represented he must be advised of the onus which rests on him or her when advancing a defence provided for in terms of the statutory provision.

In *Mushayandebvu* 1992 (2) ZLR 62 (S) the magistrate has misdirected himself in accepting a guilty plea from X, an unsophisticated woman, despite the fact that it was clear from the State outline that X was claiming to have acted in self-defence.

In cases where the law lays down that a mandatory minimum penalty must be imposed, unless there are special circumstances or special reasons, X must be told what the penalty is and what is meant by special circumstances or special reasons. This should be done early on in the trial: *Dube & Anor* 1988 (2) ZLR 385 (S).

In *Chaerera* 1988 (2) ZLR 226 (S), the magistrate had simply asked X whether he had any special reasons why the mandatory penalty should not be imposed. The Supreme Court said that the magistrate should have gone much further than this. He should have advised X what the minimum penalty was and how that penalty could be avoided by proof of special circumstances. He should have gone on to explain what was meant by "special circumstances", and he should have asked X whether he had considered obtaining legal representation.

In the case of *Mutizwa* HB-4-06 when X was asked to plead to a charge of theft of a vehicle, he indicated that he did not intend to deprive the owner permanently of the vehicle. The magistrate did not seem to accept this defence and embarked on further questioning of the accused, but the accused gave the impression that he was sticking to that defence. The court held that the responses proffered by an accused as a result of the inquiry conducted in terms of s 271(2)(b) CPE should amount to an irrevocable admission of the essential elements of the offence charged. Where there is uncertainty as to what accused is admitting to, the court must probe further and satisfy itself that all the essential elements of the offence have been admitted. Where the court has any doubts or the accused raises a defence, the court is obliged to alter the plea to that of not guilty and order that a trial be held to determine the contentious issues.

In *Ndlovu & Anor* HB-30-02, two accused were jointly charged with assault with intent to do grievous bodily harm and pleaded guilty. When putting questions to clarify the essential elements of the crime, the magistrate did not record any answer to the question whether they intended to cause serious bodily harm. In respect of other questions, it was not made clear whether the reply was from one or both of the accused. It was held that questions relating to the essential elements should not be regarded as questions which should be asked as a matter of course, but rather, as questions whose answers should assist the court in establishing whether the accused understands the core of the allegations against him. In view of the answers given, or not given, it was not safe to convict the accused.

In a limited number of complex cases, it may not be possible to ensure that the unrepresented accused who wishes to plead guilty receives a fair trial simply by carefully explaining all the essential elements to him or her and probing whether he or she admits to each of these elements.

This may apply where the case revolves around whether a complicated legal requirement has been satisfied, and in some cases where conviction is likely to result in long or mandatory prison sentences. In such cases, instead of accepting a guilty plea, if X cannot afford to engage his or her own lawyer, the court should certify the case so that X receives free legal representation: *Dube & Anor* 1988 (2) ZLR 385 (S); *Pongolani* S-48-89.

Clarification of statements

Other than to clarify any of the statements made by X, the court is not entitled to test the truth of the allegations made, nor to investigate whether the facts referred to by X exist or not. No question of onus arises. No one has to prove facts during this enquiry into plea: *Chirodzero* HH-14-88.

Doubts about plea

If **at any stage** during the proceedings following a guilty plea, the court is in doubt as to whether X is in law guilty of the crime to which he or she has pleaded guilty, or is not satisfied that he or she has admitted or correctly admitted to all essential elements of the crime or all the acts or omissions upon which the charge is based, or is not satisfied that he or she has no valid defence to the charge, the court must record a plea of not guilty and require that the prosecution proceed with the case as if there had been a not guilty plea: s 272 CPEA.

In *Bvunda* HH-278-90, the magistrate had entered a plea of guilty to a charge of assault with intent to do grievous bodily harm and had convicted X. The High Court ruled that the magistrate should have entered a plea of not guilty because, after pleading guilty, X made statements suggesting that there may have been provocation and that he or she may have been somewhat intoxicated. A plea of not guilty should have been entered in these circumstances so that the possible application of these partial defences could have been fully explored.

In *Manyami* HB-36-90, a magistrate decided from X's defence outline that he had no defence to the charge and told X that there was no point in having a trial since he would be found guilty on the basis of the admitted facts. This induced X to alter his plea to one of guilty. On review, it was held that the procedure adopted by the magistrate was a gross violation of the *audi alteram partem* rule and that there was no legal basis for forcing an accused to plead guilty because the magistrate was convinced that X was guilty before he had heard the evidence. The magistrate had shown complete insensitivity to the fact that X was not legally represented.

Recording of inquiry into guilty plea

The court must record its explanation of the charge and its essential elements and any statement of the acts or omissions upon which it is based, including any statement given by the prosecutor of the acts or omissions on which the charge is based, and all statements and replies made by X during this inquiry, and any statements made by X in connection with the offence to which he or she has pleaded guilty: s 271(3) CPEA.

In *Phiri* HB-62-93, in proceedings under s 271(3) CPEA, the magistrate failed to record X's answers to the questions put to him or her about the essential elements. The verdict and sentence were set aside.

Guilty pleas from jointly charged accused

Where a number of accused are charged jointly and they are all pleading guilty, the judge must be careful to explain to each accused in turn the elements of the offence and the facts upon which it is based in each individual case and to clarify exactly what it is that each accused is admitting to. Each person must be dealt with separately and the answers of each accused during the inquiry into his or her guilty plea must be recorded separately: *Dube & Anor* 1988 (2) ZLR 385 (S).

The case of *Mazanyane* HB-102-95 deals with the failure to conduct any real enquiry into the plea and facts following a guilty plea. A mother was charged with an offence under the Children's Protection and Adoption Act and on the basis of her guilty plea and after the most superficial of questioning whether she had mistreated her child, she was sentenced.

In *Ngwenya* HB-17-95, the court observed that in dealing with guilty pleas, magistrates need a systematic approach. Magistrates should go through the following steps:

Step 1

Explain the charge and the essential elements of the offence to X in a way in which he or she can understand. On charges of unlawful entry and theft the judge must explain:

- entering
- premises
- unlawfully
- intending (at that time) to steal
- stealing someone else's property
- without his or her consent
- intending permanently to deprive him or herof the property.

Step 2

The prosecutor must state the facts upon which the charge is based.

Step 3

Ask X if he or she has understood the explanation given to him or her. Only if he or she has, can he or she be asked if he or she admits each part of the offence. Each essential element must be checked separately. Thus, it is wrong to ask X in one question if he or she entered and took the property. Entry involves an unlawful breaking and the court must establish how X gained entry. It is misleading to ask an accused if he or she had a lawful right to enter and a lawful right to take the property. This suggests there is a lawful right and an unlawful right and the answer to this question cannot be taken as a genuine admission of the essential element. He or she should instead be asked simply if he or she had a right. There must also be an unequivocal admission of an intention to deprive permanently; in this case ambiguous replies were not followed up.

Step 4

The final question to X, namely whether he or she had any defence or excuse to offer, might have been answered differently if all the essential elements had been properly explained.

The court's explanation, the prosecutor's statement and X's responses must all be recorded.

In the case of *Ncube & Ors* S-56-93, the court said that magistrates must not be slap-dash in using s 271(2)(b) CPEA. In this case, the court had not recorded the individual pleas of each accused, although the magistrate said that he or she had asked each accused separately.

Difficulties with particular charges

There are particular difficulties with some charges when it comes to making sure that X properly understands the charges to which he or she is pleading guilty. One of these is assault with intent to cause grievous bodily harm. Care must be taken that X understands the difference between this crime and that of common assault and that he or she is in fact admitting to the more serious crime. Questions along these lines should therefore be asked: "Did you intend to cause serious harm to the complainant?" and "Do you understand that you are pleading guilty not just to common assault but to the more serious offence of assault with intent to inflict grievous bodily harm?": *Mavingere* 1988 (2) ZLR 318 (S).

Guilty pleas from legally represented accused

Where X is legally represented the court itself does not have to explain the charge, its essential elements and the acts or omissions upon which it is based to X. Instead, the court can rely upon a statement by X's legal representative that these things have been fully explained by the legal representative to X and that he or she understands them and is admitting to them: proviso to s 271(2)(b) CPEA.

The lawyer must be asked whether the guilty plea is in accordance with his or her instructions from his or her client. The court should also ask if he or she explained all the essential elements of the crime to his or her client and if the client is admitting to all these elements.

In *Mvurume* HH-198-02, the appellant, who was legally represented at his trial for attempted murder, pleaded guilty. The magistrate did not put the normal questions to the appellant to satisfy himself that the plea was genuine. He convicted the appellant. Some months later, in spite of the fact that there were no medical reports either on the complainant's condition or on the appellant's mental state, the magistrate sentenced the appellant. On appeal, against conviction and sentence, the court set out the correct procedure to adopt in this situation. It pointed out that the court must record that the statement on which it relies for a conviction was made by the legal practitioner because it is only for that reason that the court may decide not to give the necessary explanation. A failure to record that the legal practitioner made the statement may cast doubt on whether that statement was made at all. In any event, a statement by a legal practitioner does not preclude the court from making the enquiry itself. In cases of attempted murder involving a physical assault, the absence of a medical report as to the injuries, where the injuries are admitted to have been inflicted, is not fatal to the proceedings in regard to conviction and even to sentence, provided that the injuries are such that they would enable the court to reach, as the only reasonable inference, that the accused intended to cause the complainant's death.

Pleas from company

Unless a director or servant of the company produces a resolution of the company authorising him or her to plead guilty on behalf of the company, the court must enter a plea of not guilty for the company: s 385(3) CPEA.

Plea in absence of lawyer

In *Tuhwe* S-97-94, appellant's counsel had arranged for a remand; he or she was asked to plead in his or her counsel's absence instead, pleaded guilty, admitted the essential elements and was convicted. The appeal court was sceptical about his or her claim that he or she admitted the offence only because he or she panicked. It accepted, however, that he or she had been inadvertently denied the legal representation he or she wanted and had arranged; it set aside the proceedings and remitted the matter for the plea to be taken before a new magistrate.

Guilty plea to lesser offence than that charged

If X pleads guilty to a lesser crime than that which is charged, it is for the prosecutor, not the court, to decide whether or not to accept the plea. If the prosecutor accepts the plea, X can be convicted of that lesser crime; if the prosecutor declines to accept the plea, a plea of not guilty is entered and the trial proceeds. Where the facts indicate the commission of the crime charged, the State and the court should not accept a plea of guilty to a lesser offence merely to save time: *Mahango* HH-132-87.

Where the facts indicate the commission of the crime charged, the State and the court should not accept the plea to the lesser offence to save time in having to try the case on the basis of the more serious charge: *Matongo* HH-132-87.

Limited guilty plea

This is where X pleads guilty to some but not all of the charges. For example, if a person is charged with theft of a bicycle, theft of a television and theft of a coat and he or she pleads guilty to the first two thefts but not the last, the prosecutor will then have to decide whether to accept this limited plea and proceed on the basis only of the first two theft charges.

Unclear or equivocal pleas

Usually, it is clear that X has pleaded guilty or has denied his or her guilt. In the *Commonwealth Handbook for Magistrates*, a number of examples of ambiguous pleas are given. What if X says "I might as well plead guilty as I want to get it over today"? If, on further questioning, X continues not to say directly whether he or she is admitting that he or she is guilty, the court will have to enter a plea of not guilty. This Handbook gives some further examples.

An accused, who is charged with receiving stolen property, might say "I suppose I'm guilty. I agreed to look after my boyfriend's bike and he or she's now been arrested for stealing it". The vital question on this charge is whether X knew that the property was stolen when she took it into her possession. Only if it is clear after inquiry that she admits that she did know this should the guilty plea be accepted. Or X might say "If you say I drove through the red lights I suppose I did." The question here is whether X is admitting that the lights were red. He or she could be asked whether he or she himself or herself saw that they were red or whether any of his or her passengers told him or her that they were.

With cases of malicious injury to property, an admission that he or she broke the window is not enough; the breaking must be intentional and not merely accidental and X must therefore admit that he or she broke the window intentionally. Similarly, in a case of shoplifting it is not enough that X admits that he or she took the item out of the shop without paying; for shoplifting the taking must be intentional and if it emerges that X is saying that the taking was the result of absentmindedness on his or her part, a plea of not guilty must be entered.

Plea that previously acquitted or convicted (autrefois acquit or autrefois convict)

Reid-Rowland 16-19

An accused may only be tried once in respect of a crime. Thus, if he or she has previously been tried and either acquitted or convicted for that crime, he or she cannot be tried again for it: s 180(2)(c) and (d) CPEA. This plea must be dealt with as a preliminary matter before the evidence is led. The question is whether the facts necessary to support a conviction on the current charge are the same as those in the previous case: *Ndou & Ors* 1971 (1) SA 668 (A).

For the plea to succeed, X must show that he or she was "in jeopardy" (i.e. in danger) at the previous trial of being convicted of the charge that he or she now faces, or a substantially similar charge, i.e. that he or she was previously tried:

- on substantially the same charge;
- by a court of competent jurisdiction; and
- he or she was convicted or, if he or she was acquitted, that the acquittal was on the merits.

X must show that he or she was in jeopardy of being convicted of the charge which he or she now faces. In all such cases, it is the substance and not the mere form of the charges that must be looked at: the question is whether the charges are substantially the same.

In the case of *Moyo* HB-18-84, X raised the defence of *autrefois acquit*. He or she had previously been convicted of unlawful possession of a firearm. He or she had thereafter continued to possess it without a firearms permit. The question was whether he or she could be tried again for this offence arising out of his or her continued unlawful possession. The answer was yes.

However, s 180(2)(c) CPEA does not refer to the situation where the previous conviction has been set aside by reason of irregularity. See s 18(6)(a) and (b) of the Constitution. In such cases, a re-trial may be proper because the previous proceedings have been set aside or a re-trial has been ordered. See *Manera* 1989 (2) ZLR 92 (S); *Mlauzi* v *Attorney-General of Zimbabwe* S-48-92. In this latter case, the appellant had been convicted and sentenced for car theft. The appellant was going to appeal against these convictions. After these convictions, however, the records of the proceedings leading to his conviction were lost. Before the appeals were heard the convictions were quashed by the High Court on the grounds that the records had been lost.

The status of a deposit fine and admission of guilt should be remembered in cases of such a plea. For the purposes of a criminal charge the payment of a deposit fine is prima facie an unequivocal acknowledgement of guilt and when an acknowledgement of guilt and a deposit fine is confirmed by a magistrate, the offender will stand convicted and sentenced by a court. He or she cannot be convicted again in respect of substantially the same offence, as this will violate the *autrefois convict* rule: *Gore* 1999 (1) ZLR 177 (H).

Section 18(6) of the Constitution lays down that no person may be tried again for the same offence of which he or she was previously convicted. However, this section provided certain exceptions to this rule. The present case fell within proviso (a) to that section in that the convictions had been set aside "on the ground of any other irregularity or defect in the procedure". This proviso was intended to cover irregularities and defects arising **subsequent to** conviction and sentence. Thus, it was open to the Attorney-General to institute a fresh prosecution for the offences for which the appellant had been convicted after the convictions had been quashed on the grounds of irregularity.

X can also plead that he or she has already received a pardon from the President for the offence charged.

Not guilty plea

Reid-Rowland 16-18

If X pleads not guilty, or the court alters his or her plea to not guilty, the matter will then have to proceed to trial. Where the prosecutor has been expecting that the case will be dealt with on the basis of a guilty plea, he or she will usually ask that the case be remanded for trial. However, the prosecutor may ask the court to proceed with the trial if the witnesses and exhibits are available. Where X indicated that he or she was pleading not guilty, the prosecutor should normally be in a position to present the State case immediately.

Other pleas

Reid-Rowland 16-21

Other pleas which can be raised are that the court does not have jurisdiction to try the case or that the prosecutor has no title to prosecute: s 180(2)(f) & (g) CPEA.

There can also be a plea that he or she has already received a pardon from the President for the offence charged: s 180(2)(e) CPEA.

Change of plea before evidence led

An accused may plead guilty before one magistrate and be found guilty on the basis of the plea. The proceedings may then be adjourned. If he or she later decides to change his or her plea another magistrate is legally permitted under s 180(6)(ii) CPEA to hear this application provided that no evidence has been adduced at the first hearing: *Dube & Anor* S-126-89.

Withdrawal of charge after plea

Reid-Rowland 16-24

Once X has pleaded he or she is entitled to a verdict and, if the charge or charges are withdrawn, the court must enter a verdict of not guilty: s 9 CPEA.

The prosecutor may make the decision to withdraw where the proof of the case against X runs into considerable problems and it appears to the prosecutor that he or she will now not be able to prove the case. Thus, he or she withdraws in order to avoid wasting the time of the court.

If the prosecutor decides to withdraw the charge, the judge must acquit even if he or she disagrees with the prosecutor's decision to withdraw. The decision in this regard rests with the prosecutor, not with the judge. Sometimes, the prosecutor takes this course as a result of a suggestion from the defence lawyer. While it is perfectly in order for a defence lawyer to make such a suggestion during an adjournment, the same cannot be said of whispered comments made to the prosecutor in court.

Where prosecutor withdraws after plea, the effect is that the court has no power to continue with the trial thereafter: *Chari* 1998 (1) ZLR 180 (H).

Proof required following not guilty plea

If X has pleaded not guilty, the prosecutor will have to prove every averment in the charge in order to secure a conviction, unless the defence relieves him or her of part of the burden by admitting to certain facts.

In terms of the proviso to s 272 CPEA, any element, act or omission correctly admitted by X up to the stage that a not guilty plea is entered by the court following a not guilty plea and which has been recorded in terms of s 271(3) CPEA, is sufficient proof of the element, act or omission.

State and defence outlines

Reid-Rowland 16-21; 16-34

If X pleads not guilty, or a plea of not guilty is recorded because he or she refuses to plead to the charge or to plead directly thereto, the next stage is to call upon the prosecutor and X or his or her lawyer to give their outlines: s 188(a) and (b) CPEA.

First, the prosecutor **must** make a statement outlining the nature of his or her case and the material facts upon which he or she relies.

In *Dube* S-25-92, the court said that although the state outline should be an accurate summary of the police docket, discrepancies between it and the evidence of state witnesses are not given the same weight as discrepancies between the defence outline and X's evidence, because it is not prepared by or on behalf of the witness. If there are discrepancies on an essential matter, a satisfactory explanation must be given, or the State will not prove its case beyond reasonable doubt.

X must then be requested to make a statement outlining the nature of his or her defence and the material facts on which he or she relies. If he or she is legally represented his or her lawyer will make this statement on his or her behalf. If he or she is not legally represented he or she must be warned that if at this stage he or she fails to mention any fact relevant to his or her defence, which in the circumstances existing at the time he or she could reasonably have been expected to have mentioned, the court may draw adverse inferences from this failure when determining his or her guilt for the offence charged or any other crime which he or she may be convicted of on that charge and the failure may be treated as evidence corroborating any other evidence against him or her: s 189(2) CPEA.

Allowing accused to present his or her defence

In *Muleya* 1992 (1) ZLR 68(4), X had pleaded not guilty to a charge. At the end of the cross-examination of the complainant by X, the magistrate found X guilty without giving him or hera chance to present his or her defence. He or she did so because he or she was of the opinion that there was no triable issue. On review, the High Court held that this was a serious irregularity. An accused has a right to receive a fair trial and he or she is always entitled to present his or her defence no matter how untenable or unreasonable it might appear to be. It is a serious miscarriage of justice to stop the trial in the middle like this. It is only where X changes his or her plea or makes certain admissions that a full trial may become unnecessary.

Calling of witnesses by accused

X must be allowed to call his or her witnesses. If his or her witnesses are not available when he or she wishes to call them, the proceedings must be adjourned so that he or she can be given a reasonable opportunity to contact them and ensure that they are available at the resumed hearing.

However, in the case of *Nyathi* HB-90-03 the court pointed out that not every refusal of an adjournment or postponement of a trial to give the defence time to call a witness who is not available at court constitutes a gross irregularity. The question is whether in refusing the adjournment all the material facts were taken into consideration. In this case, the accused abandoned his or her intention to call his or her witness after two postponements failed to secure the attendance of the witness.

In the case of *Samakomva* HH-8-05 the court ruled the right granted to an accused person under s 18(3)(e) of the Constitution to facilities to obtain the attendance and carry out the examination of witnesses to testify on his or her behalf before the court did not mean that a request to have defence witnesses compelled by the court could be had just for the asking. The accused must demonstrate that the testimony of such witnesses will be both material and favourable.

In *Yusuf* 1997 (1) ZLR 102 (H), X, who was not legally represented, had intimated to the magistrate that he would like a handwriting expert to be called to testify as to the authorship of certain key documents in a fraud case. The prosecutor undertook to arrange for handwriting tests to be carried out. The matter was remanded on a number of occasions because the prosecutor failed to honour his or her undertaking. Finally, the accused indicated that he wished the matter to be finalised because he had been on remand too long. The magistrate proceeded to give judgment in which he found the accused guilty. On review it was held that when a person is on trial for a criminal offence he must be given a full opportunity to give evidence in his defence and to call such witnesses as he may wish. This right is laid down in s 18(3)(e) of the Constitution and is a fundamental principle of natural justice. Section 18(3)(e) provides that the accused is entitled to obtain the attendance of witnesses on the same conditions as those applying to witnesses called by the prosecution. This includes the right to the subpoenaing of reluctant witnesses. The failure to call the handwriting evidence constituted an irregularity. The indication by the accused that he wished the proceedings to be finalised did not amount to a waiver of his right to call the witness. It was not expressed as such and meant no more than he did not want a further postponement. Where the accused is faced with the inability or reluctance of the State to provide necessary facilities or rights, the powerlessness of the unrepresented accused should not be taken as acceptance of that default. Even if the magistrate erroneously took the accused's statement that he or she did not want a further postponement to be a waiver, this would not have cured the irregularity as the accused was in no way to blame for the irregularity or for any misunderstanding on the part of the magistrate. Even if the accused had consented to be tried without the witness, there still would have been a fatal irregularity, as such consent would truly have been no more than an impotent acquiescence in the face of the failure or refusal by the state to comply with its undertaking and obligation to secure the attendance of the witness. The accused was entitled to have his or her witness's attendance enforced by the machinery of the State and the judicial process. The bumbling and ineffectual measures taken by the prosecutor and his or her unexplained broken promises fall far short of affording the accused his or her right to a fair hearing.

Questioning of witnesses

Examination-in-chief

Reid-Rowland 18-28

Where the parties are legally represented, counsel will elicit the evidence of the witnesses by asking them questions. The reason why the witnesses are not just simply put in the witness box and asked to relate their stories is that only evidence that is relevant and admissible may be put before the court. Most witnesses are not aware of the rules of evidence and therefore appropriate questions are asked in order to adduce relevant and admissible evidence. Legal counsel will also try to extract the evidence in a clear and orderly fashion rather than allowing witnesses to give their testimony in a confused and haphazard fashion.

Nonetheless, the witnesses must be allowed to give their own description of the events. Questions may be put to help the witnesses to relate their own version of events but the witnesses must not be told what to say or questioned in such a way as to suggest the answers to the questions. The judge must therefore ensure that leading questions are not asked and that the prosecutor, defence lawyer or accused does not end up cross-examining his or her own witness. Leading questions may, however, be asked in order to elicit undisputed information of a routine nature such as the names and addresses of witnesses.

Where an accused is not legally represented, the court may have to assist X in eliciting the relevant information from witnesses he or she may call in his or her defence.

There are some questions which the witness cannot legally be compelled to answer. These include such things as disclosure of communications between married people, communications between lawyers and clients and so on. The circumstances in which a person may not be compelled to answer questions are set out in ss 290-297 CPEA.

If the witness steadfastly refuses to answer a question which he or she is legally obliged to answer (or to produce a document or thing which he or she is legally obliged to produce), the judge should intervene and order the witness to answer the question (or produce the document etc.) and warn him or her that if he or she refuses, he or she will be sent to prison. If he or she still declines, in terms of s 233(1) CPEA the judge may adjourn the proceedings and order the committal of the person to prison for up to eight days. If, at the resumed hearing, the person persists in his or her refusal the person can again be imprisoned for up to eight days. This process can continue until the person agrees to do what he or she has been ordered to do by the judge.

Cross-examination

Reid-Rowland 16-31

This is the process of questioning of witnesses by the other side or any co-accused after the testimony has been adduced in the examination-in-chief.

The purpose of cross-examination is to try to get the witness to alter, qualify, amend or retract evidence given, to discredit his or her evidence or to elicit from him or her evidence favourable to the party cross-examining. Leading questions are allowed in cross-examination and the court should normally allow greater latitude than in examination-in-chief to the questioner, particularly where the questioner is an undefended accused.

The failure to cross-examine a witness on any matter generally implies an acceptance of his or her evidence on that point. If the point is disputed the questioner would be expected to put questions to the witness suggesting that the witness is mistaken or is lying on that point. However, where an accused has already asserted facts in his or her defence outline which contradict the witness, the judge should not normally draw an adverse inference if X omits to cross-examine on the point. The judge (if the prosecutor has not already covered the point) may put the conflict to the witness and invite his or her comments. Where evidence proving an essential element is missing, the issue that the appellant did not challenge it in cross-examination does not arise. He or she cannot challenge what is not there: *Manyika* HH-215-02.

If evidence has already been given or will be given subsequently which is to a different effect from that stated by the witness, the effect of that evidence must be put to him or herin cross-examination to enable him or her to admit, deny or explain it.

A person may not cross-examine his or her own witness. During his or her testimony, a State witness may say something in evidence which may mean that X has some defence. He or she might say, for instance, that X was very drunk. It is impermissible for the prosecutor to cross-examine his or her own witness on this point in order to rebut this aspect of the evidence of the witness. The judge must stop the prosecutor if he or she does this. If the prosecutor thinks that his or her witness has become hostile, he or she must apply to the court to declare him or heror her to be a hostile witness, and only after the witness has been so declared is the prosecutor entitled to cross-examine him or her. This topic is dealt with more fully in the section on "Evidence — inconsistent previous statements and impeachment".

With the undefended accused the judge should inform him or her of his or her right to cross-examine State witnesses and explain to him or her what cross-examination is for. He or she should also explain to X the necessity for him or her to ensure that where he or she disagrees with their evidence his or her version must be put to them so that they can comment thereon. The judge must make sure X understands that if he or she disagrees with any evidence they have given, he or she must challenge it in cross-examination since failure to do so might be held against him.

As stated previously, the undefended accused should be given as much leeway as possible when he or she is cross-examining. After all he or she is not a trained lawyer and is not schooled in the rules relating to evidence and cross-examination of witnesses. Instead of the judge telling X in peremptory terms that his or her questions are irrelevant or simply telling him or her angrily that he or she is wasting the court's time, the judge should bring to his or her attention the aspects of the State witness testimony which are damning and which need to be brought into issue. Where X does not do so, the judge should ask pertinent questions of State witnesses so that lines of defence raised by X in his or her outline are explored with the State witnesses.

Re-examination

Reid-Rowland 18-28

After a witness has been cross-examined, the party originally calling him or her may put further questions to him. There are, however, strict limits to the type of questions which may be put and the judge must ensure that these limits are not exceeded by the questioner. Only questions relevant to matters raised within cross-examination may be put; leading questions may not be put. New matters may only be introduced if the judge grants leave to do so. If the matter was not raised in cross-examination due to an oversight, it may only be raised in re-examination if the court grants special leave for the point then to be raised.

In the South African case of *Ramalope* 1995 (1) SACR 616 (A), the court said that generally speaking, the object of re-examination is to clear up any point or misunderstanding which may have occurred during cross-examination; to correct wrong impressions or false perceptions which may have been created in the course of cross-examination; to give the witness a fair opportunity to explain answers given by him or her under cross-examination which, if unexplained, may create a wrong impression or be used to arrive at false deductions; to put before the court the full context of fact elicited during cross-examination; or to give the witness an opportunity to correct patent mistakes made under cross-examination. These examples are not a *numerus clausus*. Re-examination can be, and frequently is, a very important mechanism for presenting a full and fair picture of the evidence of a witness and thus of arriving at the truth. Of course, if counsel wishes to deal with new matter (i.e. not arising from the cross-examination) he or she requires the leave of the court to do so. Re-examination should be allowed on all matters raised during cross-examination, whether they have been raised in examination-in-chief or not. The court should invite counsel to re-examine a witness, not wait for counsel to apply for the right to do so.

In this case, where a magistrate had refused to allow counsel to re-examine his or her witness except on points which had been raised for the first time in cross-examination, the appeal court found that his or her refusal amounted to an irregularity.

Questioning by judge

Reid-Rowland 16-5

The judge's role is to try to ascertain the truth. He or she is therefore entitled, and indeed duty bound, to ask questions of both State and defence witnesses in order to clarify points and to ascertain the true facts. Where the case involves an accused who is not legally represented, the judge may often have to put questions to the witnesses so that facts favourable to X emerge. The judge must not, however, assume the role of prosecutor and put a barrage of questions to witnesses to try to ensure that X is convicted.

In *Denhere & Anor* S-39-91, the Supreme Court found that although the magistrate had admittedly asked many questions of the defence witnesses and none of the State witnesses, none of the questions were improper and he had explained in his or her judgment that he needed to resolve all contradictions and also make it clear to those witnesses that, for good reason, he did not believe them, giving them a chance to convince him. He was simply probing the defence to ascertain the truth. He had not approached the trial with a closed mind regarding the possible innocence of X. See also *Wright* S-183-89; *Hove* S-64-88.

In the case of *Ndhlovu* 1992 (2) ZLR 231 (S), the Supreme Court observed that the trial court should ask State witnesses to comment on points clearly mentioned by X in his or her defence outline if a legally unrepresented accused does not put these points to the witnesses during cross-examination; the court should not simply draw an adverse inference from the X's failure to raise these points in cross-examination. By doing this, the court is not taking sides or entering the arena; it is simply ensuring that X's defence case is properly commented upon by the witnesses.

Juvenile witnesses

Reid-Rowland 13-12

Although there is no legal requirement that the parents or guardian of a juvenile must be advised when that juvenile is required to give evidence in court so that they can be present if they so wish, where a young child is called upon to testify, especially where the child is a complainant in a sexual case, it is most advisable that the parents or guardians be informed so that they can be present. The judge may also make use of the vulnerable witnesses' provisions in the Criminal Procedure and Evidence Act. (See below).

In terms of s 194(8) CPEA, a judge may direct that persons other than the lawyers and the parents or guardian be excluded from the courtroom when a person under eighteen is testifying.

Vulnerable witnesses

In terms of Part XIVA CPEA magistrates are given the power to take various measures to protect vulnerable witnesses when they testify.

A vulnerable witness is a witness who is likely:

- to suffer emotional stress from giving evidence;
- to be intimidated by the accused or another person or by the nature of the proceedings or the place where they are taking place so as not to be able to give evidence fully and truthfully.

Where the judge believes that a person is such a vulnerable witness the judge may take certain measures either at his or her own instigation or on application from a party to the proceedings. The judge may appoint an intermediary or a support person for the witness or direct that the witness will give evidence in a position or place, either out of or in the accused's presence, that the judge considers will reduce the stress or intimidation.

If the evidence is to be given out of the presence of the accused, the judge must ensure that the accused and his or her legal representative are able to see and hear the person giving evidence by appropriate means, such as through a screen or by means of closed-circuit television.

If the problem is with the place where the proceedings are being conducted, the judge can adjourn the proceedings to some other place, where the court considers the person will be less likely to be subjected to stress or intimidation.

Another alternative measure is for the judge to make an order in terms of the Courts and Adjudicating Authorities (Publicity Restriction) Act excluding all persons or any class of persons from the proceedings while the person is giving evidence.

In deciding whether these measures should be invoked the judge is enjoined to take into account these factors:

- the vulnerable witness's age, mental and physical condition and cultural background; and
- the relationship, if any, between the vulnerable witness and any other party to the proceedings; and
- the nature of the proceedings; and
- the feasibility of taking the measure concerned; and
- any views expressed by the parties to the proceedings; and
- the interests of justice.

The court may also interview the vulnerable witness concerned out of the sight and hearing of the parties to the proceedings, but may not in this interview discuss the merits of the case.

Before it takes these measures, the judge must afford the parties to the proceedings an opportunity to make representations in the matter.

Except where there are special circumstances, the person appointed as an intermediary must be an interpreter or a person who had undergone approved training as an intermediary.

The judge may appoint as a support person a parent, guardian or other relative of the witness or any other person whom the judge considers will provide moral support whilst the witness gives evidence.

Where an intermediary is appointed, a party to the proceedings may only put questions to the witness through the intermediary. However, the judge may put questions to the witness directly or through the intermediary.

Subject to any directions from the judge, the intermediary must convey to the witness only the substance and effect of any question put to the witness and will relay the answer of the witness, using as far as possible, precise words of the witness.

Where a support person has been appointed for a vulnerable witness, the support person will be entitled to sit or stand near the witness whilst the witness is giving evidence in order to provide moral support for the witness, and will perform such other functions for that purpose as the court may direct.

When determining what weight to attach to the evidence of a vulnerable witness for whom an intermediary or a support person has been appointed, the judge must pay due regard to the effect of the appointment on the witness's evidence and on any cross-examination of the witness.

Allowing witnesses to be seated

Where a witness is frail, infirm or ill or for some other reason it will be uncomfortable for him or herto testify while standing, he or she should be allowed to be seated while he or she testifies. This would apply to elderly witnesses and pregnant women.

Statements made by accused to police

Reid-Rowland Chapter 20

Types of statement

All statements made by accused persons outside the court during investigations, including written and oral statements, confessions and statements made to the police during indications are subject to special rules in terms of the Criminal Procedure and Evidence Act. Regarding indications made to the police: see *Ndlovu* 1988 (2) ZLR 465 (S).

The same rules as to admissibility apply to all statements made by the accused, whether oral or in writing, whether constituting a confession or not, and whether inculpatory or exculpatory (or partly one or the other). These rules also apply to indications made to the police.

In *Toms* S-200-93, the court stated that a policeman is only required to warn and caution a suspect before recording a statement. A policeman attending a vehicle accident does not have to caution the motorists involved in the accident before recording their statements in a Traffic Accident Book. A motorist's statement was admissible unless she was a suspect at the time and was improperly induced, threatened or forced to make the statement.

In *Muchindu & Ors* 1994 (2) SACR 179 (C), the court stated that in a trial within a trial to determine whether indications made by X were freely and voluntarily made, photographs of X making indications may be produced in order to show that he or she made them freely and voluntarily.

In *Mlambo* HB-72-03, X signed an admission of guilt and paid a deposit fine for a traffic offence. The circumstances in which he or she did so were questionable, and it appeared that the police coerced him. He was later charged in court with the offence. It was held that the admission could not be held against him. The trial should be continued without regard to the admission.

Method of production

The method of production of an accused's statement depends upon whether or not the statement has previously been confirmed before a magistrate.

Confirmed by Magistrate

A statement which has been confirmed by a magistrate under s 113 CPEA must be admitted by the court into evidence on its mere production by the prosecution without any further proof under s 256(2) CPEA. If X challenges the admissibility of the statement the onus is upon him or her to prove its inadmissibility.

Not Confirmed by Magistrate

If the statement has not been confirmed before a magistrate and X challenges the admissibility of that statement, a trial within a trial must be held to determine the admissibility of the statement. The statement must not be admitted into evidence and does not become an exhibit until the State has proved that it is admissible.

If X denies making the statement to the police, the making of the statement becomes a factual issue. The prosecutor will have to call the police officers who recorded the statement to seek to prove that X did indeed make the statement. X or his or her lawyer is entitled to cross-examine these police witnesses.

If X admits he or she made the statement, but asserts that the statement was not made freely and voluntarily, the prosecutor will have to call the police officers who interrogated X and who recorded his or her statement in order to try to prove that the statement was freely and voluntarily made.

The correct procedure for producing an unconfirmed statement is as follows:

1. When a policeman is giving evidence and is about to relate what X said to him or heror her, he or she should say "X made a statement to me".

2. He or she should then stop. If he or she does not stop, he or she should be stopped. If the prosecutor does not stop him or her, the judge should.

3. If he or she says, "X then admitted", he or she should be stopped at once, told of his or her error, and the judge should record 'X then made a statement' to this witness.

4. The prosecutor should then ask the witness the standard questions:
   (a) Was X in his or her sound and sober senses at the time?
   (b) Did he or she make the statement freely and voluntarily?
   (c) Was any undue influence brought to bear on him or her to make the statement?

5. The prosecutor should then say to the court, "The State proposes to tender this statement in evidence", or words to that effect.

6. If all the questions set out in 4. have been answered satisfactorily, the court should then ascertain from X whether he or she wishes to challenge the admissibility of the statement, and should explain, if he or she is not represented, what is meant by challenging its admissibility.

7. If X does not challenge, the witness may then be invited to produce the written statement or recite the oral statement, as the case may be.

8. If X does properly challenge the admissibility of the statement, then a trial within a trial must ensue if the prosecutor still wishes to produce the statement.

Taken from the case of *BC & Anor* HH-255-84; see also *Nkomo & Anor* 1989 (3) ZLR 117 (S).

Required explanation

Some statutory provisions require X to give an explanation such as in relation to his or her possession of property in respect of which there was a reasonable suspicion that it was stolen (e.g. s 14 of the Miscellaneous Offences Act [*Chapter 9:15*] and s 10 of the Copper Control Act [*Chapter 14:06*]). If X's required explanation was in written form, the procedure for adducing a warned and cautioned statement does not have to be followed in regard to this statement as X is obliged by statute to advance an explanation; such a statement can be produced without formality like any other statement.

Onus of proof when challenged

Reid-Rowland 20-17

Different rules apply depending upon whether or not the statement under challenge had previously been confirmed before a magistrate

Confirmed by Magistrate

Where a statement of an accused person has been properly confirmed in terms of s 113 CPEA, the onus is on X under the proviso to s 256(2) CPEA to prove on a balance of probabilities that the statement was not made by him or her or that it was not made freely and voluntarily and without undue influence. It is not necessary for the court to believe his or her story beyond any doubt; if the court comes to the conclusion, despite certain reservations, that X is telling the truth, then he or she has discharged the onus: *Ndlovu* 1983 (4) SA 507 (ZS); *Mthombeni* S-80-90.

In *Tshumba & Anor* S-137-94, the appellants challenged the validity of the proceedings in which their statements were confirmed. The onus was on the State to prove that there was no irregularity; no record of the proceedings was produced at the trial and the magistrate was not called, so the onus was not discharged and the statement had to be treated as unconfirmed.

The onus was then on the State to prove beyond reasonable doubt, in a trial within a trial, that the statement was made freely and voluntarily and without undue influence. The State did not call the witnesses who allegedly confronted the appellant so there was no proven legitimate explanation for his or her change from denials to confession. The policeman admitted he or she recorded only what he or she thought was relevant, not the whole statement; and the wording of the statement was highly improbable. It should not have been allowed into evidence. The court again emphasised that it was a misdirection to put the statement before the judge during the trial within a trial, or to cross-examine as to its truth.

Not confirmed by magistrate

Where the statement has not been confirmed in terms of s 113 CPEA, the onus rests squarely on the State to prove that it was made freely and voluntarily and without undue influence. The State must prove this beyond reasonable doubt. The reasons why the statement was not confirmed must obviously be probed: *Slatter & Ors* 1983 ZLR 144 (H).

Trial within a trial

Reid-Rowland 20-17 – 20-19

When X challenges the admissibility of his or her statement it is permissible for the judge to ask X to give details of his or her reasons for challenging the statement. Before doing so, however, the police detail who dealt with the case must be asked to leave the court so that there is no danger of members of the detail adapting their later testimony in the light of the nature of X's challenge. At the start of the trial within a trial the prosecutor is entitled to ask the judge that X be called upon to indicate how he or she was assaulted or pressurised, where this was done and by whom: *Musekiwa & Ors* 1965 RLR 225 (A). See *Prosecutors Handbook* Chapter 23.

Where there is more than one accused person challenging the admissibility of an extra-curial statement, the admissibility of all the challenged statements should be determined at one trial within trial, rather than dealing with the statements piecemeal. This practice is calculated to ensure that the judicial officer has all relevant evidence before him or her when giving his or her rulings on admissibility. It may happen that the necessity for holding a trial within a trial arises quite unexpectedly or at a time when it would be inconvenient or impracticable to consolidate such a trial within similar trials. Departures from the general practice must be left to the good sense and judicial discretion of the presiding officer. *Gumbo & Ors* HB-46-06.

Where X denies that he or she made the statement, it is not necessary to hold a trial within a trial unless this denial turns out to be a disguised form of challenge to the admissibility of the statement: *Chamba & Ors* A-43-79. A straight denial by X that he or she made the statement can be dealt with as a factual matter in respect of which the State can call evidence to try to rebut this denial.

There is no legal basis for holding a trial within a trial where a State witness alleges that his or her statement to the police was extracted from him or herby undue influence. In *Million* HH-53-92, the holding of such a trial within a trial was highly irregular, as was the allowing of the prosecutor at this trial within a trial to cross-examine his or her own witnesses as if he or she were the accused person at the trial within a trial.

In *Donga & Anor* S-169-93, the court pointed out that a confession may be truthful but may still be inadmissible, e.g. where it has been obtained by duress or other improper means. In a trial within a trial therefore, it does not seem to be advisable for the judicial officer to see the confession itself because if the statement is ruled to be inadmissible, there is a danger of unconscious prejudice. Additionally, the contents show its truth but it was difficult to see how its contents can help prove its admissibility. Further, cross-examination on the truth of a confession is not permitted during investigation into its admissibility.

In *Donga & Anor* S-169-93, the court pointed out that a confession may be truthful but may still be inadmissible, e.g. where it has been obtained by duress or other improper means. In a trial within a trial therefore it does not seem to be advisable for the judicial officer to see the confession itself because if the statement is ruled to be inadmissible, there is a danger of unconscious prejudice. Additionally, the contents show its truth but it was difficult to see how its contents can help prove its admissibility. Further, cross-examination on the truth of a confession is not permitted during investigation into its admissibility.

In cases of multiple accused challenging the admissibility of an extra-curial statement, it is desirable to determine admissibility of all challenged statements in one trial within a trial rather than piecemeal. In *Gumbo & Ors* HB-46-06, it was held that where there is more than one accused person challenging the admissibility of an extra-curial statement, the admissibility of all the challenged statements should be determined at one trial within trial, rather than dealing with the statements piecemeal. This practice is calculated to ensure that the judicial officer has all relevant evidence before him or her when giving his or her rulings on admissibility. It may happen that the necessity for holding a trial within a trial arises quite unexpectedly or at a time when it would be inconvenient or impracticable to consolidate such a trial within similar trials. Departures from the general practice must be left to the good sense and judicial discretion of the presiding officer.

State witnesses alleging that police assaulted them to extract statements

If X says that he or she was beaten by the police but that he or she was not influenced by this beating to make a statement, it will be unnecessary to hold a trial within a trial if the judge is satisfied that X did make the statement without being influenced by the beating as he or she asserts: *Mujuru* 1976 (2) SA 900 (RA).

When statement inadmissible

Reid-Rowland 20-2 – 20-8

A confession or a statement made by X is admissible in terms of s 256 CPEA if it is "freely and voluntarily made by X without his or her having been unduly influenced thereto".

The statement will not have been made freely and voluntarily and without undue influence if X made the statement because:

- he or she was tortured, beaten up or physically maltreated in some other way, such as by being deprived of sleep or food and drink for long periods in order to force him or herto confess;
- he or she was threatened with death or with torture or physical brutality unless he or she made the statement;
- he or she was told that dire consequences would occur to members of his or her family unless he or she made the statement;
- he or she was offered some benefit or advantage if he or she confessed to the crime, such as that he or she would be released from custody as soon as he or she confessed or that if he or she confessed he or she would receive only a light sentence such as a fine;
- he or she had been kept in solitary confinement for a long period and no one had been allowed to visit him or her and he or she confessed simply because he or she could no longer bear this isolation;
- he or she had been denied access to his or her lawyer after requesting access to him or her and had been pressured into making a statement in the absence of his or her lawyer;
- he or she had been subjected to such intensive, hostile and prolonged questioning that his or her freedom of volition had been overborne as a result of this psychological pressure.

The reason why such evidence is not admissible is that the contents of a statement made in these circumstances will be highly unreliable.

See *Ananias* 1963 R&N 938 (SR); *Hlupe* 1964 RLR 333 (GD); *Murambiwa* 1951 SR 271 (SR); *Michael & Anor* 1962 R&N 374; *Dube* 1965 RLR 177 (A); *Hackwell* 1965 RLR 1 (A); *Edward* 1966 (2) SA 359 (R); *Mfungelwa* 1967 RLR 308; *Schaube-Kuffler* 1969 (1) RLR 78 (A); *Attorney-General* v *Slatter & Ors* 1984 (1) ZLR 306 (S); *Mthombeni* S-80-90; *Nkomo & Anor* 1989 (3) ZLR 117 (S); *Jana* S-172-88; *Ndlovu* 1988 (2) ZLR 465 (S).

A confirmed statement can be introduced in evidence on mere production. If X challenges such a statement the onus is on him or her to prove on a balance of probabilities that or she did not make it or did not make it freely and voluntarily.

If challenged, unconfirmed statements may not be produced until their admissibility has been determined at a trial within a trial. The onus is on the State to prove that, despite X's protestations to the contrary, it was made by X and was made freely and voluntarily.

In the case of *Woods* 1993 (2) ZLR 258 (S), the Supreme Court commented upon the effect of refusal of the police to allow access by prisoners to their lawyers. It said that the court cannot condone a blatant refusal of access to their lawyers of prisoners held in police custody. Such refusal violates the fundamental right granted by s 13(3) of the Constitution and brings the administration of justice into disrepute. Where there has been a wilful and flagrant denial of access, this will warrant the exclusion of evidence in any extra-curial statement or indication made prior to the allowing of access to the lawyers.

On the other hand, confrontation by the police does not amount to duress Confrontation is a permissible element of police interrogation procedures, provided it is not improper or persistent. It is not improper to tell a suspect that his or her co-accused has confessed where that indeed has happened, nor is it improper for the police to tell the suspect that they know about an incident connected with the alleged crime. See *Nkomo & Anor* 1993 (2) ZLR 131 (S).

In the case of *Woods & Ors* S-60-93, the court dealt with a challenge to a warned and cautioned statement. The court said that if the defence is able to raise a potentially sustainable challenge to the propriety of the confirmation proceedings under Part VIII CPEA when the prosecutor tenders a confirmed extra-curial statement, the court must decide the validity of that challenge as a separate preliminary issue of fact, before the statements are introduced. The impropriety need not be apparent in the transcript of the confirmation proceedings. The defence can rely on external factors, such as a denial of legal representation or a police threat. The onus is on the State to prove the absence of any irregularity. If the challenge is rejected, s 42(1)(a) of Chapter 9:07 is satisfied and the statement is provisionally accepted with the onus then on X to rebut the presumption of admissibility, on a balance of probabilities. If the challenge is upheld, then the separate issue of admissibility must be decided with the onus on the State to prove beyond reasonable doubt that X made the statement, freely and voluntarily and without undue influence. A rolled-up approach to deciding the validity of confirmation proceedings and the admissibility of the statements can be inappropriate and fraught with possible prejudice. The return of an accused person to police custody after confirmation proceedings should be avoided wherever possible, to avoid abuse. In this case, the Supreme Court found that the statements of 2 appellants were validly confirmed, and could have been provisionally admitted with the onus on those appellants to prove their inadmissibility. It then found that the defence had proved the inadmissibility of all the statements made while the police denied all 3 prisoners access to their lawyers.

If an accused is legally represented at proceedings under Part VIIA CPEA to confirm his or her extra-curial statement, the judge can expect the legal practitioner to raise any complaint and need not be on guard to the same degree as he or she should be if X is unrepresented.

A challenge to the propriety of confirmation proceedings can be based on factors not shown in the record of those proceedings, and must be decided as a separate preliminary issue, with the onus on the State. During a separate issue, no adverse inference can be drawn from the refusal of an accused to answer questions about the contents of the statements, because their truth or falsity is irrelevant; it is only their admissibility that is to be decided. Statements made while the appellants were being deliberately denied access to a lawyer were inadmissible, whether properly confirmed or not.

Extra-curial statements made by accused while pointing out

If the accused testifies that the indications made by him or her to the police were made under duress, the court must hold a trial within a trial

In *Ndlovu* 1988 (2) ZLR 465 (S), the court commented upon the provision now contained in s 258(2) CPEA. This section renders admissible anything that was pointed out by the accused or any fact discovered in consequence of information given by the accused, even if the pointing out or information forms part of a confession or statement that is not admissible. The section does not, however, render admissible the statements or remarks made by the accused while he or she is pointing out the object or scene in question, nor does it cover statements he or she may make on the way to the scene. If the police wish to give evidence about what the accused said in these circumstances, he or she must be given the usual opportunity to say whether or not he or she made the statements freely and voluntarily and without undue influence. If he or she puts the matter in issue, and if the statements have not been confirmed, there must be a "trial within a trial".

In *Mazono & Anor* 2000 (1) ZLR 347 (H), the accused stated at their trial that indications made by them to the police were made under duress. The magistrate admitted these statements and decided that they had been made voluntarily, without holding a trial within a trial. The High Court decided that the magistrate had been wrong in admitting these statements. Where there is a dispute as to whether a statement by an accused person was made freely and voluntarily, a separate issue or trial within a trial must be held before such a statement can be admitted in evidence.

See also *S* v *David* HH-204-94.

However, any evidence, such as the murder weapon, discovered as a result of his or her indication or of information given by X is still admissible even if X did not make the indications freely and voluntarily: *Nkomo* 1989 (3) ZLR 117 (S); *Jana* S-172-88; *Ndlovu* 1988 (2) ZLR 465 (S).

Whether accuseds' extra-curial statement admissible in evidence against a co-accused

In *Sibanda* 1993 (1) SACR 691 (ZS), the court said that it is only in two exceptional situations that an extra-curial statement may be admitted as evidence not only against its maker but also against a co-accused. The first is where the co-accused, by words or conduct, accepts the truth of the statement so as to make all or part of it his or her own. The second exception applies in the case of conspiracy or any crime committed in furtherance of a conspiracy; statements of any conspiracy made in the execution or furtherance of the common design are admissible in evidence against any other conspirator. Statements made after the conspiracy has ceased to exist are not so admissible, however.

As a result, an extra-curial statement made to the police by one conspirator cannot be regarded as corroborating the evidence of a witness implicating a co-conspirator.

In *Chatanga* HH-19-90, X alleged that he was forced to make the unconfirmed warned and cautioned statement. Without dealing with that challenge by holding a trial within a trial, the policeman who recorded the statement was called and he or she produced the statement as if it had not been challenged. The review court said that the magistrate should have determined whether the statement was admissible by holding a trial within a trial.

If X admits that he or she made the statement and that it was made freely and voluntarily, then it may be produced in evidence.

Summary

A confirmed statement may be introduced in evidence on mere production. If the defence challenges such a statement the onus is on it to prove on a balance of probabilities that X did not make it or did not make it freely and voluntarily.

If the defence challenges an unconfirmed statement the statement may not be produced until its admissibility has been determined at a trial within a trial. The onus is on the State to prove that, despite X's protestations to the contrary, it was made by X and was made freely and voluntarily.

Formal admissions by defence or State

Reid-Rowland 18-4 – 18-5

During the course of his or her trial, X may admit to any fact relevant to the issue. The prosecutor may also make such admissions: s 314 CPEA. Any such admission "shall be sufficient evidence of that fact".
This provision only applies to admissions during the trial following upon a plea of not guilty or the entering of such a plea by the judge: *Dhliwayo* 1987 (1) ZLR 1 (H).

This procedure allows for admissions to be made thereby dispensing with the need for that fact to be proved. Where an undefended accused purports to make an admission of fact, the court must ensure that X properly understands what he or she is admitting and that he or she is competent to make the admission. X's legal representative may make admissions on his or her behalf. Admissions are usually only made by the defence on relatively minor matters which do not go to the heart of the issue.

In *Tashu* HH-172-94, the court said that when an accused is unrepresented and the prosecutor wants admissions from him or her in terms of s 314 CPEA, the prosecutor must ask the court to seek the admissions, setting out each one clearly and separately. The court must then explain to X that he or she is not obliged to make any admissions, before asking him or her about each point. He or she is not to be pressured, nor to be cross-examined or even questioned by the prosecutor.

In *Chirimuuta* S-3-95, an unrepresented accused was asked to agree to the production of a policeman's Traffic Accident Book without calling the policeman. Such a person should never be asked to consent to the production of a document unless it is made quite clear to him or her what his or her consent involves - particularly when his or her defence outline already shows its contents are in issue. Also consent to the production of a document is not an admission that its contents are true and correct.

In *Mubaya* S-5-93, a blood alcohol level slightly above the legal limit is something outside X's knowledge; the driver is not shown to have been incapable of proper control. The prosecutor must place forensic evidence before the court in proof of the alleged concentration, or the court must ask for such evidence. The omission to do this and simply relying upon questions under s 271(2)(b) was a fatal defect.

Section 314(2) CPEA further provides that if the judge considers it desirable, for the purpose of clarifying the facts in issue or obviating the production of evidence on facts which do not appear to be in dispute, he or she may **on the application** of the prosecutor, X or his or her lawyer ask the prosecutor, X or his or her lawyer whether a fact relevant to the issue is admitted.

In the case of *Kajokoto* HH-32-05 X had pleaded not guilty and outlined the basis for his defence. The prosecutor applied for admissions. When the application was granted, the prosecutor proceeded to interrogate the accused, as a result of which the accused made various admissions. The court held that the magistrate did not comply with the requirements of s 314(2) CPE. The magistrate should have ascertained from the prosecutor what facts it was intended to be sought as admissions. It was the duty of the magistrate, not the prosecutor, to ask the accused person if he was willing to admit the facts concerned in order to obviate the need to adduce evidence. The admissions envisaged by the section are for purposes of clarifying the facts in issue or those facts which do not appear to be in dispute. It is not intended under this section to give the prosecutor an opportunity to cross-examine the accused and force him to make admissions in the absence of any evidence from the State.

Care must be taken to ensure that admissions are correctly recorded as disputes may later arise as to what exactly was admitted.

Production of Exhibits

Generally

The way in which exhibits are produced is set out in Chapter 17 of the *Prosecutors Handbook*.

If the size or condition of an exhibit, such as a knife, is material, the prosecutor will ask the judge to examine the exhibit and note on record the result of his or her observations. If the judge examines an exhibit and makes observations about its size, condition, etc. he or she must state his or her observations e.g. that a knife has a blade which is about 20cm and appears to have blood stains on it. It is important that all observations are noted in the record. Exhibits are not sent to the High Court on review so the review judge must be able to ascertain details of exhibits from the record. This is also important for the purposes of appeals.

All exhibits produced must be properly proved by evidence on oath from witnesses unless there is statutory authority for handing them in from the bar, that is, for the production of them by the prosecutor. There are a number of documentary exhibits which are usually produced by handing them in from the Bar. These are dealt with below.

All exhibits should be marked as they are produced in court.

Documentary exhibits

Reid-Rowland Chapter 19

Subject to certain exceptions dealt with below, documentary exhibits must be proved by evidence on oath from witnesses.

A court should not put itself in the position where a party to a dispute may perceive it as having acted unfairly. In *Austin & Anor* v *Minister of State (Security) & Anor; Bull* v *Minister of State (Security) & Anor* 1986 (2) ZLR 28 (S), the reliance placed upon a document by the judge was contrary to the *audi alteram partem* rule and to the protection of law enacted in the Constitution because it was handed to the judge in chambers without access of the other party and not under cover of affidavit or Ministerial certificate. This was held to be irregular.

Photographs and plans

To prove photographs and plans, the State must call the person who made the indications or observations upon the basis of which the photograph was taken or the plan made: s 279 CPEA. The plan or photograph may be handed in to the court by the prosecutor without having to call the witness to prove it if there is consent from the defence to its production without the witness being called: s 279(2)(b) CPEA.

Notes in police notebooks

Police witnesses may wish to refer to notes in their notebooks taken soon after the incident about which they are being asked to testify. The judge is entitled to examine these notes, as is the defence.

In the *Prosecutors Handbook* Chapter 18, it is stated that police notebooks are frequently used to record unconfirmed warned and cautioned statements. Magistrates should not ask that the relevant pages from the notebook be torn out to put them in the court record as an exhibit. The correct procedure is for the policeman to read the statement from the notebook in evidence and for the judge to record in the court record whatever is read out. The judge should examine the notebook to check the accuracy of the evidence, but should, generally, return the notebook to the witness.

In more general terms, if a witness refreshes his or her memory from contemporaneous notes, the document used to refresh his or her memory should be produced and once produced the witness may be cross-examined on the document. However, the document only becomes an exhibit if the witness is cross-examined on parts of the document other than those he or she used to refresh his or her memory.

Documents admissible in affidavit form

Reid-Rowland Chapter 19

There are statutory provisions allowing for the handing in of certain types of documentary exhibits without calling the persons who made them to testify in court.

Section 278 CPEA allows the production of certain documents from the persons who compiled these documents provided that these are in affidavit form. These are:

Medical Reports from doctors
ss 278, 279 and 280 CPEA.
In cases such as assault with intent to cause grievous bodily harm, culpable homicide, attempted murder, infanticide and rape the State will often want to introduce medical evidence. If the State wishes to produce that evidence in affidavit form certain formalities must be followed.

Section 278(11) CPEA provides that X must be given three days' notice of the intended production of the report. A written medical report is not admissible unless X has been given three days' notice of the intended production of the medical report or X waived his or her right to be given three day's notice. Where X is unrepresented the implications of consenting to the production of a medical report in affidavit form should be fully explained to him. The proper procedure is for the affidavit which is to be adduced in evidence to be read out to X, and for the explanation then to be given to him or her that he or she has a right to have the doctor called for cross-examination and, if he or she consents to the admission of the report, he or she will be consenting to the truth and accuracy of its contents. See *Anock* 1973 RLR 154 (A).

The court has the discretion in terms of s 280 proviso (ii) CPEA to order that the doctor be summoned to give oral evidence at the trial. It may also send written questions to him or herto which he or she must reply.

It will be necessary to use the power to ask the doctor to give oral testimony when the original affidavit is inadequate and the court is unable to arrive at a just decision on the basis of this report. If the information is very scanty or vital information is omitted, or the information in the report seems to be contradictory, this power should be exercised. But if it contains all the necessary information there will be no need to summon the doctor: *Anock* 1973 RLR 154 (A); *Sibanda* A-10-72; *Melrose* 1984 (2) ZLR 217 (S).

It is further provided that at the request of the prosecutor or X, made not less than three days before the trial, the medical practitioner shall be summoned to give oral evidence: proviso (iii) to s 280 CPEA.

Reports from nurses, ambulance drivers and carriers
s 278(5) CPEA.

Reports from Vehicle Inspectors
s 278(4) CPEA.

Photocopies of extracts from accused's diary
In *Dube* S-53-95, the court said that a photocopy which was allegedly a part of the appellant's diary was produced in evidence under s 281 CPEA. No-one knew who had made the copy, and although appellant admitted that he or she kept a diary, he or she denied that this was a true extract from it. The copy had not:

- been made or kept by him
- been in the course of transmission to him
- been in his or her custody or control.

It was not admissible in evidence under that section. It could have been admitted if some witness had testified to making it and properly identified its source.

Photographs at scene of traffic accident
In *Mposi* S-22-94, the appellant's agents took photographs of the accident site three weeks after the accident and introduced them unproved and unexplained during cross-examination of the complainant. This should not have been allowed: photographs are secondary evidence and are inadmissible unless a proper foundation is laid, or they are admitted by agreement. Great care should be taken before allowing them to supplant the evidence of eye witnesses. Photographs can be taken at angles that distort the truth; the angles from which they were taken should be clearly determined. They should be taken by someone impartial. Their proximity in time is often crucial, especially for traffic accidents on a busy road. Where these photographs conflicted with the eye-witness testimony and the police observations soon after the accident, they had to be rejected.

Certified Documents

Reid-Rowland Chapter 19

In various statutes, there is provision for documents to be certified so that they can be produced in court. These include documents certified under s 319 of the Companies Act

[*Chapter 24:03*], under s 196 of the Insolvency Act [*Chapter 6:04*] and under s 23(6) of the Maintenance Act [*Chapter 5:09*].

The procedure for the production of certified copies of official and public documents is set out in ss 275-277 CPEA.

Bankers' books

Sections 285-289 CPEA provide an easy method of proving entries in bankers' books. This special procedure is necessary because it would be impossible for banks to function efficiently if their officials had to attend the various courts in the country and produce the bank's books to prove the entries therein.

Under this procedure, a copy of an extract from bank books can be produced without having to call someone from the bank to prove that extract in court, provided that an official from the bank (such as the bank's accountant) has sworn an affidavit to the effect that the entries in question were made in the ordinary course of the business of the bank and that the copy is a true copy of the original entry.

This procedure applies in respect of commercial banks and other financial institutions registered under the Banking Act [*Chapter 24:01*], the Post Office Savings Bank, the Agricultural Finance Corporation and building societies. The same procedure applies in respect of foreign banks.

It can be used in relation to bankers' books and documents such as ledgers, day-books, cash books, deposit slips and letters of transfer.

Under this procedure, X is served with a copy of an extract from the bank's books. The papers from the prosecutor in this regard must be served on X at least ten days in advance of the criminal proceedings, unless he or she agrees to waive this period of notice.

If he or she wishes to do so, X will be given the opportunity of comparing this copy with the original entries in the bank book. In order to do this, X must make an application to a judge who may make an order that X be permitted to inspect the relevant bank books and take copies from the books which relate to the matter in question. Three days' notice must be given to the bank should the court grant such an application.

The certified copies of the extracts are *prima facie* evidence of the matters, transactions and accounts recorded in them. It is not conclusive proof and the court may decide not to accept the documents as evidence of those transactions where, for instance, there is doubt regarding the accuracy of the entries, or where a bank official has been charged with an offence which involves the alteration of the bank's books of account.

Documents made in course of business

Sections 281-284 CPEA provide for the production of documents made during the course of business or trade.

In terms of s 282(2) CPEA, records relating to any transactions in connection with any trade, business or occupation are admissible on mere production, provided that the facts contained in them would have been admissible as direct oral evidence. The transaction can be either inside or outside Zimbabwe. This provision provides a way for the State to overcome the difficulty of having to call the person who originally made these records.

Section 281(2) CPEA can be used by the State to produce documents such as documents made and kept by an employee or agent of X, as proof of the facts contained in that document, provided that those facts would have been admissible as direct oral evidence.

Section 284 CPEA deals with stamps, signatures and writing on negotiable instruments which were purportedly made by personnel in banks outside Zimbabwe. Until the contrary is proved, these marks on the instruments are deemed to have been made by these bank personnel.

Documents executed outside Zimbabwe

For documents executed outside Zimbabwe to be admissible in evidence the document must be properly authenticated. This is dealt with in rule 3 of the High Court (Authentication of Documents) Rules, 1971 [RGN 995 of 1971]. This lays down that any document executed outside Zimbabwe is deemed to be sufficiently authenticated for the purpose of production in any court if it is authenticated by a notary public, a mayor or a person holding judicial office or by certain specified Zimbabwean diplomatic or consular officials in countries which have such officials.

Evidence on commission

There is provision for taking evidence on commission from witnesses where the attendance of the witness cannot be procured without unreasonable delay, expense or inconvenience: ss 281-284 CPEA. The judge may authorise the taking of evidence on commission in certain limited circumstances. When he or she does this it means that someone else, usually another judicial officer or a legal practitioner, will take and record the evidence and send the record to the trial court. It is the responsibility of the judge to ensure that the papers are forwarded to the person who will take the evidence on commission.

This procedure is very rarely used and is usually only done when the witness is outside Zimbabwe in some distant country. It must only be resorted to in respect of evidence of a formal nature and not evidence which could be the subject matter of serious cross-examination directed towards attacking the credibility or accuracy of the evidence. If he or she so wishes, X is entitled to be legally represented at the proceedings before the person commissioned to take the evidence, at State expense.

This subject is extensively dealt with in Chapter 29 of the *Prosecutors Handbook*.

Inspection in loco

Reid-Rowland 9-12 – 9-13

In *Toms* S-200-93, the court said that the facts found at an inspection *in loco* must be placed on record and the agreement of both parties to those facts should also be placed on record.

Adjournment

Reid-Rowland 15-5

Magistrates are given the discretion to decide to adjourn a case on the grounds that this is necessary or expedient. A case can be adjourned at any stage of the trial, whether or not evidence has been given. The period of adjournment must not exceed fourteen days unless X consents to a longer period of adjournment.

A case may be adjourned more than once for sufficient cause: s 166 CPEA.

Magistrates must obviously refrain from adjourning court for frivolous personal reasons.

Where a case is adjourned or postponed the court may release X on bail or extend his or her previous bail: s 167 CPEA. On Adjournment, see Appendix to this Handbook.

Court calling of further evidence

Reid-Rowland 16-6

It is a fundamental principle of our law that an accused person is entitled to a fair trial. The trial should be fair in substance as well as form. Where the accused is unrepresented, a trial judge has a duty to assist the accused, and to ensure that relevant evidence is called: *Garande* HH-46-02. Because the objective is to ensure that justice is achieved and because the liberty of X is often at stake in a criminal case, a judge in a criminal case has the right to call witnesses not called by either party. He or she may also recall and re-examine any witness already examined. He or she may do these things if the evidence appears to be essential for arriving at a just decision in the case: s 232 CPEA. This right, however, must be sparingly exercised. In defended cases it should not be exercised, save in exceptional circumstances, so as to interfere with the discretion of counsel in their choice of evidence they wish to be placed before the court: *Zakeyu* 1963 SR 434 (FS); *Buitendag* 1976 (1) RLR 345 (A); *Wright* S-183-89; *Shezi* 1994 (1) SACR 575 (A).

After the prosecution and defence had closed their cases and counsel had delivered their addresses, the court recalled a policeman who had given evidence at a trial within a trial to testify that X's confession referred to the offence with which X was charged. On appeal, it was argued that the court had improperly exercised its discretion under the South African equivalent of s 218 CPEA in recalling the witness.

It was held that the section confers a wide discretion on the court to recall a witness at any stage, and the court's decision in this case could not be faulted. The policeman's evidence was inherently formal, concise and uncontroversial.

Section 232 CPEA can also be used when the State by oversight has failed to prove a purely formal element. In *Mavingere* 1988 (2) ZLR 318 (S) it was stated that if the prosecutor at the trial fails to call the evidence necessary to prove a mere technicality or purely formal element, the judge should call the evidence himself acting in terms of s 232 CPEA. This provision should be sparingly used in respect of a missing element in the State case which is more than purely technical and which is of a contentious nature: *Mavingere* 1988 (2) ZLR 318 (S); *Nyamayaro* 1987 (2) ZLR 318 (S).

Discharge at end of State case

Reid-Rowland 16-32; 8-3

Section 198(3) CPEA provides that the court may return a verdict of not guilty after the State has closed its case and before the defence case has commenced. It may only return such a verdict if it considers that there is no evidence that X committed the offence charged or any other offence of which he or she might be convicted thereon.

X or his or her lawyer may apply for discharge at the close of the State case. But where X is unrepresented, even if he or she has not applied for discharge at the end of the State case, the court should consider whether he or she has a case to answer or whether he or she should be discharged without being put to his or her defence: *Ruzani* HB-63-84.

Under this provision, X may be discharged if there is no evidence either that he or she committed the offence charged **or** that he or she committed any other offence of which it is competent to convict him or heron the basis of the crime charged. If there is no evidence that X has committed the crime charged, the court must still consider what other crimes it is competent to convict X of on the basis of the crime charged and whether, in the light of the evidence produced by the State, there is evidence that X committed any of these other crimes. If there is such evidence X must be put to his or her defence.

When considering discharge, the judge must consider whether the State has made out a *prima facie* case against X, not whether the State has proved guilt beyond all reasonable doubt.

X must obviously be discharged if the State has been unable to lead any evidence whatsoever of the commission of the crime charged. This would be a very rare situation. If the entire case against X has collapsed, one would expect the prosecutor to withdraw the charge. The court in *Tsvangirai & Ors* HH-119-03 was alive to the rarity of such circumstances. The court summarized the circumstances in which discharge will be granted, as follows:

> " The court shall return a verdict of not guilty if at the close of the State case the court considers that there is no evidence that the accused committed the offence charged (or any other offence with which he or she could be convicted on that charge). Thus, the court must discharge the accused at the close of the case for the prosecution where: (a) there is no evidence to prove an essential element of the offence; (b) there is no evidence on which a reasonable court, acting carefully, might properly convict; (c) the evidence adduced on behalf of the State is so manifestly unreliable that no reasonable court could safely act on it. Instances of the last such cases will be rare; it would only in the most exceptional case where the credibility of a witness is so utterly destroyed that no part of his or her material evidence can possibly be believed."

Usually, some evidence will have been advanced by the State. Where this is the case the test to be applied is whether a reasonable court might convict X on the basis of that evidence. In the case of *Hartlebury & Anor* 1985 (1) ZLR 1 (H), the court elaborated further on the application of this test. It said that a court may order discharge where there is no evidence on which a reasonable court may convict. It may also order discharge where the evidence adduced by the prosecution is so discredited or manifestly unreliable that no reasonable court could safely act upon it or where there is no evidence to prove an essential element of the offence. These latter two grounds for discharge seem only to be particular illustrations of where the evidence adduced would not allow a reasonable court to convict. A reasonable court could not convict where the evidence led is totally unreliable or the State has failed to prove one of the essential elements of the crime charged.

In *Attorney-General* v *Bvuma* 1987 (2) ZLR 96 (S), the Supreme Court decided that, if the evidence led by the State is insufficient for a reasonable court to convict, the trial court should not refuse to discharge X at the close of the State case because it thinks that if X is put to his or her defence he or she could possibly provide a missing link in the State case. In other words, the onus is on the State to prove the guilt of X and if the State fails to produce evidence upon which a reasonable court could convict, the court should discharge X. It should not speculate on the possibility that the gaps in the State case might be plugged during the course of the defence case.

Where X is jointly tried together with others and the State has failed to adduce evidence upon which a reasonable court could convict X, it is not a proper basis for refusing to discharge X: *Attorney-General* v *Bvuma* 1987 (2) ZLR 96 (S).

In *Mpofu* S-192-90, two persons were jointly charged with theft of money. The State failed to prove which of the two had stolen the money. The magistrate put the two on their defence as they "were throwing stones at each other" so as to enable the State to discover through cross-examination who committed the offence and who did not. At the end of the case the magistrate then convicted one of the two accused. The Supreme Court said this was a wrong approach. The magistrate should not have put X to their defence in the hope that one might be condemned by his or her co-accused. The State must choose before the trial who to prosecute and who to use as a witness.

In the South African case of *Nzimande* 1993 (2) SACR 218 (N), the court said that if at the close of the State case an accused person who is not legally represented has no case to meet, the presiding judicial officer should discharge him or her *mero motu.* A failure to do so is an irregularity which will amount to a failure of justice if proof of guilt is adduced at some subsequent stage which ought never to have been reached.

The court should exercise its discretion to discharge X at the close of the State case if no *prima facie* case has been made out and no reasonable court could convict X of the crime charged on the basis of the evidence led by the State.

However, it must not so discharge X if the evidence led could lead to the conviction of X of some other charge which is a competent verdict for the crime charged.

It must be noted that the accused has no right of appeal against refusal to discharge at the close of the state's case until after conviction: *Hunzvi* 2000 (1) ZLR 540 (S)

Summary

The defence can apply for discharge of X at the close of the State case if no *prima facie* case has been made out and no reasonable court could convict X of the crime charged on the basis of the evidence led by the State.

However, the court will not discharge X if the evidence led could lead to the conviction of X of some other charge which is a competent verdict for the crime charged.

Defences

Explicitly raised or suggested by evidence

If X is legally represented his or her lawyer may specifically plead a particular defence on his or her behalf. With unrepresented accused, X may not explicitly raise a defence but in his or her evidence he or she may say things which suggest that a certain defence might apply. He or she may, for instance, testify that he or she was extremely drunk at the time he or she committed the crime. Here the judge must carefully investigate whether in fact the defence does apply.

Onus of proof

Once there is sufficient evidence to put a defence in issue, the rule is that the State must disprove the defence. The only exceptions to this rule are:

- the defence of insanity, where the onus is on the defence to prove on a balance of probabilities that X was insane at the time of the crime;
- where a statutory provision provides for defence to an offence but the onus is on X to establish the existence of the defence.

In the case of *Mapfumo & Ors* 1983 (1) ZLR 250 (S), the court said that, subject to the exceptions set out above, there is no onus on X to establish his or her defence. Once there is some evidence suggesting a defence the court must consider this evidence. That evidence may have been adduced by the defence or it may emerge from what has been said by the defence or prosecution witnesses.

Evidence in rebuttal of defence by State

Sometimes, the examination or re-examination of a defence witness may reveal a line of defence that could not reasonably have been foreseen by the prosecutor and which was not indicated during the questions put in cross-examination of State witnesses. In such cases, the prosecutor may ask the leave of the court to call evidence in rebuttal of the defence. The court has a discretion on whether to grant leave. It should normally not grant leave if, by the exercise of due diligence, the prosecutor could have called the evidence before closing his or her case. There must have been something in the nature of a surprise or an unexpected new issue introduced by the defence.

This situation is most likely to arise with an accused who is not legally represented. Such an accused may not have indicated this point in his or her defence outline and he or she may not have realised that it was necessary to put this line of defence to the State witnesses.

Questioning of accused by prosecutor or judge

If X gives evidence in his or her defence the prosecutor can cross-examine him or her and he or she may be questioned by the judge.

Even if he or she declines to give evidence, under s 198(9) CPEA the prosecutor and the judge may still put questions to him or her. If he or she refuses to answer the questions put to him or heror her, adverse inferences may be drawn by the court from this refusal.

Re-opening of State case

Reid-Rowland 16-37

It is not just and proper for the State to be allowed to re-open its case to lead evidence that was available to it from the beginning of the proceedings. To allow such evidence to be led after the close of the defence case is unjust to the defendant, as it gives the State an opportunity to rebuild its case. In *Munyaradzi* S-74-89, at the close of the State case against the appellant on a charge of receiving stolen property, there was no evidence that X had known that the property, which he admitted buying from the thief, was stolen. At the close of the defence case either the court itself or the State called a witness in an attempt to prove that the prices the thief demanded for the property were so low as to have given the appellant ground for suspicion that the property was stolen. This witness should not have been called.

Addresses at conclusion of defence case

Reid-Rowland 16-38 – 16-39

In terms of s 200 CPEA, both the prosecutor and X or his or her legal representative have the right to address the court at the conclusion of the defence.

Where the parties wish to exercise this right to address, the prosecutor must address first and then X or his or her lawyer will address. If X or his or her lawyer raises any point of law during the address, the prosecutor then has the right to reply to this point. In other words, the defence has the last word on the facts and the prosecutor has the last word on the law.

The court will normally require the parties to address immediately after the defence case is closed. However, in very complicated cases where the evidence is highly contradictory or where there are complex points of law involved, the parties may request an adjournment to prepare their addresses. Such requests for adjournment should normally be granted.

A judge will sometimes tell the prosecutor that it is unnecessary for him or her to address the court. This may be because the judge is quite satisfied of the guilt of X and he or she feels it is a waste of time to hear an address from the State. If this is done it must be made clear to the prosecutor that this is the reason why he or she does not need to hear argument from him. However, in a complex case it is far better always to hear what the prosecutor has to say by way of summarisation and argument. The summation will help the judge to crystallise his or her reasoning.

Even in a simple and straightforward matter if the prosecutor insists on addressing, he or she has a legal right to do so and the judge cannot refuse to allow him or her to do so. If the judge has decided that he or she is going to acquit X, he or she should not seek to prevent the prosecutor from addressing on the basis that anything the prosecutor has to say will change his or her mind. The prosecutor may believe that he or she has made out a reasonable case against X and is entitled to try to persuade the court that its inclination towards acquittal is based upon flawed reasoning or misinterpretation or misassessment of the evidence.

Stopping trial and referral of case to Attorney-General

Reid-Rowland 23-3

At any time during the trial, a magistrate may, in terms of s 58 of the Magistrates Court Act as read with ss 225-228 CPEA, stop the proceedings and refer the case to the Attorney-General.

Where a magistrate has already arrived at his or her verdict, but considers that the offence deserves a sentence in excess of his or her jurisdiction, the case can be referred to the High Court for sentence if the Attorney-General decides that this should be done. This aspect is dealt with in detail in the section on sentence.

Before verdict the proceedings may also be stopped and the case can be referred to the Attorney-General. This procedure is designed primarily to deal with situations which arise unexpectedly where the evidence discloses that X has committed a more serious crime than that charged and the magistrate does not have jurisdiction to deal with the more serious crime. For instance, an accused has been charged with indecent assault before an ordinary magistrate and during the course of the case it emerges that X's acts really constituted rape. As only a regional magistrate can try rape cases, the magistrate should stop the proceedings here, adjourn the case, remand X and submit the case to the Attorney-General who can take the remedial step under s 225 CPEA of directing that the proceedings commence afresh before a regional magistrate if he or she agrees that X should have been charged with rape, or ordering the original magistrate to continue to deal with the case if he or she does not.

The prosecutor may also under these provisions request the magistrate to stop the trial. If he or she does so, the magistrate must stop the trial and refer the matter to the Attorney-General who must decide which course of action to take under the powers given to him or her under s 225 CPEA. The State should take care to charge the correct charge on the facts and to bring the case before the magistrate with appropriate jurisdiction in the first place. The prosecutor should not request the magistrate to stop the proceedings because, some time after the proceedings have commenced, he or she changes his or her mind about the charge and decides that he or she should have charged a more serious crime, even though he or she originally decided on those same facts that a lesser charge should be brought. But he or she can legitimately make this request if the evidence discloses the commission of a more serious crime than the police investigations originally disclosed: *Moyo (2)* 1978 RLR 469 (GD); *Collett* 1978 RLR 288 (GD) at 291.

This procedure should be sparingly used as it involves expense and inconvenience, especially if X is in custody: *Moyo* (2) 1978 RLR 469 (GD).

This topic is dealt with in more detail in Chapter 39 of the *Prosecutors Handbook*. This Chapter points out the circumstances in which prosecutors can request the magistrate to stop the trial if the magistrate has refused to stop the trial on his or her own initiative, or where the magistrate has refused to allow the charge to be amended, or to allow the State to recall witnesses or re-open its case.

Change of plea before verdict

Reid-Rowland 16-24

Where an accused applies to withdraw a plea of guilty before verdict, the presumption of innocence still applies. X must give an explanation as to why he or she initially pleaded guilty and why he or she now wishes to change his or her plea. Once he or she gives an explanation, however, it will suffice; there is no onus on him or her to convince the court of the veracity of his or her explanation. If he or she fails altogether to give an explanation for the withdrawal of the original plea the court is entitled to hold him or her to his or her plea.

Even though X's explanation may be improbable, the court is not entitled to refuse the application unless it is satisfied that the explanation is not only improbable but false beyond reasonable doubt. If the application is one to which s 272 CPEA applies, the question of onus cannot arise: *Nyathi & Anor* 1988 (1) ZLR 221 (H).

If X alleges that his or her plea of guilty was the result of improper conduct by those in authority over him, the court must stop the proceedings and investigate this allegation.

Change of plea after conviction

In the case of *Jackson* HH-201-02 X, together with a colleague, stole a car in Chinhoyi. While driving it away, the accused lost control. His or her companion was killed and the vehicle was badly damaged. At his or her trial in a regional magistrates court, the accused pleaded guilty and was convicted. The matter was referred to the High Court for sentence.

Before the hearing, the accused's legal representative indicated that the accused wished to change his or her plea to one of not guilty. The reason given was threats by the police. The question was whether the High Court could remit the matter to the lower court for the accused to change his or her plea. The court held the application to change the plea should be directed to the trial court. Although there is no onus on the accused – all he or she must do is offer a reasonable explanation for having pleaded guilty – less is required of him or her when he or she applies to the High Court for remittal to change his or her plea. All he or she must show is that he or she has an explanation which *prima facie* shows that he or she has a reasonable explanation for a change of plea to give to the trial court. Sections 227 and 271(2)(b) CPE apply in this regard.

Section 4

Common Problems of Evidence

Rules of evidence apply to both sides

The same rules of evidence apply to both defence evidence and state evidence.

Onus of proof

Reid-Rowland 15-13

Proof of guilt

In our system of law all persons accused of crimes are presumed innocent until their guilt has been proved beyond reasonable doubt. The rule in our system of law is that the burden or onus of proof is on the State to prove the guilt of X. X does not have to prove his or her innocence.

The same rule, namely that the onus is upon the State to prove the guilt of X, applies in respect of statutory crimes. However, sometimes in statutes the onus is placed upon X to prove certain things. The most glaring examples of such shifting of the onus of proof to X are to be found in the some of the security offences contained in the Criminal Law (Codification and Reform) Act. Normally, however, the shifting of onus is done as a matter of convenience and the onus is only placed on X to prove something peculiarly within his or her knowledge on a balance of probabilities. See, for example, s 40 as read with s 61(7) of Road Traffic Act, [*Chapter 13:11*] s 78(1) of Road Traffic Act and s 385(5) CPEA.

Proof beyond reasonable doubt

In our system, the State has to prove the guilt of X beyond reasonable doubt. Proof beyond reasonable doubt cannot be subject to exact measurement. For judges and magistrates it becomes a matter of experience and intuition rather than analysis. It is a matter of degree. Proof beyond reasonable doubt does not mean proof to an absolute degree of certainty. It means that there should be such proof as leaves no reasonable doubt in the mind of an ordinary man capable of sound judgment and of appreciating human motivations. It means a high degree of probability, not proof beyond a shadow of a doubt. The State does not have to close every avenue of escape and fanciful or remote possibilities can be discounted as these do not lead to reasonable doubt. See *Isolano* 1985 (1) ZLR 62 (S) at 64-65. To be a reasonable doubt, the doubt must not be based on pure speculation but must be based upon a reasonable and solid foundation created either from the positive evidence or gathered from reasonable inferences not in conflict with or outweighed by the proved facts. (It is sometimes said that X should not be convicted unless there is moral certainty as to his or her guilt.) However, it is not necessary for the State to prove every single individual fact in a criminal case beyond reasonable doubt although the State must prove beyond reasonable doubt a fact which is particularly vital and upon which the whole State case hinges. The question which needs to be asked is: do all the facts taken together prove guilt beyond reasonable doubt? Even a number of lines of inference, none of which would be decisive, may in their total effect lead to there being proof beyond reasonable doubt.

If X gives some explanation, he or she must be acquitted even if the court is not satisfied that his or her explanation is true if, nonetheless, the explanation might reasonably be true. The onus is not on X to prove that his or her story is true. Even if he or she gives an explanation which is improbable, X cannot be convicted unless the court is satisfied beyond reasonable doubt that it is false. Again, X must be acquitted. Even if his or her story is not believed in all of its details, X must be acquitted if there is a reasonable possibility that his or her story is substantially true.

Defences

With all defences except insanity, once the evidential onus of introducing sufficient evidence of the defence to put the defence in issue is discharged (or to put it another way as soon as a foundation has been laid for the defence), the substantive onus to disprove the defence rests squarely on the prosecution.

The case of *Mapfumo & Ors* 1983 (1) ZLR 250 (S) at 253 (ZS), clarified further the matter of onus in relation to defences. It pointed out that there was no onus as such upon X to establish some defence. Once there is some material, **whether adduced by the defence or emerging from the prosecution case**, suggesting that such certain defence may be available the Court must consider the defence. Evidence sufficient to raise a defence does not have to be evidence sufficient to establish the factual basis on a balance of probabilities; all that is required is that there be sufficient material evidence to make it a realistic issue and this evidence could emerge from the State case, from X's confession, from the cross-examination of State witnesses or from evidence from the defence. Thus once there is a sufficient foundation for the defence from whatever quarter this evidence comes, the onus rested squarely on the prosecution to prove that the defence does not apply. In *Machakaire* S-30-92, the court held that the magistrate had wrongly cast the onus on X to prove his or her defence.

Insanity is the one exception to the rule that the onus rests upon the State throughout to disprove X's defence. In respect of the defence of insanity, it is laid down that the defence must prove on a balance of probabilities that X was insane at the time he or she committed the crime. In practice this means that the defence lawyer must call psychiatric evidence to prove this defence on a balance of probabilities. However, State and the court may decide to request psychiatric examination of X person if there seems to be doubt as to the mental stability of X when he or she committed the crime or when he or she is about to stand trial.

Corroboration

Reid-Rowland 21-5 – 21-9

Corroboration means evidence, other than that of the complainant, which is consistent with the complainant's version of the facts and which tends to show the guilt of X. To be of evidential weight, the fact or facts corroborated must be material ones.

In the situations dealt with below, what is important is for there to be "implicatory corroboration". This means evidence that implicates X in the commission of the offence.

The corroboration can come from evidence adduced by another witness or from the evidence of X. The confession of an accused can be used as evidence corroborating other evidence. Even the failure of X to tell the truth can sometimes be a corroborative factor: *Katerere* S-55-91.

In certain situations dealt with below, there is a cautionary rule which applies. In these situations, the court must be alive to the dangers which arise from accepting certain types of evidence, especially if that evidence is uncorroborated. It is not enough that the court warn itself on a token basis of the dangers of accepting these types of evidence. This warning must be put into practice exercising great caution before accepting this evidence.

It should be noted that a witness cannot corroborate himself.

Single witness evidence

Reid-Rowland 18-25; 21-4

Where there is only one single witness to the crime certain special evidential rules apply.

A single witness may or may not also be a "suspect witness". If the single witness is also a "suspect witness" then the court must apply the special rules relating to single suspect witnesses. These rules are dealt with later. This present section deals with single witnesses who are not also suspect witnesses.

The entire State case against X may rest upon the evidence given by one single State witness. The State may only have been able to produce one witness against X or may have called more than one witness but it is clear that the only evidence on which the guilt of X is going to depend is that of one witness alone. This situation has been referred to as a "boxing ring" situation because the outcome of the "contest" hinges on which of the two contestants is believed, namely the State witness or X.

With crimes other than perjury and treason, the court may convict an accused on the basis of the uncorroborated evidence of a single competent and credible State witness: s 269 CPEA.

There is obviously a risk which attaches to convicting X on the basis of the uncorroborated testimony of a single witness. There is a scarcity of evidence in the case and the testimony of the witness is the sole proof of X's guilt. In this situation, the court must be particularly alive to the dangers of poor observation, faulty recollection, reconstruction of evidence after the event, bias and any other risk that the circumstances of the case suggest. The quality of evidence must make up for the lack of quantity.

In the South African case of *Mokoena* 1956 (3) SA 81 (A) at 85-86, it was laid down that the uncorroborated evidence of a single witness should only be relied upon if the evidence was clear and satisfactory in every material respect. Slight imperfections would not rule out reliance on that evidence but material imperfections would. The court stated that single witness evidence should not be relied upon where, for example, the witness had an interest adverse to X, has made a previous inconsistent statement, has given contradictory evidence or had no proper opportunity for observation. However, in the later case of *Sauls & Ors* 1981 (3) SA 172 (A) the South African Appellate Division stated that there was no rule of thumb to be applied when deciding upon the credibility of single witness testimony. The court must simply weigh the evidence and consider its merits and demerits. It must then decide whether it is satisfied that the testimony is truthful, despite any shortcomings, defects or contradictions in it. The approach adopted in the *Sauls* case was followed in the case of *Nyabvure* S-23-88. See also *Worswick* S-27-88; *Mukonda* HH-15-87; *Nemachera* S-89-86.

Judge Beck in his article in *Prosecutors Bulletin* Vol. 1 No. 1 at p 18, advises that in assessing the quality of the single witness' evidence in order to decide whether X should be convicted on the basis of this evidence, the court should take the most attentive note of the witness. It should take particular note of his or her apparent character, his or her intelligence, his or her capacity for observation, his or her powers of recall, his or her objectivity and things like that. The evidence should be carefully weighed against the objective probabilities of the case, and against all the other evidence which is at variance with it. The court must have rational grounds to conclude that the evidence of the single witness is reliable and trustworthy and is a safe basis for convicting X. In *Worswick* S-27-88, it was said that the evidence of an accomplice must be examined critically and with caution.

Judge Beck points out that proper investigation of criminal cases will usually uncover corroborating evidence and that it is seldom necessary to rest the entire State case upon single uncorroborated testimony. The police and prosecutors should be discouraged from being content with the production of only such evidence. In appropriate cases the court itself should use its powers to call other witnesses if it appears there are such witnesses.

In *Muzonza & Ors* S-217-88, the Supreme Court stated that as a general rule it is undesirable to rely solely and entirely on the evidence of the complainant, particularly in assault cases and more particularly where there are counter allegations of provocation, self-defence or justification in one form or another. The complainant in such cases has a clear bias and a reason to place himself in a favourable light and X in an unfavourable light.

In *Tamba* S-81-91, the Supreme Court stated that in assault cases where there are other witnesses to the incident in addition to the complainant, these witnesses should be called and the case against X should not be left to rest only upon the testimony of the complainant alone. It is wrong to deal with such cases as if they were a "boxing match" between the complainant and X. These two protagonists should not, as it were, be thrown into the ring with the magistrate as referee who, at the end of the bout, having awarded points for demeanour and probability, would name the winner who would usually be the complainant. It is even worse if the magistrate is, as often seems to be the case, a biased referee who works on the unspoken assumption that the police would not have charged X if he or she was not the guilty one. This approach, said the Supreme Court, was dangerous, especially in assault cases where almost invariably the parties give conflicting versions of what was the cause of the fight. Without evidence from bystanders, it was almost impossible to determine which version of the facts was the true one although often both versions are partially untrue or exaggerated.

In *Zimbowora* S-7-92, the appellant had been convicted of three counts of contravening the Labour Relations Act, 1985. The State case had rested entirely on the evidence of the complainant. On appeal, the Supreme Court said that although the trial court was entitled to convict the appellant on the single evidence of the complainant, it was necessary for such evidence to be clear and satisfactory in every material respect. As the complainant was a witness with an interest to serve, the trial court was not only required to approach her evidence with caution but should also have sought corroboration of her evidence. The conviction was set aside by the Supreme Court as the complainant's evidence was not satisfactory in all material respects and no evidence was led to corroborate her assertions.

An accused can be convicted on the basis of the uncorroborated testimony of a single competent and credible State witness, but not if the crime charged is perjury or treason.

The credibility and reliability of this witness must be very carefully assessed to see whether it is safe to convict on the basis of his or her testimony alone. In *Nduna & Anor* HB-48-03 it was held that where a conviction relies on the evidence of a single witness, discrepancies in the witness's evidence are not necessarily fatal. The discrepancies must be of such magnitude and value that it goes to the root of the matter to such an extent that their presence would no doubt give a different complexion of the matter altogether. Discrepancies that do not affect the change should be regarded as immaterial and as such of no value in the determination of the truth or otherwise of the matter at hand.

The fact that the single witness is himself guilty of some unlawful conduct does not make him or her an accomplice in the crime which is charged. Where the accused, who were policemen, arrested and robbed a person who was crossing the border illegally, that person was not an accomplice.

Complainant evidence in sexual cases

In rape and other cases of a sexual nature, such as aggravated indecent assault, indecent assault and sexual relations with a person under the age of 16, the courts used to adopt the approach that because of the danger of false incrimination in such cases, a cautionary rule applies. Essentially this cautionary rule meant that in sexual cases the court had not only to believe the complainant, but in addition it had to be satisfied, by an application of the cautionary rule, whether it might still not have been deceived by a plausible witness. It therefore must seek corroboration or evidence tending to exclude the danger of false incrimination. This was laid down in a series of cases: *Mupfudza* 1982 (1) ZLR 271 (S); *Chitiyo* 1989 (2) ZLR 144 (S); *Chigova* 1992 (2) ZLR 206 (S); *Makanyanga* 1996 (2) ZLR 231 (H); *Zaranyika* 1997 (1) ZLR 539 (H).

However, in the case of *Banana* 2000 (1) ZLR 607 (S), the Supreme Court ruled that the cautionary rule in sexual cases is based on an irrational and outdated perception, and has outlived its usefulness. It unjustly stereotypes complainants in sexual assault cases (overwhelmingly women) as particularly unreliable. There were no convincing reasons for its continued application. It exemplified a rule of practice that placed an additional burden on victims in sexual cases which could lead to grave injustice to the victims involved. It is no longer warranted to rely on the cautionary rule of practice in sexual cases. Despite the abandonment of the cautionary rule, however, the courts must still consider carefully the nature and circumstances of alleged sexual offences.

In the context of sexual cases, usually the strongest evidence which the State will be able to lead will be medical evidence. If the accused has admitted that he or she had sexual relations with the complainant but maintains that the complainant was a consenting party, medical evidence of injuries consistent with forced sexual relations will be cogent evidence of the complainant's allegation of rape. Where, on the other hand, the accused denies sexual relations, medical evidence indicating that the complainant was raped or at least that the complainant has had sexual relations with someone does not prove the identification of the accused as the culprit. Corroboration often takes the form of testimony from the complainant's mother or sister. As regards the corroborative evidence, its cumulative effect must be considered. *V* v *A* 1984 (2) ZLR 139 (S).

Evidence from children

Reid-Rowland 21-9

Children often have vivid imaginations and have a tendency to fantasize. They may believe their fantasies and relate them as reality because they believe them. Immature children are also susceptible to suggestions made by others. In cases of sexual molestation of children, parents may jump to wrong conclusions about the culprits and may prompt or intimidate their children in the direction of implicating innocent persons. Or the persons doing the prompting of children may want maliciously to get other people into trouble.

In *Sibanda* S-55-94, the court set out the dangers inherent in testimony from children as follows: The court accepted that the 6 main objections to a child's evidence are:

(a) Children's memories are unreliable — particularly for detail;

(b) Children are egocentric and not likely to consider the effect of their statements on others — particularly pre-school children;

(c) Children are highly suggestible;

(d) Children have difficulty distinguishing fact from fantasy;

(e) Children make false allegations, particularly of sexual assault; and

(f) Children do not understand the duty to tell the truth.

Judge Beck advises these steps to reduce the risks arising out of evidence from children:

1. The judge and prosecutor must put the child at ease in the court. Efforts must be made to make the child feel relaxed rather than feeling that the atmosphere is threatening and strange.

2. The judge must use his or her authority to control the examination and especially the cross-examination of child witnesses. There must be no unfair questioning aimed at overbearing, overpowering or confusing the child or trying to prompt the child unduly. The child should be allowed to respond naturally and spontaneously.

3. The child's mental development and maturity must be assessed very carefully. One has to be careful in applying the normal tests of credibility such as demeanour,

consistency and probabilities to child witnesses. A seven-year-old cannot be expected to behave in the same rational way as an adult. When assessing the probabilities the judge should take into account the child witness' age and maturity. The child should not be expected to behave like a mature, adult witness.

In *Musasa* HH-52-02, Hlatshwayo J held that while the evidence of child witnesses must be approached with caution, such caution must be creative or positive caution, where a judicial officer uses knowledge of psychology or other relevant disciplines in order to maximise the value of such testimony. Psychological research has established that young children do not fantasize about being raped and other unusual, horrific occurrences but that their fantasies and play are characterized by their daily experiences.

To overcome the dangers which are inherent in testimony from children such as the danger arising out of their tendency to fantasize, the court should see whether from the evidence the events related by the child really did happen.

Wherever possible, corroboration of the child's evidence implicating X should be looked for. The existence of corroborative evidence is the safest assurance against wrong conviction. There is, however, no rigid requirement that a child's evidence must be corroborated. The court can convict on the basis of the uncorroborated testimony of the child witness, provided it is satisfied that the dangers inherent in founding a conviction on the child's uncorroborated evidence have been eliminated. *Ponder* 1989 (1) ZLR 235 (S); *J* 1958 (3) SA 689 (SR); *Sikurlite* 1964 (3) SA 151 (SR).

Because of the dangers of children giving false testimony their testimony must be approached with great caution and care. Wherever possible there should be corroboration of their testimony. In the absence of such corroboration, the court should convict on the basis of a child's evidence only if it is satisfied that the evidence is reliable and the dangers inherent in such testimony have been eliminated.

Evidence from wrongdoer against person catching him or her

In *Elsworth* S-55-95 a number of women who had been caught by a farm guard stealing firewood lodged a complaint with the police that the farmer had stripped them of their clothes. The appeal court said that the trial court should have approached their evidence with caution.

The initial allegation on remand was that they were released by the farmer to go home stark naked; the charge alleged that they were ordered to remain in a state of nudity or semi-nudity; the women's evidence was merely allegations of partial undress. This was coupled with the fact that no two witnesses gave the same account of the brief order the farmer allegedly issued, to be weighed against the consistency and credibility of his or her own account and the support of an impartial witness. "Where a wrongdoer, caught red handed, turns around to make a counter allegation of a more serious offence against the person whom he or she has wronged, his or her testimony against that other must be received with the utmost caution."

The trial court took the variety of allegations made by the complainants and stuck them together with the mortar provided by a biased and discredited witness — a proven liar to whose evidence he or she should have accorded no weight. Conviction and sentence were set aside.

Accomplice evidence

Reid-Rowland 21-3 – 21-5

What are accomplices?

An accomplice is a person who has participated or assisted in the commission of a crime together with others.

The accomplice who is testifying against others may or may not be on trial himself. A person who is jointly charged with others may deny that he or she was involved in the crime at all and testify that he or she witnessed one or more of those jointly charged commit the crime or he or she may admit that he or she was involved but claim that his or her involvement was minor and that the major role was played by his or her fellow criminals. The other type of case is where an accomplice testifies after the authorities have dropped charges against him or her in return for his or her giving evidence against his or her fellow criminals.

Dangers of accomplice evidence

There are a number of cogent reasons for treating accomplice evidence with considerable caution such as follows:

- An accomplice is a person who is himself guilty of criminal conduct and might easily be a person of bad character who does not have a high regard for the truth.
- The accomplice may tell lies about another person in the hope that, by testifying against another person, he or she will secure an indemnity from prosecution or he or she will receive a lighter sentence or, if he or she has already been sentenced, that he or she will receive clemency. He or she may have received promises from the police that they will go easy on him or her provided that he or she testifies against another person.
- The accomplice may wish to implicate another falsely to shield someone else. He or she may do this, for instance, because he or she is afraid of the real

culprit or he or she may greatly exaggerate the role played by a fellow criminal in order to minimise his or her own role in the crime.

- The inside knowledge of the accomplice of how, when and where and by whom the offence was committed gives him or her a golden opportunity to engage in convincing deception when giving evidence. The only thing he or she has to change in what is otherwise an entirely true version of the facts is the identity of his or her accomplice. By virtue of his or her inside knowledge, he or she is peculiarly equipped to convince the unwary that his or her lies are true: *Ngara* 1987 (1) ZLR 91 (S).

However, it should be noted that there are varying types of accomplices. Some are more culpable than others and thus some are more dangerous to believe than others. In *Moyo* S-170-90, the Supreme Court said that the accomplice was simply a person caught up in an evil system and was not trying to shift the blame from his or her shoulders and therefore there was no danger in relying upon his or her testimony.

Because of the danger of false incrimination which exists with accomplice evidence, this evidence must be approached with extreme caution. The court must be satisfied that the inherent dangers of relying on this testimony have been eliminated and that the evidence can safely be relied on. There are special rules which apply in respect of single accomplice evidence. These are dealt with later.

Warning to accomplices

It is obligatory for magistrates to warn accomplices who are testifying in conformity with the direction given in *Simakonda* 1956 R&N 463 (SR) at 465B-C. See also *Ncube & Anor* 1975 (2) RLR 150 (A) at 151H-152A and *Ngara* 1987 (1) ZLR 91 (S) at 96G. The court should warn the accomplice that what is expected of him or her is to tell the truth.

The warning that X must answer questions "to the satisfaction of the court" can be misleading when translated into the vernacular as it may give the impression to the accomplice witness that the evidence required of him or her to satisfy the court is evidence which incriminates X, even if this evidence is not the truth. The judge, in warning the accomplice, must emphasise that the court is interested only in the truth, whether it incriminates or exculpates X.

As regards the accomplice who has already been convicted and who is presently serving his or her sentence, he or she should be advised that exaggerating the part allegedly played by X or minimising his or her own role will not affect the sentence in any way.

As regards the unconvicted accomplice in line with s 267 CPEA, he or she must be advised that:

- he or she is not obliged to give evidence;

- if he or she testifies, questions may be put to him or her which might incriminate him or herin regard to the specified offence;
- he or she will be obliged to answer any question that may be put to him or her despite the fact that the answer might incriminate him or her in respect of the specified offence (or some other offence for which he or she could be found guilty on the basis of the charge relating to the specified offence);
- if he or she answers all questions put to him or her frankly and honestly he or she will be discharged from prosecution in respect of the specified offence (or from any other offence for which he or she could be found guilty on the basis of that charge).

See Hoffmann and Zeffertt *South African Law of Evidence* 3ed pp 196-197.

Single accomplice evidence

Where the case against X rests on the evidence of one single accomplice s 270 CPEA (not s 269) applies. This says that a court may convict an accused on the basis of the evidence of a single accomplice, provided there is competent evidence other than the single and unconfirmed evidence of the accomplice which proves to the satisfaction of the court that the crime was actually committed.

The courts have interpreted this provision to mean that even where there is no proof *aliunde* (from another source than the evidence of the accomplice) of the commission of the offence, X can still be convicted if there is corroboration in a material respect of the evidence of the accomplice. In *Mubaiwa* 1980 ZLR 477 (A) at 479H-480A, this is stated as follows:

> " The purpose of this section is that the court must be satisfied that the crime to which the accomplice testifies has, in fact, been committed. If not, there can be no conviction at all. Even where there is no proof *aliunde* that the crime has been committed, the statutory requirement can still be satisfied if there is corroboration in a material respect which convinces the court that the accomplice can safely be relied on when he or she says the crime was committed, though it need not directly implicate X. In such a case, the requirement is satisfied because, despite the lack of proof *aliunde* of the commission of the offence, the accomplice is no longer 'single and unconfirmed'."

In *Lawrence & Anor* 1989 (1) ZLR 29 (S) the Supreme Court laid down that with single accomplice testimony there should be a two-pronged inquiry. The court must first satisfy itself that the offence with which X is charged has been committed before convicting. Secondly, the court must look for corroboration, for if there is no evidence *aliunde* proving the commission of the offence, then there can still be a conviction if the court is satisfied that there is corroboration of the evidence of the accomplice sufficient to satisfy the court that the witness is to be believed. See also *Moyo* 1989 (3) ZLR 250 (S).

Thus, if the evidence of the accomplice is single and unconfirmed there must be proof *aliunde* of the commission of the offence. If, on the other hand, there is material corroboration of the testimony of the accomplice, the evidence is no longer single and unconfirmed and there need not be proof *aliunde* of the commission of the offence.

Imperfections in evidence of accomplice

Where there are imperfections in an accomplice's evidence and there is no corroboration of his or her evidence implicating X, the question remains whether there are other features which reduce the dangers of false incrimination and, if there are, whether they reduce it to the point where there is no reasonable possibility that X has been falsely incriminated: *Juwaki & Anor* 1964 RLR 604 (A).

In *Lawrence & Anor* 1989 (1) ZLR 29 (S) despite the imperfections in the accomplice's evidence there was sufficient corroboration to eliminate the danger of false incrimination.

In *Vengesayi* S-26-93 the court said the warning administered to an accomplice witness is not for the benefit of X but is a promise to the witness. Failure to give it is an irregularity but does not make the witness's evidence wholly inadmissible. Even if there is ample corroborative evidence of an accomplice's testimony, the court must warn itself of the danger inherent in basing a conviction solely on the evidence of a suspect witness; but the conviction will only be quashed if there has been a substantial miscarriage of justice.

In *Chitongo* HH-53-95, the court found that although there were some unsatisfactory aspects in the accomplices' evidence, they were credible and their evidence was corroborated. On the other hand, X's testimony was wildly improbable and his or her testimony was not credible. Thus although there was a need for caution in respect of the evidence of accomplices, everything pointed to the overall truth of their testimony.

Co-accused implicating one another

Where two or more persons are jointly charged with an offence and each gives evidence blaming the other for the offence, the evidence of each is admissible against the other, but the court must approach the evidence with care since there is a risk that either or both may be seeking to protect himself by telling lies: *Sambo* S-22-90.

Note that the statement of X in reply to police questions is only evidence against the maker of the statement and is not evidence against any other person: s 259 CPEA. This is because there is no opportunity for cross-examination of the person who made this statement when he or she makes his or her statement. But if the maker goes into the witness box and repeats on oath what he or she said in the statement, he or she renders himself liable to cross-examination by an accused who is jointly charged with him or her and thus such evidence on oath is admissible against the co-accused.

In *Nyathi & Ors* S-52-95, first appellant's fingerprint was found at the scene of a housebreaking/murder. He or she had an absolute need to shift the blame, and named the two other appellants. Strong corroboration was essential. The involvement of one was corroborated by his or her possession of a lot of the stolen property and by his or her own evidence. But the accomplice evidence implicating the other was only supported by the latter's possession of a cheap disposable lighter and his about how he to be in possession of it. The second accomplice did not mention him. This was not sufficiently strong corroboration to prove his beyond reasonable doubt; his or her conviction was set aside.

What should a judicial officer do where co-accused have not been warned? Where a prosecutor fails to inform court that witness is to be treated as an unconvicted accomplice or where witness not warned he or she would be discharged from liability if he or she gave his or her evidence satisfactorily and that he or she could decline to answer questions which might tend to incriminate him, it was held that it would be contrary to interests of justice for him or her not be discharged. The witness had admitted to further crimes with which he or she was subsequently charged and the effect was held to be to deprive witness of the right to fair hearing contrary to s 18(2) of Constitution: *Sivako* v *A-G* 1999 (2) ZLR 271 (S).

Reducing the dangers

The safest way to eliminate the risk of false incrimination of another by an accomplice is to look for corroborative evidence implicating X. In *Ngara* 1987 (1) ZLR 91 (S), the Supreme Court said, however, that the corroborative evidence need not necessarily show that X is the offender. It said that the corroboration looked for was corroboration in some material respect which shows, or tends to show, that the accomplice is reliable, though it does not necessarily have to show that X is the offender.

The evidence of one accomplice can corroborate the evidence of another. The court, however, must be satisfied that the testimony of both accomplices is credible and that there has not been an opportunity for the accomplices to conspire together before testifying in order to concoct a false story to implicate X.

In *Zata* S-64-91, a visitor to Zimbabwe alleged that he or she had paid a bribe on demand to a junior customs officer who had handed it over to the appellant. The junior officer confirmed his story. As the visitor was a stranger to the customs official and they did not have the same interests to serve, their evidence could be given credence and could be used to corroborate each other's testimony.

Where there are several counts, each testified to by a single witness, the evidence on one count may be taken to corroborate the evidence on others, provided that the acts spoken of by each accomplice bear a striking similarity to one another: *Ngara* 1987 (1) ZLR 91 (S).

It is usually dangerous to convict without corroboration of the accomplice's evidence. Thus in *Machakata* S-106-89, there was no corroboration and the court quashed the conviction. The appellant had been found guilty of stock theft. It was alleged that he had instructed two of his employees to go and steal cattle for him. One of these employees, P, gave evidence for the State and the entire State case rested on this testimony which was not corroborated. The appellant denied that he had given such an instruction to the two employees and another of his employees, E, corroborated his or her testimony. The Appeal Court found that the trial court had only paid lip service to the cautionary rule. P's evidence had not been rigorously examined to ascertain whether or not he may have falsely implicated the appellant. P's uncorroborated evidence was open to question.

However, sometimes even without corroborative evidence, the court can convict a person on the basis of the evidence of even a single accomplice if the circumstances are such that the court can properly be quite satisfied that the accomplice is telling the truth. For example, if the accomplice gives convincing evidence against another and X adamantly refuses to give evidence and maintains his or her right to silence, there is a reduced risk of relying on the evidence of the accomplice in convicting X because if X is innocent one would have expected him or herto have vigorously denied the false testimony against him. So too, there is a reduced risk of reliance on testimony by an accomplice against a person with whom he or she has a very close relationship and with whom he or she has been on good terms previously because here it would be unlikely that the accomplice would implicate this person falsely.

Disclosure of inducements to testify

In *Lawrence & Anor* 1989 (1) ZLR 29 (S), the Supreme Court indicated that it is desirable that the court be informed of any inducement or promise made to an accomplice when the accomplice is called upon to testify because the danger of the false incrimination is greater when an accomplice has been promised a pardon or remission. It further pointed out that it is the court, not the Attorney-General, which should decide whether or not the accomplice has given satisfactory evidence justifying fulfilment of the undertaking to recommend remission.

Before the accomplice gives evidence the State should advise the court that the witness who is being called is either a convicted or unconvicted accomplice.

Accomplice evidence must be approached with extreme caution because of the dangers of false incrimination by the accomplice. Although it is not essential that the accomplice evidence be corroborated, the presence of corroborative evidence is usually the best safeguard against false incrimination. Slight imperfections in the accomplice's evidence do not necessarily discredit it, especially if the material portions of that evidence are corroborated. The evidence of one accomplice can corroborate the evidence of another, provided that the court is satisfied that the accomplices did not conspire together to give an agreed false story against X.

Accomplices must be given a warning when they are testifying.

With single accomplice evidence the judge should ask himself:

1. Are you satisfied that the crime charged has been committed?
   If no, acquit;
   If yes, proceed to next stage.

2. Is there material corroboration for the witness' testimony?
   If yes, may convict even if no proof *aliunde* of commission of crime;
   If no, may only convict if proof *aliunde* that crime committed.

Lies told by accused as corroboration

For a lie told by X in or out of court to be capable of amounting to corroboration of the testimony of a State witness, the following criteria apply:

- the lie must be deliberate;
- it must relate to a material issue;
- the motive for the lie must be a realisation of guilt and a fear of the truth;
- the statement must be clearly shown to be a lie by evidence other than that of the witness who is to be corroborated.

Caution should be adopted in this regard. Too much weight should not be attached to lies told by X. The court must guard against drawing an inference of X's guilt solely on the basis of lies told by an accused person: *Nyoni* S-118-90.

In *Masawi & Anor* HH-111-94, two persons were charged with the kidnap-murder of a woman. They told lies about their involvement with her, the whereabouts of their car and themselves over the crucial period and other matters. The court found that their lies, transversing all the crucial parts of the case, could only be indicative of guilt. They could not be explained by fear or other reasons. Both were convicted of murder.

Summary

The courts are obliged to approach accomplice evidence with extreme caution because of the dangers of false incrimination by the accomplice. Although it is not essential that the accomplice evidence be corroborated, the presence of corroborative evidence is usually the best safeguard against false incrimination. Slight imperfections in the accomplice's evidence do not necessarily discredit it, especially if the material portions of that evidence are corroborated. The evidence of one accomplice can corroborate the evidence of another, provided that the court is satisfied that the accomplices did not conspire together to give an agreed false story against the accused.

Where the evidence of a single accomplice is relied on, the judicial officer is obliged to consider whether there is material corroboration for the witness' testimony. If there is such corroboration, the court may convict even if there is no proof *aliunde* of commission of crime. If there is not, it may convict the accused only if there is evidence *aliunde* that the crime was committed.

Conviction on basis of confession

It is provided in s 273 CPEA that a court may convict X on the basis of a confession proved to have been made by him, although the confession is not confirmed by any other evidence, provided that the offence has been proved to have been committed by competent evidence other than such confession.

The court may thus convict on the basis of a confession either:

- where there is proof that the crime was committed, although there is no evidence other than the confession to connect X with the crime; or
- where there is direct evidence to confirm X's confession, even though there is no direct proof of the commission of the crime:

Tsorayi 1985 (1) ZLR 138 (H).

Exculpatory portions of plea

In *Cloete* 1994 (1) SACR 420 (A), the court stated that the rule in *Valacia* 1945 AD 826, that a judicial officer must take into consideration everything contained in an extra-curial statement made by X, including exculpatory portions, applies equally to statements made by X in explanation of his or her plea under s 163(4) CPEA.

Similar fact evidence

General rule

Similar fact evidence is evidence of similar acts done previously by the accused. Similar fact evidence is not admissible if its only relevance is to show that the accused is of bad character and is therefore likely to have committed the offence. It is, however, admissible if it is relevant and is of sufficient probative force to warrant its reception despite its apparently prejudicial nature.

Previously, the approach of the courts was that the similar facts had to bear a striking resemblance to the case in hand. See *Mutsinziri* 1997 (1) ZLR 6 (H); *Ngara* 1987 (1) ZLR 91 (S). However, in *Banana* 2000 (1) ZLR 607 (S) the Supreme Court said that the test for the admissibility of similar fact evidence used to be whether the similar facts were of such a striking similarity that it would be an affront to common sense to assume that the similarity was explicable on the basis of coincidence. However, the courts have moved away from this test. Striking similarity is not a pre-requisite to admissibility. What has to be assessed is the probative force of the evidence in question; there is no single manner in which this can be achieved. Like corroboration, this is a matter of logic and common sense.

This is in contrast to the position in South Africa. In the South African case of *M & Ors* 1995 (1) SACR 667 (BA) contains an exhaustive review of the authorities on the admissibility of similar fact evidence. In the course of its review, the court agreed with authorities which held that for such evidence to be admissible, the similar facts must bear a striking similarity to the evidence adduced in relation to the offence charged: "The use of the word 'striking' — strengthens the concept that the admission of similar fact evidence requires a 'strong degree of probative force', bearing in mind the basic principle that its admission is out of the ordinary and unusual".

In *Mutsinziri* 1997 (1) ZLR 6 (H), the court pointed out that where there are multiple counts, the fact that each one must be looked at separately does not prevent material which could be admissible under the rules relating to similar fact evidence from being received. Even evidence on one count which ultimately leads to an acquittal may be used but, for such evidence to be receivable and acted upon by a court of law, those discreditable acts of the accused must share with the discreditable conduct in issue, features of such an unusual nature and striking similarity that it would be an offence to common sense to assert that the similarity was explicable on the basis of coincidence. Similar fact evidence may be admitted on one count in order to bolster evidence on another count, where there is an issue as to identity.

In *Mupah* 1989 (1) ZLR 279 (S), the court said that evidence of a previous offence is admissible to rebut a defence of accident or innocent intent and to show a systematic course of conduct by X. This is so whether or not X has been convicted of that offence. There must not only be similarity between the previous acts and those in issue, but such a concurrence of common features that the various acts are naturally to be explained as caused by a general plan of which they are the individual manifestations. The discreditable acts of X must share with the discreditable conduct in issue, features of such an unusual nature and striking similarity that it would be an affront to common sense to assert that the similarity was explicable on the basis of coincidence. Where X has been acquitted in one case, it would be wrong, in order to obtain a conviction in a later case, to seek to show that X was guilty in the first case. This does not mean that evidence relating to the first case may not be called to show what X's intent was in the second; it means that it is impermissible, in the second case, to rely on X's guilt in the first if he or she has been acquitted in the first case.

Exceptions

In the case *Mupah* 1989 (1) ZLR 299 (S), the Supreme Court set out when similar fact evidence is admissible. It stated that:

- Evidence as to previous conduct is admissible to prove that the acts alleged to constitute the crime charged were intentional or part of a systematic course of conduct or to rebut a defence of accident or innocent intent;
- The conduct must demonstrate such an underlying unity or such a concurrence of common features that it would be an affront to common sense to assert that the similarity was explicable on the basis of coincidence;
- X person need not have been convicted of an offence in relation to the previous conduct before such conduct becomes admissible as similar fact evidence;
- On the other hand, if X has been acquitted of an offence in relation to the previous conduct, evidence as to that conduct is not admissible as similar fact evidence as its admission would require the court to assume that X was guilty of the offence of which he or she was acquitted; such evidence may be admissible, however, to show, for example, what X's intent was in relation to his or her subsequent conduct.

In *Tirivanhu* S-170-91, the Supreme Court stated that where an accused faces several charges, the evidence on one count cannot be taken as evidence on another unless it would have either been relevant to that other charge if it were the only charge against him, and justify an inference about it, or it shows a certain peculiar course of conduct.

In this case, the appellant was charged with the theft of five pumps, all of which were found in his or her possession, three shortly after the theft, and he or she gave a false explanation for each. The Supreme Court said that it would be an affront to common sense to accept that the possession of all these stolen pumps by him or her was explicable on the basis of coincidence.

Expert evidence

In order for a person to give expert evidence, his or her special expertise must first be established. The professional qualifications and the professional experience of the person concerned must be established: *Makuni* HH-75-84.

Identification Evidence

Visual identification of persons

Human observation is very fallible and experience has shown that genuine errors can easily be made by witnesses who have identified culprits. In a number of cases in Britain it emerged that X were wrongly convicted on the basis of mistaken identification evidence.

Whenever the State case depends wholly or mainly on evidence of visual identification special caution must be exercised, especially if there is only a single witness who has made the visual identification. Even if the court decides that the witness is entirely honest and truthful in his or her testimony and he or she has asserted that he or she is completely certain that he or she has identified the correct person as the culprit, it must nonetheless ask itself whether there is a danger that the witness was mistaken: *Mutters & Anor* S-66-89; *Makoni & Ors* S-67-89.

It should also be borne in mind that ordinary members of the public are not trained in accurate observation as are policemen. The ability of different people to observe carefully and recollect later varies widely. Also memories fade over time and accurate identification long after the event is difficult.

The quality and reliability of the identification evidence must be most carefully assessed. The court must look at the circumstances in which the identification was made and whether the witness has the capacity for careful observation. Factors which should be taken into account include the following:

- the amount of time that the witness had X under observation;
- the distance between the witness and X at the time of observation;
- the lighting conditions at the time;
- whether there were any objects in the way which would have prevented or obscured observation;
- whether the witness has good or poor eyesight;
- whether the witness was able to see clearly the face of X as well as the rest of his or her body;
- whether or not the witness had known X previously and, if he or she had, how well had he or she known him or her;
- whether there is any special reason why the witness would have been likely to have remembered X, such as the fact that X has distinct facial scars or a pronounced limp or is extraordinarily tall or short;
- whether the person identified belonged to a different ethnic group to the witness because if he or she did there may be doubt that the witness was able to distinguish accurately between different persons in that other ethnic group.

See *Mutters & Anor* S-66-89; *Nkomo & Anor* 1989 (3) ZLR 117 (S).

The identification will be unreliable if, for instance, the witness caught only a fleeting glimpse of a person from a considerable distance in poor light. The identification in these circumstances would be dubious, whether or not the person was a person he or she had known previously. On the other hand, close-range observation for a reasonable period of time in good lighting conditions where the witness clearly saw and carefully studied the person's facial features will be far more reliable, particularly if the person was well known to the witness or had some very distinctive features which made him or her easy to identify: *Nkomo & Anor* 1989 (3) ZLR 117 (S).

In *Musakwa* S-1-95, the complainant was conned out of money by two men. One chatted to her for 10 minutes and she saw X at the same spot shortly afterwards and identified him. He denied any involvement and said that he or she had been elsewhere. The police did not check his alibi. The trial court believed the complainant and accepted her identification. The appeal court held that mistakes happen; the question is not simply whether there was the opportunity for reliable recognition: the State must disprove the *alibi.*

The bald assertion by the witness that he or she is certain that he or she has identified the right person should not be accepted at face value. The objective basis of his or her identification must be carefully probed.

Witnesses should be asked by what features they made their identification. The witness should be questioned as to the height, build, complexion and apparel of the person observed. Where X is undefended, the court should carefully examine the circumstances of the identification and test its reliability.

The dangers of wrong identification are reduced if several witnesses independently identify X.

In *Madziwa* S-191-90, it was pointed out that weak evidence of identification is not made any more reliable by the mere fact that appellant was in the vicinity at the time and lied about this fact, as even an innocent person can lie out of a sense of panic.

Identification evidence can be very unreliable. In order to ensure that it is safe to rely upon the identification evidence the circumstances of the identification must be carefully probed and the powers of accurate observation and recall of the witness properly tested.

Identification from photographs

If the police decide to ask the witness to identify the culprit by looking at photographs, this exercise must be fairly conducted if any identification based thereon is to have reliable evidential value. For the identification process to be fair:

- the witness should be asked to look at a reasonable number of photographs and should not be shown only one photograph and asked whether this is the culprit;

- the names of the persons photographed should not be on the photographs and the photograph of a person whom the police already suspect should not be ringed or specially marked and that photograph should not be of an entirely different size from all the others;
- the police should allow the witness to make his or her own independent selection and should not prompt the witness in the direction of selecting one particular photograph;
- only photographs of reasonable quality should be shown because there is an increased danger of wrong identification from poor quality photographs;
- the identification process will not, however, be vitiated simply because the witness sees a label on the cover of the album indicating that the photographs in the album are of persons convicted of crimes similar to those for which the culprit is presently being sought:

Nkomo & Anor 1989 (3) ZLR 117 (S).

A witness to a crime is sometimes asked to identify the culprit from photographs so that the police can then make an arrest. In cases where police investigations have hitherto failed to lead to the arrest of a suspect, the police may ask a witness to a crime to look through an album containing photographs of persons with previous convictions to see if he or she can identify the culprit. If the witness is able to make an identification in this way, the police can investigate the case and possibly discover tangible evidence which can be produced in court. If this happens, the case against X will not have to be based solely on identification evidence.

However, if they cannot uncover such further evidence, and it is intended to proceed on the basis of identification evidence, it is best to hold an identification parade to see whether the witness will pick out the same person originally identified from photographs: *Nkomo & Anor* 1989 (3) ZLR 117 (S).

If, however, the police already have a suspect, the best way to test whether the person is the one the witness saw is to hold an identification parade, rather than asking the witness to look at photographs. The effect of showing the witness photographs upon his or her subsequent identification of X at a parade or in court needs to be considered. A witness who is first shown photographs may be predisposed towards identifying a person at a parade or in court on the basis of the photographic image he or she has selected rather than on the basis of his or her original observation at the time of the crime. This danger is reduced if the witness has made his or her selection from a large number of photographs. But even here there is a danger of false identification. The witness may have only caught a fleeting glimpse of the criminal committing the crime. He or she may then be asked by the police a long time later to pick out the culprit from photographs in an album. If, with only a hazy recollection of the culprit, he or she selects one of the photographs as being that of the culprit, he or she will obviously have looked carefully at the photograph. He or she will thus see in close-up all the person's facial features. That image will then stick in his or her mind and when he or she is called to identify the culprit at a parade or in court, he or she will be making his or her selection mostly on the basis of the photograph. This is not always so. Where the witness had a good opportunity to observe the face of the culprit at the scene of the crime he or she may be able to make a positive and reliable identification from both a photograph and at a later identification parade.

The State should always disclose if the witness previously identified the culprit from police photographs because this will have a bearing on the reliability of the witness' subsequent identification of the culprit at a parade or in court: *Ndlovu* S-3-88.

There is a difficulty in the State producing in evidence the photograph album which the witness examined to make an identification. The State may want to produce this to show that the identification process was a fair one and that the witness was asked to go through a large number of photographs. Because of the way in which the album is labelled its production to the court may have the effect of revealing that X has at least one previous conviction for the crime. If this is the case it cannot be produced because this would be prejudicial to X. If, however, X raises the matter of his or her identification from photographs and alleges that the process was unfairly conducted, then the State is at liberty to produce the album to prove the fairness of the process. See 1978 *Criminal Law Review* 343.

In examining the reliability of evidence of identification from photographs, the judge must ascertain whether the identification exercise was fairly conducted. The selection should have been made from a substantial number of photographs and there must have been no special markings on the photograph of X. The witness must be allowed to make his or her own independent selection without any prompting. After identifying a suspect from photographs, the witness should normally have been asked to confirm his or her identification at an identification parade.

In *Mutsinziri* 1997 (1) ZLR 6 (H), the court said that, where identity is in issue and X is identified by means of a photograph of him or her in the possession of the police, it is not inevitable in all cases that the witness would thereby conclude that X is known to the police and has a known or suspected criminal record. The police may come by photographs of the suspect in perfectly innocent circumstances and it is not necessarily harmful to X, where a policeman does no more than say that he or she was able to identify the accused from a photograph or to say that he or she tried to locate X by distributing photographs.

Summary

The reliability of evidence of identification from photographs can be attacked either on the basis that the witness' identification is unreliable or on the basis that the photographic identification exercise was unfairly conducted.

Identification in court

In *Mutsinziri* 1997 (1) ZLR 6 (H), the court pointed out that a "dock identification", where a witness is asked whether the person in the dock is the offender, suffers from considerable disadvantages. Everything about the atmosphere of the court proceedings points to the accused, and to him or her alone, as the person who is to be identified by the witness. These circumstances are inevitable unless one insists that any dock identification take the form of an identity parade. The manner in which a dock identification is elicited from witnesses by the prosecutor can be done the right way or the wrong way. The wrong way is one which makes it virtually impossible for the witness to say anything other than that the accused is the culprit. This way constitutes an irregularity. The better way is to get the witness to recount all the events without reference to the accused in the dock, and only when the witness has said all he or she has to say about the events should he or she be asked whether any person in the court is recognised. This form of identification still carries the defective feature of a dock identification, that the accused is obviously the person who is suspected of committing the offence, but it avoids leading questions and putting the identification into the witness's mouth.

In the South African case of *Maradu* 1994 (2) SACR 410 (W), the court held that the danger of a dock identification is the same as that created by a leading question in examination-in-chief: it suggests the answer desired. As the latter type of question is inadmissible, there is no reason why a dock identification should also not be inadmissible, save in special circumstances. (The court found that the witness's dock identification of the appellant was unreliable for a number of reasons.)

Identity parades

If the State case is likely to hinge on identification evidence identification parades should be held wherever possible. This should be done in order to overcome the obvious dangers of the witness being left simply to identify the person in the dock as the culprit. In identifying the person in the dock, the witness will be likely to assume that the police have got hold of the right person and, if there is any similarity between this person and the person he or she saw commit the crime, he or she will be inclined to assume that the person in the dock is the person he or she saw commit the crime.

To produce reliable evidence an identification parade must be carried out fairly. It must be carefully carried out to obviate errors. These are the basic requirements for a fair parade:

- It must be conducted by an officer who has had nothing to do with the investigations into the case;
- The officer conducting the parade should not call the witness to the parade;
- A sufficient number of persons, say ten, should form the parade;

- The persons on the parade must be approximately the same build, height and complexion and they should all wear similar clothing and, preferably, clothing similar to that worn when the crime was committed;
- The witness must be kept somewhere where he or she cannot see the prisoner being guarded by police officers or the parade being assembled;
- The witness should not be told that the suspect is on the parade but should only be asked if the person he or she saw commit that crime is on the parade;
- The witness must be left to pick out the person he or she saw commit the crime, if he or she can, without out any form of assistance or prompting;
- The police should not attempt to point out or suggest someone either before or during the parade;
- It is also important that the identification parade be held as soon after the commission of the crime as possible to avoid memory impairment occurring with the passage of time: *Mavunga* 1982 (1) ZLR 63 (S).

In *Gomo* HH-21-93, the court stated that evidence must be led showing the proper conduct of an identification parade in accordance with the established police procedures, with all its safeguards. Unless these essential requirements are complied with, any evidence of identification at a parade must not be relied on.

In *Masawi & Anor* HH-111-94, a woman saw her daughter being kidnapped at gunpoint at 7 am. She made no immediate statement to anyone present or to the police that she had recognised the assailant, who was 30 paces off and wore dark glasses and a hat pulled down over his or her face. Despite her claim in evidence that she recognised the man immediately as someone she had met two weeks before, it was obviously an *ex post facto* identification after she had had time to think about it. This was not inherently objectionable, but the particular circumstances made her identification unreliable, so it could only be accepted as evidence that the assailant was someone who looked very like X. Other circumstantial evidence then convinced the court that it was in fact X.

X, on legal advice, declined to participate in an identification parade. The police then organised an 'informal parade' in which the witness was invited to look around the police station and identify the suspect if she saw him. She did so. The police and the court accepted that, because of the handcuffs and his dishevelled state, this procedure did not enhance the identification but simply excluded the possibility that she would say it was not him.

In determining the reliability of the evidence derived from identification of a suspect at an identification parade, the judge must explore whether the parade was fairly conducted. A sufficient number of persons of similar build and appearance and similarly dressed should have formed the parade and the witness must have made his or her identification independently and without any prompting.

Fingerprints and handprints

Where the State case rests exclusively or substantially on evidence that the prints found at the scene of the crime matched those taken from X, an expert must testify as to the basis upon which he or she reached his or her conclusion that the prints belonged to one and the same person.

In *Mutsinziri* 1997 (1) ZLR 6 (H), the court said that where fingerprint evidence is given by an expert, the court ought not insist on its own ability to make a fingerprint identification by study of a comparison chart between the latent print (that found at the scene) and the inked print (that recorded from the suspect). Nevertheless, the court is still faced with a decision as to whether or not to accept the expert's evidence when he or she purports to find sufficient points of identity between the latent and the inked print. The court must take into account the witness's experience and the apparent weight and reliability of his or her opinion. The court may, if it considers it necessary, insist on a study of the comparison chart; and where the court is in a position to make its own examination of the comparison, it may, to the extent which it considers proper, attempt of its own accord to confirm the validity of the expert's opinion. In an appropriate case it may depart from the expert's opinion, if it is unable to find on the chart the points of similarity which so impressed the expert.

Fingerprint or handprint evidence is led in order to show that X was present at the place where the crime was committed. It is damning evidence if, for instance, it is established that X's fingerprints were found inside a house which had been burglarised and into which X had no right of entry. On the other hand, there is nothing incriminating for the fingerprints of X to be found inside the same house if he or she is a domestic worker who enters the house on a daily basis to carry out his or her work. The same would apply to the finding of the fingerprints of an accused who is a messenger, in offices into which he or she has free access in connection with his or her work.

Footprints and shoeprints

When dealing with the issue of identification, it is permissible for the court to rely on evidence relating to bare footprints. However, a number of precautions have to be observed before such evidence can be accepted. It is certainly not enough for a witness to make a bald assertion that the footprints were those of X, even if he or she says he or she had lived together with X in the same area for some time and he or she knew those prints well. The witness must be asked by what characteristics or peculiarities, marks or indications he or she recognised the footprints as being those of X. The ability to give a precise and detailed description and to point to features of unique distinction will point in the direction of reliable identification.

In *Menzou* HH-90-93, the court said there should be details of the length of the trail, its clarity and the expertise of the witnesses who followed it. The identification of a footprint as belonging to an accused must be precise and set out enough unusual features to convince the court beyond reasonable doubt.

In cases in which the identity of the footprints of the suspect forms a vital part of the evidence upon which the State relies for conviction, the police should, whenever possible, take a cast or other impression of the footprint at the scene of the crime and a comparative footprint from X. These should then be produced in court as exhibits so that comparisons can be made. See *Menzou* HH-90-93.

In respect of bare footprints an expert in handprints may also have the expertise to conduct an expert comparison between the two sets of footprints.

Reliance on shoeprints is obviously fraught with danger, especially where the shoeprint is from a type of footwear which is in widespread use: *Mavunga* 1982 (1) ZLR 63 (S).

Tyre marks and tool marks

Casts and photographic evidence should be produced and a scientific expert must testify as to the common features.

Voice identification

There is obviously substantial risk of error if identification is made on the basis of witness testimony that the voice of the suspect is the same as that of the culprit. This sort of evidence would need to be probed extremely carefully. The court should approach this sort of evidence in the same way as it does visual identification evidence. Questions such as the following must be put to the witness:

- What was there about the voice heard which made him or her sure that it was a particular person's voice?
- Did the voice have a timbre or quality that set it apart from the voice of others and, if so, what was this quality?
- Were the words spoken when the crime was committed spoken in a soft or loud voice and for how long did the culprit speak?
- How good is the witness's hearing?
- Were there other background noises at the time which would have made it difficult to hear the voice properly?
- Did the witness know X previously and was he or she familiar with his or her voice?

See *Denhere & Ors* GS-235-80; *Chitate* 1966 RLR 251 (A), 1966 (2) SA 690 (RA).

Matching of blood, DNA, bodily secretions and hair fibres

Expert medical and scientific evidence is obviously required.

Identification of property

When assessing the reliability of a person's identification of property such as a stolen motor vehicle, the court does not look at each feature or point of identification in isolation but has regard to the cumulative effect of the various features by which the person has identified the property: *Nyamaro* 1987 (2) ZLR 222 (S).

Dead bodies

As regards the identification of dead bodies see s 278(6) CPEA and as regards evidence on the physical condition of the deceased; see s 278(5) CPEA.

Handwriting

There is provision for handwriting evidence to be given in terms of s 261 CPEA. An expert may be called to testify as to whether the handwriting in a document produced in court is that of X. The person usually called to give evidence is the Questioned Documents Examiner of the Police Forensic Science Laboratory. The expert will testify as to the results of the comparison between the handwriting on the questioned document with the handwriting of X.

It is desirable that the handwriting expert should produce photographs supporting his or her evidence to show points of similarity between X's handwriting and the handwriting on the questioned document. The expert should point out the similarities and the significance of these.

The vital question is whether the similarities are so strong as to exclude any reasonable possibility that the handwriting is that of any one other than X.

It is the duty of the court to satisfy itself that the handwritings are those of the same person, X. In doing this, the court is entitled to take account of its own observations regarding the similarities and dissimilarities between the handwritings.

See *Chidota* 1966 RLR 178 (A); *Chibi* v *Minister of Internal Affairs* 1970 (1) RLR 88 (GD); *Mayahle* 1968 (1) RLR 133 (A); *Sibanda (2)* 1963 R&N 601 (SR); *Dedza* v *Ekblad* S-196-91. See also *Questioned Documents Examiners Evidence in Court* by E. Dzvairo in (1988) *Legal Forum* Vol. 1, No. 1, p 16.

Ballistics

In (1987) *Prosecutors Bulletin* Vol. 1, No. 3, p 12, there is a useful article by Chief Inspector Haley of the Police Forensic Firearms Identification Office entitled "Ballistics Evidence in Court". This article deals with the procedure for obtaining a ballistics report and also with the problems encountered when presenting ballistics evidence in a criminal case.

Presumption in relation to crimes only committed by those possessing particular qualification or acting in particular capacity

In terms of s 315 CPEA, where a crime can only be committed by a person possessing a particular qualification or vested with a particular authority or acting in a particular capacity it will be presumed that X had the qualification or authority or was acting in that capacity until the contrary is proven.

Circumstantial evidence

In the *Commonwealth Magistrates Handbook*, this advice is to be found on circumstantial evidence:

> " Means, motive and opportunity are all examples of what is called circumstantial evidence. Where direct evidence of a particular act or state of affairs is not available, one may, and indeed must, have resort to indirect means of establishing the facts ... Since the direct evidence of a witness is open to all the weaknesses of observation and recollection, ... evidence of a circumstantial kind may be less contestable and more easily relied on. To show that a defendant had the means, a motive and the opportunity may go some way towards convincing us of his or her guilt. It may raise a *prima facie* case against him or herwhich he or she is called upon to answer."

Where the conviction of an accused depends upon circumstantial evidence and the drawing of inferences from all the established facts, then the inference sought to be drawn must be consistent with the proved facts and the facts should be such that they exclude every reasonable inference from them, save the one sought to be drawn: *Edwards* 1949 SR 30.

Hearsay evidence

Reid-Rowland 18-20

Hearsay evidence is testimony not of what the witness himself saw, heard or otherwise observed, but what he or she heard others tell him or her or say about the matter under investigation. The general rule is that hearsay evidence is not admissible. The reason for this is that it is not the best evidence in that the actual observer is not giving the evidence and therefore the credibility of his or her evidence cannot be tested by cross-examination. There is also the risk that a second-hand report of what the actual observer said may be garbled or inaccurate.

There are many exceptions to the rule against hearsay evidence and the relevant textbooks should be consulted if there is a dispute as to whether the case falls within a particular exception. The main exceptions are statements made in the course of duty and dying declarations. As regards statements made in the course of duty this is provided for in s 253 CPEA. The provision applies where the person who made the statement is dead or unfit to give evidence due to bodily injury or mental condition or he or she cannot, with reasonable diligence, be identified or found or brought to court and the person made the statement in the ordinary course of duty, contemporaneously with the facts stated and without motive to misrepresent. See "Hearsay Evidence in Outline" by W.A. Hope in 1961 *Rhodesia and Nyasaland Law Journal* 130.

Evidence of confession elicited by cross-examination of State witness

In *Mvambo* 1995 (1) SACR 180 (W), the court said that where an accused or his or her legal representative, in the course of cross-examining a State witness, elicits evidence of a confession made by X, the evidence is admissible, provided that:

- the witness's answer constitutes a direct and fair answer to the cross-examination; and
- in the case of an unrepresented accused, the court is satisfied that X is fully aware of the risk attached to the question.

Considerations of fairness to X require that the courts should be vigilant to enforce these provisos. Furthermore the presumption underlying the second proviso, that legal practitioners know what they are about and are aware of the risks attaching to the questions, is not always true — particularly with inexperienced *pro deo* counsel. In such cases, the court should be vigilant, when counsel puts a dangerous question, or seems about to do so, to warn of the dangers and to permit its withdrawal before it is answered.

Evidence during trial within a trial

In *Gquma & Ors (2)* 1994 (2) SACR 182 (C), the court said it is a settled general principle that the issue of the admissibility of a statement or confession must be kept clearly distinct from the issue of guilt, which object is achieved by insulating the inquiry into voluntariness (the trial within the trial) in a compartment separate from the main trial. But once the statement has been ruled admissible X and his or her witnesses, if they give evidence in the main trial, may be cross-examined on the evidence given by them in the trial within a trial.

In *Shezi* 1994 (1) SACR 575 (A), the SA court stated that an accused person has the right to have the question of the admissibility of his or her statement tried as a separate and distinct issue. Hence, the evidence at a trial within a trial to determine the admissibility of a statement cannot be relied upon in reference to the ultimate verdict. A trial within a trial and the main trial are separate in substance as well as form, and the former is restricted to evidence relating to the admissibility of X's statement.

Drawing adverse inferences from accused's silence

Reid-Rowland 16-37; 20-8

Adverse inferences

In terms of the CPEA, the court can draw certain adverse inferences from X's silence at different stages. The court may draw such adverse inferences from silence at these different stages as appear proper. Also, on the basis of such inferences, the silence may be treated as evidence corroborating any other evidence given against X.

Confirmation proceedings

Adverse inferences can be draw at the trial if, at proceedings to confirm a statement allegedly made by X to the police, X remains silent and does not mention any fact which, in the circumstances, he or she could reasonably have been expected to have mentioned. If then at his or her trial he or she challenges the statement on the basis that he or she did not in fact make it or he or she did not make it freely and voluntarily, the court may draw adverse inferences from his or her earlier failure to mention the facts: s 115 CPEA.

Defence outline

Adverse inferences can be drawn if X pleads not guilty or the judge enters a plea of not guilty because X refuses to plead to the charge, and on being called upon to give his or her defence outline he or she fails to mention any fact relevant to his or her defence which, in the circumstances existing at the time, he or she could reasonably have been expected to have mentioned. Such adverse inferences can be drawn by the court from his or her earlier failure to mention these facts when it determines his or her guilt for the offence charged or any other crime which he or she may be convicted of on that charge: s 189(2) CPEA.

This provision must not, however, be taken too far in relation to X who is not legally represented. In *Pandehuni* 1982 (2) ZLR 133 (S), the Supreme Court stated that even where X has been properly warned of the fact that adverse inferences may be drawn from his or her failure to mention relevant facts in his or her defence outline, it must still be borne in mind that an accused who is required to give an *ex tempore* summary of the features of his or her defence may very easily fail to marshal his or her thoughts so as to include in the outline everything that should be included. The outline is after all only that; it is not a detailed and comprehensive exposition such as would be expected in the course of evidence in chief. X must therefore be allowed to add facts to his or her evidence in chief which are not in his or her initial outline. This is why it is wrong to use the shortcut device of prompting X simply to adhere to his or her initial outline when giving evidence in chief before cross-examination commences. This applies even when he or she is asked if he or she wishes to add anything to that outline. By circumscribing, X in this way he or she is not able to give a full exposition of his or her case in his or her evidence in chief and this means that he or she does not have a proper opportunity to give full evidence covering in detail the additional facts not in his or her initial outline.

If X is circumscribed in this way, the scepticism which arises from the fact that he or she has mentioned salient facts for the first time only when under cross-examination may be entirely unjustified.

When giving evidence

If X refuses to answer any questions put to him or her when he or she gives evidence in his or her defence, and his or her refusal is not for a just cause (on the grounds of privilege), adverse inferences may be drawn by the court from the failure to answer the questions: s 199 CPEA.

In *Masawi & Anor* HH-111-94, the facts were that at 7 am on 15 December 1992 a woman was kidnapped; in late December a second suspect was arrested and after being warned and cautioned simply said he denied the charge. The court drew an adverse inference from his failure to give any indication that his defence was an alibi or any details of what he was doing during the crucial period. Although the court accepted that he had been assaulted by police at the time of his arrest and then denied both a timeous remand and access by a lawyer for some days, it was found to be an insufficient justification for giving no facts at all.

Questions put by prosecutor or court

Even if X has declined to give evidence in his or her defence he or she can nonetheless be questioned by the prosecutor or the court. If, without just cause, he or she refuses to answer such questions adverse inferences may be drawn by the court from the failure to answer the questions: s 199 CPEA.

Statements by accused to police

If X's statement to the police is admissible, the statement needs to be carefully examined to see what sort of a statement it is. In the *Prosecutors Handbook*, it is pointed out that the statement may amount to:

- a complete admission (in which case if X has not challenged the admissibility of the statement he or she probably will have pleaded guilty);

- a partial admission (as where X admits to stealing two of the four items which he or she is alleged to have stolen);
- a complete denial;
- a partial denial;
- an innocent explanation.

Partial admissions and partial denials need to be particularly carefully treated. If X is charged with attempted murder and says that he or she admits to having stabbed the complainant, this does not mean that he or she has admitted that he or she did so with the intention to kill; if a person is charged with assault with intent to do grievous bodily harm and denies that he or she used a knife as alleged, he or she may nonetheless have admitted in his or her statement to the police that he or she did have a fight with the complainant.

Note that the statement of X in reply to police questions is only evidence against the maker of the statement: s 259 CPEA. This is because there is no opportunity for cross-examination of the person who made this statement when he or she makes his or her statement. But if the maker goes into the witness box and repeats on oath what he or she said in the statement, he or she renders himself liable to cross-examination by an accused who is jointly charged with him or her and thus such evidence on oath is admissible against the co-accused.

Inconsistencies and contradictions in witness testimony

The mere fact that there are some minor discrepancies in the testimony of a witness does not mean that that testimony must be rejected. The mere fact that there are some minor contradictions in the testimony of the various witnesses testifying for either the State or the defence does not mean that the testimony of all those witnesses must be rejected. The nature and extent of the discrepancies and contradictions must be probed, together with the overall question of credibility of the various witnesses.

A witness statement may be entirely or substantially true, entirely or substantially false, partially true or partially false. The witness may also have a reason for altering his or her testimony in favour of X or may have a reason such as a grudge for falsifying his or her evidence against X.

Previous inconsistent statements by State witnesses

Reid-Rowland 18-19

Hostile witness

A State witness may have made a statement to the police which was against X. However, when the case gets to court, because of his or her relationship to X or for some other reason, he or she may depart from his or her statement and give evidence favourable to X and become a hostile witness against the State case.

Impeachment of witness

When a witness has become hostile the State has the option to apply to impeach the witness in terms of s 316 CPEA. The object of impeachment is not to persuade the judge to accept the evidence he or she gave in his or her original statement, but to destroy his or her reliability for either side.

To have his or her own witness impeached by the court, the correct procedure is as follows:

- The State must first produce the previous apparently conflicting statement from the witness and the prosecutor should give the witness sufficient particulars of the statement to identify the occasion on which it was allegedly made.
- The witness must then be asked whether he or she made the alleged statement. If the statement is signed, he or she may be asked to admit to the signature.
- If the witness admits to having made the statement on the specified occasion, the statement should be put to him or her and he or she should be asked to admit or deny using the words alleged.
- If the witness denies using the words alleged, the prosecutor may apply to adjourn the case so that he or she can call witnesses to prove that the statement was made by this witness. Where the statement has been interpreted, the interpreter must be called.
- If the witness admits using the words alleged, the statement may be used without further proof.

The witness must then be asked to explain the discrepancies between the statement on the occasion specified and his or her present testimony, and what the truth of the matter really is.

See *Muhlaba & Ors* 1973 (1) RLR 178 (GD) and C Goredema "Procedural aspects relating to the impeachment of witnesses" (1989) *Legal Forum* Vol. 1 No. 6, p 8.

The witness' explanation of the apparent conflict may be entirely acceptable. If it is not, it may be appropriate to impeach him or her in terms of s 316 [293] CPEA. In *Chari* 1989 (1) ZLR 231 (S), after a State witness had given evidence inconsistent with a previous sworn statement, the prosecutor had produced this statement as an exhibit. Without further ado the magistrate summarily dismissed the witness and excused him or her from further attendance. The Supreme Court held that this amounted to a gross irregularity. The prosecution should have laid a proper foundation for the impeachment and the defence should have had an opportunity to cross-examine the witness.

If the State decides to apply to have the witness declared hostile and the judge declares him or her to be adverse, the State can then proceed to cross-examine the witness. It is an irregularity for the State to be permitted to cross-examine its own witness before the court has declared the witness to be hostile. Before the witness has been declared hostile, the prosecutor may not go beyond putting the discrepancies and eliciting an explanation from the witness; he or she may not proceed with full blooded cross-examination of the witness.

Although the object of this cross-examination may be to discredit all aspects of his or her testimony, this witness may say some things under cross-examination which, in fact, implicate X. As seen below the State can then seek to rely on those portions of the testimony of this hostile witness which assist the State case.

Reliance on portion of evidence of impeached witness

Where a witness has been impeached after departing from his or her statement to the police and it is obvious that the witness is favourably inclined towards X, it is permissible to accept and rely on that part of his or her evidence which tends to incriminate X: *Millar* 1971 RLR 159 (A) and *Mpofu & Anor* S-150-89. In *Millar* at 160, it is stated that "it is quite illogical to say that, because the witness is trying to help X to the utmost extent, he or she must not be believed when he or she gives evidence which does not help X, but which tends to incriminate him or her ... There is no ground in law ... for rejecting out of hand those portions of evidence ... which implicate him."

Inconsistent statements at another trial

In *Mutters & Anor* S-66-89, defence counsel had been allowed to put to State witnesses previous inconsistent statements they were alleged to have made in a previous trial. However, the magistrate had refused to admit as evidence the record of the previous trial. The Supreme Court held that by refusing to admit the record as evidence, the magistrate had precluded the defence from proving inconsistencies in the testimony of the witnesses, and had disabled himself from adjudicating on their credibility. The record was perfectly admissible and should have been admitted in evidence.

If a State witness makes a statement which is apparently inconsistent with a previous statement made during investigations before trial, this witness must be asked if he or she made the previous statement and whether he or she has any explanation for the inconsistency.

The prosecutor can only cross-examine his or her own witness after the court has, on application, declared him or her to be hostile.

The entire testimony of an impeached witness does not have to be disregarded. The prosecutor may ask the court to take into account portions of the testimony which are prejudicial to X.

Summary

If a witness makes a statement which is apparently inconsistent with a previous statement made during investigations before trial, the party calling the witness may ask his or her witness if he or she made the previous statement and whether he or she had any explanation for the inconsistency.

The party calling a witness can only cross-examine its own witness if the court has on application first declared him or her to be hostile.

The entire testimony of an impeached witness does not have to be disregarded. The State may ask the court to take into account portions of the testimony which are prejudicial to the accused.

Previous consistent statements

A statement made by a State witness in a criminal case to the police, whether as an affidavit or otherwise, is not normally admissible in evidence unless he or she departs from it in a material respect and is impeached. A witness, as a rule, is not permitted to confirm or strengthen his or her evidence by testifying that he or she had made a similar statement on a previous occasion.

There are, however some exceptions to this rule.

If X puts to the witness under cross-examination that his or her story is a recent fabrication, the witness' previous statement becomes admissible in order to show that he or she had made a previous consistent statement at a time sufficiently early to be inconsistent with the suggestion that the present account was a recent invention.

Complaints in sexual cases are admissible to show consistency and to deny a defence of consent but not to prove its content or to corroborate the evidence of the complainant;

Other previous statements which are admissible are statements forming part of the *res gestae*, statements relating to previous identification, to show consistency in the identification and previous statements by accused persons.

(The *res gestae* consists of the facts constituting and immediately accompanying the matter which is in issue. It includes facts leading up to, explaining and following continuously from the facts in issue. Thus evidence by a hearer of what the victim shouted when assaulted is admissible as part of the *res gestae*.)

Blood samples

In *Jesse* v *Attorney-General & Ors* HH-213-94, it was pointed out that the police have a right to require a blood sample from an accused to ascertain any fact material to their investigations. This implies a right to use force if necessary to obtain it, if consent is withheld. The sample has to be taken by a medical officer at the written request of a police superintendent or above. X is entitled to be told who is to take the blood sample, where and when, and the facts sought to be established, i.e. why it is to be taken; and should be given a copy of the request to a named medical officer. Applicant had the right to ignore a demand that did not comply with this, and should not have been threatened with force until the correct procedure had been followed. However, his or her fear of false incrimination had not been justified.

In *Mandwe* S-142-93, it was stated that a blood test must be taken on the orders of an inspector or above. Thus, a blood test taken on the orders of a sergeant is incurably defective and is inadmissible.

Incompetent witnesses

Certain witnesses are not competent to give evidence according to the rules of evidence. For example, under s 246 CPEA "no person appearing or proved to be afflicted with a mental disorder or defect or labouring under any imbecility of mind arising from intoxication or otherwise, shall be competent to give evidence while under the influence of any such malady or disability".

Where an allegation that a witness is mentally disordered is made during a criminal trial and the witness appears to be mentally disordered, the court must properly investigate whether the witness is competent in terms of this provision.

In *Ndiweni* S-149-89, the court failed to probe an assertion by the defence that a State witness was labouring under some mental disorder. The State did not challenge this assertion. The appeal court said that this was an irregularity.

Pre-conviction disclosure of previous convictions of accused

Normally, it is totally impermissible for the State to prove the previous convictions of X before he or she has been convicted of the offence with which he or she is being charged. The prosecutor may not refer to the previous convictions of X prior to X being found guilty of the charge. Nor may the prosecutor ask X when he or she is testifying whether he or she has previous convictions: s 324 CPEA. The reason for this is obvious. The judge should be solely concerned with whether X has committed the present offence. If he or she knows that X has a string of previous convictions, this might mean that the judge will be biased against him or her and will find him or her guilty on the basis of his or her previous criminal tendencies rather than because his or her guilt on the current offence has been proved beyond reasonable doubt. For this reason, if the previous convictions are disclosed before he or she has been found guilty this will constitute a gross irregularity which will lead to the proceedings being set aside.

There are however some exceptions to this general rule.

1. Accused charged with receiving of stolen property.

   If X is charged with receiving, in terms of ss 305 and 306 CPEA the State is permitted at any time during the trial to lead evidence that the person was found in possession of stolen property within the period of twelve months preceding the time when the person was first charged with the current offence and evidence that within the preceding five years he or she has been convicted of an offence involving fraud or dishonesty. X must be given three days written notice before such evidence is introduced.

   This evidence can then be taken into account by the court in deciding whether or not X knew that the property he or she had in his or her possession on the present occasion was in fact stolen.

2. Although evidence of previous convictions or bad character of X may not normally be introduced before conviction, in terms of s 290 CPEA such evidence can be introduced before conviction if:

   - X has given evidence of his or her own good character or he or she or his or her lawyer has asked a witness questions to try to establish his or her good character;
   - aspersions are cast upon the character of the prosecutor or State witnesses by the defence; and
   - X has given evidence against another person charged with the same offence;

In *Jesse v Pratt & Anor* 2001 (1) ZLR 48 (H), it was held that the magistrate had permitted a serious irregularity to take place, the adduction of evidence of the X's bad character, even though X's cross-examination of the complainant had not even exposed himself to cross-examination as to his or her character. Although s 290 CPEA allows X to be cross-examined as to his or her character, the scope of the section is limited. X must have some latitude to examine on credibility without exposing himself to the extremely damaging prospect of being examined on his or her character. He or she should only be vulnerable to such an attack where he or she has attacked the credibility of a State witness, by attempting to impeach character, on an issue not being an essential element of the charge or offence, and to a degree not adjudged warranted, and where the court in its discretion permits such an attack upon the accused.

Illegally obtained evidence

In *Tswangira* S-184-95, the police had detained X for more than the permitted 48 hour period. He confessed to the crime 63 hours after his arrest. In such a case, the court has the discretion to decide whether to admit the evidence despite the illegality. Factors that the court would take into account included:

- whether the illegality was intentional or inadvertent
- whether the illegality was trivial or technical or whether it involved serious invasion of important rights, the recurrence of which would involve a real danger to such rights
- whether it was a situation of urgency or emergency which provided some excuse for the illegality.

In this case, the only illegality shown was detaining X beyond the permitted period without taking him or her before a magistrate. The illegality was inadvertent as X had surrendered himself at one police station and was collected and dealt with by an investigating officer from another station, who did not notice the time of his or her arrest. The policeman's dereliction of duty was condemned, but the Appeal Court decided that the trial court had properly admitted the statement.

See also *Hammer & Ors* 1994 (2) SACR 496 (C) where the court said that it has a discretion to exclude evidence that has been illegally or improperly obtained.

Treason cases

Section 269 CPEA provides that it is not lawful for a court to convict a person charged with treason "except upon the evidence of two witnesses where one overt act is charged in the indictment or, where two or more such overt acts are so charged, upon the evidence of one witness to each such overt act."

This rule is a safeguard against false accusations of treason.

In *S* v *Tsvangirai & Ors* HH-119-03, Garwe JP set out the special evidential rules relating to treason as follows:

> " It is not competent for a court to convict a person of treason except on the evidence of two witnesses for each 'overt act' charged or, where two or more overt acts are charged, one witness for each overt act. There would be no compliance with the Act if, in a case where more than one overt act is charged and there is only one witness, the same witness were to give evidence on each of the overt acts. Where one overt act is charged at least two witnesses must give evidence on the overt act, although the evidence need not overlap. Where the court is relying on the evidence of only two witnesses to prove the whole overt act, the evidence of each of those witnesses must be such that, standing alone, it would, if believed, be adequate to establish that the accused committed the overt act of treason with which he is charged.
>
> An overt act is any act manifesting the criminal intention and tending towards the accomplishment of the criminal object. It is generally a composite thing, passing through distinct stages and made up of various circumstances. Several witnesses speaking to those different stages and circumstances may be necessary."

Witness recollection about traffic accident

In *Mupanedungu* S-197-94, the court pointed out that traffic accidents happen suddenly and unexpectedly. Those involved, and the bystanders, are shocked. Their recollections are impressionistic and often inaccurate. The facts on the ground will often show that witnesses' recollections of details are unreliable. This does not mean they are lying. It means only that their memory of a sudden, unexpected, fast-moving and fast-changing series of events is faulty. Judicial officers need to use common sense to sort out fact from imagination and self-justification. The parties in particular usually intended to act sensibly and are often convinced from their recollection or reconstruction of events that they did.

Rape cases

In *Khupe & Anor* HB 30-83, the court pointed out that penetration in legal terms means the slightest entry into the female body. It is not necessary that the hymen be ruptured. Doctors compiling medical reports understandably fail to appreciate this; and hence often state that there has been no penetration, while the complainant's evidence shows that there was some. The court should not be unduly influenced by the medical report.

In *Dube* S-216-93, after giving evidence a young girl who had accused her father of 12 counts of rape had allegedly recanted her story in a letter to a church minister. The trial court refused to allow the letter to be introduced as hearsay and refused to allow the complainant to be recalled because it preferred finality in trials. This was wrongful exclusion of possibly material evidence, and the conviction was quashed.

In *Zaranyika & Ors* HH-41-95, the court said that magistrates should carefully compare the medical report against the evidence of the complainant in a rape case, not accept the report with an unquestioning mind unless it clearly and conclusively supports her evidence; and call the doctor if there is any possible ambiguity. This can have a significant effect on assessing the complainant's credibility.

In *Dube* S-139-95, the court decided that two affidavits concerning medical examinations of the complainant were inadmissible, as X had not been given 3 days' notice and had not consented to their production. The other evidence was insufficient to sustain the conviction, with the trial court ignoring accused's requests for a medical examination to prove he did not have any sexually transmitted disease. If affidavits had been admissible they would still have needed to be elucidated by *viva voce* evidence because a number of questions arose from them, and it was not clear whether the doctors had been advised of facts that could have provided alternative explanations for the young complainant's vaginal warts and injuries. Both doctors had left the country. The conviction was set aside.

In *Rembani* S-141-95, the court said that the medical report produced in this case was confusing; appellant argued that it suggested complainant was promiscuous and not a virgin as she claimed; but medical reports should not be taken at face value; there were other inferences that could reasonably be drawn from the report. Without oral testimony from the doctor, the court could not draw the inference suggested by the appellant. The complainant's story was credible and corroborated by other evidence.

Intercourse with "imbecile"

In *Matekukamizora* HH-192-94, the court said that in a case where X is charged with having sexual intercourse with an "imbecile" in contravention of the Criminal Law Amendment Act, there must be medical investigation and evidence essential to establish imbecility.

In *Mbizi* S-184-84, the court said that whether the requisite state of mental defectiveness has been reached in a particular case is a question of fact to be determined on the basis of expert medical testimony.

See also *Chamukwanda* HB-17-90.

Abortion cases

In *Chiunye* HH-153-94, the court pointed out that even when an accused pleads guilty to abortion or unlawful termination of pregnancy, the court must establish that her actions actually caused the abortion and that it was not spontaneous or coincidental.

Assault cases

In *Tamba* S-81-91, the court criticised the "boxing match" approach especially in assault cases arising from an affray. In such cases, the State tends to throw the two protagonists into the ring with the magistrate as referee. At the end of the bout, the magistrate awards points for demeanour and probability, and names the winner, who is usually the complainant. Usually, neither version is entirely true. Each party will tend to minimise his or her own role and exaggerate that of his or her opponent. So it is not just a question of who is telling the truth, but how much of the truth is being told by each of them. The complainant in a case of this nature must be regarded in many ways as the courts regard an accomplice. It is unsafe to rely on his or her unsupported word. In the present case the conviction was quashed because of the State's failure to lead evidence from others present or involved in the incident.

In *Chatyoka* S-75-92, the Supreme Court pointed out that judicial officers should not forget that a complainant with a legitimate complaint may still exaggerate his or her own virtue and gloss over his or her faults; disbelieving X does not mean that the court should believe every word of the complainant. Usually, neither party has a monopoly of the truth.

In *Chiweshe* S-38-93, the court pointed out that in assault cases, often neither side has a monopoly of the truth, and the court must analyse the evidence to reconstruct the facts; not simply decide which story is more credible and accept it entirely.

In *Moyo & Anor* S-12-93, the court said that in assault cases the two common faults are:

- choosing and believing one or the other version of a fight, without considering whether both parties are improving their versions; and
- deciding the case against co-accused jointly – the court must weigh up the evidence against one accused and reach its conclusion for him, then weigh up the evidence against the next person, etc.

A court also cannot decide on the basis of whose story is more probable and credible because of the burden of proof; if the defence version could reasonably possibly be true, although improbable, X must be acquitted.

A complainant is often a single witness with an interest strongly adverse to X's. Her evidence should be treated with great caution. Where it conflicts with the defence evidence it should be accepted only where it is corroborated or overwhelmingly probable.

Theft – general deficiency

In *Chikasha* S-94-94, appellant was a postal clerk; he recorded he had received $3 000 one day when he had received $3 200, and his books did not account for the extra $200, leaving him with a general deficiency for that amount that day. Appellant alleged some receipts were really carried over from the previous day, creating the appearance of a deficiency, and a surplus on that day plus the sale of stamps accounted for the apparent deficiency on the day in question. The page for the previous day was not produced in court; the postmistress simply said that the previous day balanced. The best evidence rule required that the book itself be produced so the court could judge for itself whether there was any truth in the appellant's claim, not simply rely on a witness's testimony and conclusion on the point. As with fingerprints, the court must look at the evidence itself on which the witness's opinion is based. The appeal was allowed and the conviction and sentence were quashed.

Section 5

Criminal Law Code

The Criminal Law (Codification and Reform) Act brings together in one single statute all the major aspects of the Criminal Law. It codifies all the major aspects of the common law Criminal Law and incorporates many of the offences that were previously contained in various statutes. It does not, however, codify statutory offences that are integral to the statutes in which they are contained such as the offences in the Road Traffic Act.

The Code however does not simply incorporate the existing law; it also effects many changes which are intended to improve and reform the existing law.

The Code also codifies the various defences that can be raised to criminal liability. From the standpoint of criminal defence lawyers, these provisions are of major importance.

It should be noted that although the Code does not eliminate case law precedents. Zimbabwean case law remains relevant in relation to offences and defences that have simply been incorporated into the Code without change. South African case law remains persuasive authority.

Defence lawyers need to familiarise themselves with this Code. In this regard they should refer to the Feltoe Commentary on the Code published by the Legal Resources Foundation.

Some of the important changes to the existing law are these:

Culpable homicide (s 49)
This crime has been extended to cover situations where there is 'conscious negligence'

Inciting or assisting suicide (s 50)

A new crime has been created which consists of inciting another to commit suicide or assisting a person to commit suicide.

Rape (s 65)
The crime has been extended to cover a situation where a male has non-consensual anal intercourse with a female.

Aggravated indecent assault (s 66)
This new crime covers cases where a male or female commits an indecent assault involving non-consensual penetration with indecent intent.

Sodomy (s 73)
This crime now includes acts of physical contact between males that would be regarded by a reasonable person as an indecent act.

Incest (s 75)
The crime now incorporates customary law notions of incest.

Assault (s 89)
There is no longer a distinction between common assault and assault with intent to do grievous bodily harm with seriousness only affecting sentence. Administration of noxious substances is now treated as a species of assault.

Negligent assault (s 90)
This new crime covers situations were harm has been negligently inflicted.

Pledging a female person (s 94)
This crime now prohibits the customary practice of handing over a female person to settle a debt.

Witchcraft and witch finding (ss 97 162)
The Code recognises the distinction between witchcraft and witch finding. Witch finding is only criminalised in certain circumstances where this practice socially disruptive or result in an injustice.

Unauthorised borrowing (s 116)
This new crime outlaws the borrowing or use of someone's property without their authorisation.

Making off without payment (s 117)
This new crime covers situations where services rather than goods are stolen. It also covers situations were there has been consumption of goods but payment has been refused.

Computer related crimes (ss 162 – 168)
A whole range of 'cyber-crimes' has been created.

Threatening to commit specified crimes (s 184)
This covers the new crime of threatening to commit a serious crime, such as threatening to murder or rape

Malicious damage to property (s 140)
The common law crimes of arson and malicious injury to property have been merged.

Unlawful entry into premises (s 131)
This crime reformulates this crime to do away with the artificial requirements of this offence.

There are a number of other new crimes:

Corruptly concealing from principal a personal interest in a transaction (s 173)

Obstructing a Public official (s 178)

Impersonating a police officer, peace officer or public official (s 179)

Deliberately supplying false information to a public authority (s 180)

Negligently causing serious damage to property (s 141)

Some crimes have been merged into other crimes or are now charged as other crimes:

The crimes of theft by false pretences and uttering are now simply treated as species of fraud.

Subornation of perjury is now treated as incitement to perjury or, if the perjury is committed as a result of the incitement, then the person who incited is charged as an accomplice to perjury. (Fifth Schedule)

Commenting upon a pending court case is now charged as defeating or obstructing the course of justice and no longer is charged as contempt of court. (s184(1))

The Code in drastically changes the common law by providing that theft or stock theft continues to be committed regardless of whether the thief has lost possession of the stolen property (s121).

Section 189 extends circumstances upon which an attempt could be said to occur. The accused is now guilty of an attempt if he or she or she does or omits to do anything intending to commit the crime (or realising that there is a real risk that the crime may be committed) with the proviso that what the accused has done or omitted to do can be said to have reached at least the commencement of the execution of the crime.

> As relates participation or assistance, every joint or co-perpetrator is liable as if he or she was the actual perpetrator.

Another important development is highlighted in s 54(2). The High Court now has the power to order the removal of a person from a life support system. This species of euthanasia is now part of our law.

As regards defences, the one major change is to the defence of voluntary intoxications. Previously voluntary intoxication could be a partial defence having the effect of reducing the crime charged with to a lesser one e.g. murder to culpable homicide. There has now been created a new strict liability crime of "Voluntary Intoxication leading to unlawful conduct". This allows the court to find an accused guilty of this crime instead of the one originally charged and sentence the accused to the same punishment to which the accused would have been liable if he or she or she had been found guilty of the crime originally charged and intoxication had been assessed as a mitigatory circumstance (s 222).

Section 6

Judgment Process

Deciding on verdict

After all the evidence has been led the judge must make up his or her mind as to whether the State has proved the case against X beyond reasonable doubt. This involves deciding whether all the essential ingredients of the crime have been proved on the version of the facts accepted by the court and whether any defences are available to X. If there is proof of all the essential elements of the crime and no defences are available on the facts, X will be found guilty.

The *Commonwealth Magistrates Handbook* advises magistrates to go through these steps before reaching a verdict:

1. Consider what are the essential ingredients of the criminal offence which have to be proved by the State before there can be a conviction.

   What does the law require the prosecution to prove in respect of the crime charged?

   Does the law require proof of a mental element?

   Must the injuries be so serious as to constitute grievous bodily harm?

   Must X have known that the goods in question were stolen, etc.?

2. Consider what facts have been proved in the case.
   In deciding what the facts of the case are, only admissible facts must be taken into account. The evidence on both sides must be considered as elucidated in cross-examination. A decision must be made regarding disputed facts. In respect of all competing or contradictory versions of facts the court must decide which version of the facts should be accepted as being the most credible. Remember that minor discrepancies in the testimony of a witness or minor contradictions between witnesses for the State or the defence will not automatically make this testimony unworthy of belief. The question will be whether the testimony appears to be substantially true.

3. Decide which of these facts are relevant. Facts which are not relevant in deciding whether each of the essential elements of the crime has been proved can then be disregarded.

4. Apply the law to the facts and decide whether all the essential ingredients are satisfied on the basis of the proved facts.

   Bearing in mind that the onus is upon the State to prove its case beyond reasonable doubt, the court will proceed to apply the relevant law to the facts and decide whether all the vital ingredients of the crime have been proved. If any have not been proved, X must be found not guilty.

There is another suggested framework in this Commonwealth book which is similar to the first. Under this the judge is advised to go though these stages:

1. Consider the charge, noting its exact wording.

2. Decide what are the essential elements of the offence which have to be proved. (Bear in mind any case law explaining the elements of statutory and common law crimes).

3. Consider what facts of the case are relevant to these elements.

4. Decide which of these facts are in issue, and which are admitted.

5. Ascertain what evidence tends to prove or disprove each of the facts in issue. In doing this:

   (a) start with what is legally presumed or assumed, what is agreed, admitted or uncontested, and work towards what is contested;

   (b) exclude all evidence which is legally inadmissible such as inadmissible hearsay;

   (c) evaluate each item of evidence in the light of credibility and consistency.

   (Inexperienced magistrates sometimes acquit accused where there is a conflict in evidence between State and defence witnesses, either because they lack the ability to resolve the conflict or because they wrongly believe that the mere existence of the conflict justifies an acquittal. Obviously, the fact of conflicting defence and State evidence is not a proper basis for acquittal; the evidence must be assessed to see which version of the facts should be accepted.)

6. Consider what defences are available to X on the facts, and the requirements for these defences and decide whether these defences have been disproved or proved, depending upon whom the onus lies in respect of the defences.

7. Consider whether each element of the offence has been proved to your satisfaction and whether the guilt of X has therefore been proved beyond reasonable doubt and is there no validly established defence.

   If yes, convict.

   If no, acquit.

Logical and systematic framework for judgments

A good way to structure judgments is to use headings to deal systematically with all the essential components of judgments. But even if headings are not used, it is useful to have some sort of check list of components and in what sequence they should be covered.

Trial cases

1. **Charge**
   Set out charge and particulars of charge.

2. **Essential elements of crime**
   Note the essential elements of crime charged.
   Decide what facts in the case are relevant to these elements.
   (Often only one element in dispute – e.g. did A intend to kill or did he or she kill in self-defence and therefore did he or she act lawfully.)

3. **Decide which facts are admitted**
   Set out the admitted facts which are salient for the decision.

4. **Evaluate evidence regarding facts in dispute**
   Summarise evidence presented by prosecution and defence on disputed facts and make findings of fact on which versions of the evidence the court is accepting and why (credibility, consistency etc). There is no need to recite every single piece of evidence produced on both sides. Concentrate on evidence which is material to the facts in dispute relating to the vital legal issues.

5. **Decide whether proof of guilt**
   Decide on the basis of findings of fact and inferences to be drawn from facts whether State has proved commission of the crime charged beyond reasonable doubt i.e. all its essential elements.

Every single fact does not have to be proved beyond reasonable doubt but facts establishing that the essential elements are satisfied must proved.

Possible defences must be considered if the evidence suggests that they may apply even if they are not specifically pleaded. The onus is on State to disprove such defences except insanity.

6. **Sentence**
   If guilty, set out factors accepted in mitigation and in aggravation and then decide upon appropriate punishment for offender. Sentence must be an informed process based on adequate information.

Good technique

Dube 1997 (1) ZLR 229 (H): A man killed a police officer who referred to him or heras "Banana's wife". The judgment was set out systematically using headings.

Bad technique

An ex-judge used to set out in exhaustive detail the prosecution and defence cases, quoting verbatim the state and defence outlines and reciting in detail the testimony given by every single witness. Without making any findings of fact regarding contradictory evidence, the judge would simply proceed to verdict. In other words, he or she would not decide which of two competing and contradictory versions of facts he or she was accepting. There was therefore no way of determining what facts he or she had used to arrive at his or her verdict.

Appeal against conviction

1. **Crime of which convicted**
   Set out crime of which A was convicted and its essential elements.

2. **Grounds for appeal**
   Set out the grounds for appeal and summarise the arguments for and against the appeal.

3. **Whether sound basis for conviction**
   Analyse basis upon which trial court convicted A.
   (a) Were findings of fact consistent with evidence? (but the Appeal Court will not normally interfere with the trial court's findings of fact);
   (b) Were correct inferences drawn from the facts?
   (c) Did the court apply the correct law to the facts?
   (d) Did the trial court correctly apply the law to the facts?
   (e) Did the State discharge the onus of proving the essential elements of the crime beyond reasonable doubt?

Making findings of fact

In some criminal cases, there is no dispute as to the facts. If X pleads guilty the court must satisfy itself that X is agreeing to the material facts of the State case. Having done so it convicts him or heron the basis of the State case as admitted by X.

Even where X pleads not guilty, he or she will sometimes not dispute the facts contained in the State case. He or she may agree that these are the correct facts but maintain that on these facts he or she has some defence to the charge. The State and the defence will sometimes put forward an agreed statement of facts.

The difficult cases from the standpoint of arriving at a judgment are those in which the facts are in dispute. This difficulty is most pronounced in a complex case where many witnesses have testified. Where the State and the defence version of the facts differ, the court has to decide which version of the facts it believes. Sometimes, and very commonly in assault cases or traffic cases, neither X nor the complainant is necessarily telling the whole truth. So it is not a question of "which party do I believe?" but "even if basically I believe the complainant, is it safe to accept everything he or she says?"

The court must decide what the true facts are before it can apply the law to the facts in order to arrive at a decision as to the guilt or innocence of X person.

There are two ways in which the court can make its findings as to what the true facts were.

1. The first technique, which is commonly used, consists of these stages:
   (a) The court first summarises the State evidence;
   (b) It then summarises the defence evidence;
   (c) It then identifies contradictions between the State and defence versions of the facts, analyses the relative strengths and weaknesses of the evidence presented and decides what version of the facts it accepts.

2. The second technique consists of going chronologically through the course of events and making findings of fact regarding each stage of the events. Under this technique, the court will not summarise the evidence on both sides. It will simply start at the beginning of the course of events and move through those events to the final event.

   In an assault case, for example, it will start with the events leading up to the incident, move on to the events at the time the complainant was injured and then move to what happened after the complainant was injured.

   As the court examines each stage of the course of events, it will carefully note what evidence there was on each event. It will note which witnesses testified on a particular event. In relation to each event:

- ➢ If there were contradictory versions of what happened at a particular stage from the State and the defence, the court will have to evaluate the strengths and weaknesses of those competing versions and decide which version is to be believed and why;
- ➢ If there was only State evidence on that event, the court will decide whether the evidence is credible and worthy of belief. It will then accept or reject that evidence.

The major advantage of the second technique is that the evidence is examined in logical sequence and the court systematically builds up a picture of what the true facts were. The first technique, on the other hand, has the disadvantage that the evidence may end up being dealt with in a rather haphazard and unsystematic way.

All too often a judgment reads like this:

> "State Witness A said this ...
> State Witness B said this ...
> State Witness C said this ...
> X said this ...
> The state witnesses gave their evidence well. X gave a very poor performance. Accordingly I find X guilty as charged."

This sort of judgment contains absolutely no reasoning, no assessment of probabilities, no consideration whether the proved facts establish the commission of the offence charged and no analysis as to what facts were proved. Yet a remarkably high percentage of magistrates court judgments follow this pattern.

Reasons for Judgment

Unless reasons are given for a judgment it is impossible to determine how the ultimate conclusion was reached and whether it was reached on a proper reasoned basis. Merely to state a conclusion, without giving reasons, creates the impression that the decision was an arbitrary one; it could have been reached on the basis of caprice or whim. By giving reasons, the judge shows that his or her decision is a reasoned one. He or she gives proof that he or she has taken into account the evidence and arguments on both sides: *Makombe & Ors* HH-120-86.

Thus, it has been repeatedly laid down that judgments must be reasoned and that the reasons for reaching the conclusion on verdict must be stated.

Without reasons for judgment it is impossible to decide on appeal whether X was properly convicted. In two appeal cases, the Supreme Court stressed the need for reasons to be given. In *Makawa & Anor* 1991 (1) ZLR 142 (S), it stated that the trial magistrate must record what he or she considered and give reasons for his or her decision otherwise there will be a gross irregularity. In *Marevesa* S-108-91, it said that the judgment must contain a brief summary of the facts found proved and the trial court's appraisal of the credibility of each witness, stating what evidence was accepted or rejected and giving its reasons for its decision. In both these cases, the Supreme Court stated that if the judgment is inadequate, the appeal may have to be allowed as it may not be possible for the appeal court to be satisfied that the convictions were warranted from the record.

In the absence of reasons, the review court will have difficulty in deciding whether the proceedings were in accordance with real and substantial justice. The absence of reasons will be an irregularity. However, it may not be a fatal irregularity and a conviction may still be upheld on review if the evidence on the record supports it: *Rusero* HH-151-86.

A full and comprehensive judgment will be more than just a recitation of the State and defence cases. It will include findings of fact, with comments on the credibility and demeanour of witnesses. It will include an analysis of the evidence and will deal with the probabilities. This will then lead up to the finding of whether the guilt of X was proved beyond reasonable doubt.

The contents of a judgment were dealt with in *Ncube & Ors* HB-61-03. The judgment should contain a brief summary of the facts found proved and the trial court's appraisal of the credibility of each witness, stating what evidence was accepted or rejected and giving reasons for its decision. For a magistrate not to record what he or she considered amounts to a gross irregularity, which will usually result in a conviction being set aside on appeal or review, although the conviction may still be upheld if the evidence on record supports it.

Public Announcement of Judgment

In terms of s 334(1) CPEA, all judgments in criminal proceedings against persons aged eighteen or above shall be pronounced in open court.

Alternative Charges

Where alternative charges have been brought against an accused and the evidence establishes that the two or more alternative charges have been committed, the judge is at liberty to convict X of the most appropriate charge, which will usually be the most serious charge levelled against him: *Mtandwa* HH-233-87.

Competent verdicts

Criminal Law (Codification and Reform) Act Chapter XV deals with the issue of permissible verdicts (i.e. competent verdicts).

A person charged with a crime may be found guilty if the facts proved establish this of ¾

- threatening, inciting, conspiring to commit or attempting to commit that crime or any other crime of which the person might be convicted on the charge; or
- assisting a perpetrator of that crime or of any other crime of which the person might be convicted on the charge.

[s 273]

If X is found not guilty of the crime charged, and the essential elements of the crime charged include the essential elements of some other crime, X may be found guilty of such other crime, if such are the facts proved. [s 274]

A person charged with an offence listed in the first column of the Fourth Schedule can be found guilty of any of the offences listed alongside that crime in the second column in the Fourth Schedule. [s 275]

A person charged with threatening, inciting, conspiring or assisting the perpetrator to commit an offence listed in the first column of the Fourth Schedule can be found guilty of any of the offences listed alongside that crime in the second column in the Fourth Schedule. [s 275]

276 Sentence imposable where person found guilty on competent verdict.
Where a person charged with a crime is found guilty of another crime in terms of this Chapter, the sentence imposed upon that person shall not exceed the maximum sentence applicable to the crime of which he or she is convicted.

Section 207 CPEA provides that where a court finds that part but not all of the facts of an offence charged have been proved, it shall nevertheless convict the accused of that offence if the facts that are proved disclose all the essential elements of that offence.

Conviction of other charge without amendment of charge

A court cannot convict a person of a charge other than that with which she was charged without the charge first being amended. In *Moyo* 1994 (2) ZLR 24 (H), X had been charged with contravening s 2 of the Concealment of Birth Act. She was, however, convicted of infanticide without the charge being amended. The court ruled that the magistrate had misdirected himself. There was no evidence that the accused had killed the child. The accused should have been convicted of the crime with which she had been charged.

Alteration of judgment

Once a judicial officer has made a written record of court proceedings, that record constitutes the exclusive memorial of the proceedings. Judicial officers, save in exceptional circumstances, are strictly bound by the written record made during the course of proceedings. They may not subsequently supplement, amend or vary the record. Once the proceedings are recorded the record speaks for itself. No one can speak on its behalf, including the author. The record should be left to speak for itself at all material times without interference or adulteration, although patent errors may be corrected or rectified: *Muendawoga* HH-10-04.

Section 201(2) CPEA provides that if, by mistake, a wrong judgment was delivered, the judgment may be altered before or **immediately after** it is recorded. But it is not every mistake which can be corrected under this provision. There must have been a genuine mistake in delivering the judgment either in the sense that the judge said something different from what he or she intended to say or that the judge did something in his or her judgment which was legally incompetent. For example, a judgment may be corrected if the judge intended to acquit X and by mistake gave a judgment convicting him or her. It would seem that ambiguous and obscure aspects of a judgment may be clarified immediately after the judgment is recorded: *Sikumbuzo* 1967 (4) SA 602 (RA).

In *Masundulwane* HB-22-06 in passing sentence on a charge of theft, a magistrate sentenced the accused to one month's imprisonment, wholly suspended on appropriate conditions, plus a fine or in default a period of imprisonment. After sentence was passed the accused asked the magistrate to consider community service because he could not afford the fine, whereupon the magistrate purported to "convert" the fine to a period of community service. The court held that a magistrate is not entitled to alter either his or her verdict or his or her sentence after is has been pronounced. The only exception is provided for in s 201(2), which allows the court to amend a wrong verdict or sentence delivered "by mistake". That implies a misunderstanding or an inadvertency resulting in an order not intended, or a wrong calculation. A verdict or sentence, however much open to criticism, cannot be altered if it was deliberately given or imposed. The correction must be done immediately on the same day, preferably before the magistrate leaves the bench. In the present case, the sentence was not delivered by mistake: it was deliberately imposed.

Change of plea after verdict but before sentence

An accused may sometimes apply to withdraw his or her plea of guilty after verdict or an application for change of plea may be made during an address from the bar.

Where an accused person, after verdict, seeks to withdraw his or her unequivocal plea of guilty, he or she is required to show, on a balance of probabilities, that the plea was not voluntarily and understandingly or correctly made: *Nyajena* 1991 (1) ZLR 175 (S).

There is no onus on X to show anything on a balance of probabilities. He or she must simply offer a reasonable explanation for having pleaded guilty. Unless the court is convinced beyond reasonable doubt that the explanation is not merely improbable but positively false, X must be allowed to change his or her plea. See *Matare* 1993 (2) ZLR 88 (S). In the *Matare* case, X, who was not legally represented at this stage, had pleaded guilty to four counts of fraud. The magistrate had questioned X to make sure that the essential elements of the crime were present. The proceedings were adjourned for a week pending sentence. When the proceedings resumed, the legal practitioner who was now appearing for X, applied for the pleas of guilty to be altered to not guilty. The grounds upon which this application was made were that X had pleaded guilty as a result of assaults and intimidation and that in any event he or she was innocent of the offences. The magistrate held a trial within a trial to determine whether X had discharged the burden of proving his or her allegation. The magistrate thus placed the onus on X to prove his or her allegations. On appeal, the majority of the court held that it was held that the magistrate was wrong in placing the onus on X to prove his or her allegations. Once X offers an explanation that is not false beyond reasonable doubt, the change of plea must be allowed. The magistrate found that X's explanation was improbable but he or she did not reject it as false. In the light of this, the magistrate should have allowed the change of plea. [The *Matare* case overruled the earlier cases of *Maseko* 1986 (2) ZLR 52 (S) and *Nyajena* 1991 (1) ZLR 175 (S).]

Where X seeks to withdraw his or her plea at this stage, the court has the discretion to allow the withdrawal of the plea. This discretion will be exercised very sparingly and only in clear cases. Most applications for change of plea are based on allegations of undue influence from the police. X will usually maintain that the police threatened reprisals if, during the trial, he or she said anything about the treatment previously meted out to him or herby the police.

Where an allegation has been made of mistreatment of X by the police, the judge must hold a trial within a trial to determine the veracity of X's allegations. If the judge finds that there is substance in the allegations, he or she will then change the plea: *Maseko* 1986 (2) ZLR 52 (S).

Where, however, a magistrate has convicted X and has then stopped the trial and the Attorney-General has directed that the matter be referred to the High Court for sentence, the magistrate is then *functus officio* and has no jurisdiction to hear an application by X to change his or her plea. Such an application can only be heard by the High Court. See *Dube* HB-65-93 and *Kaiwona* S-192-93.

Subsequent facts establishing innocence

Occasionally, after convicting X but before sentence is imposed, evidence comes to light which proves conclusively that he or she did not commit the offence, such as that he or she was in prison when the offence was committed. Or the magistrate may discover a superior court decision which reveals conclusively that he or she misconstrued the law and wrongly convicted X. In such situations, the proceedings may be sent for review to the High Court before the case is completed, for it is clearly undesirable that an accused be sentenced if inevitably the conviction will later be quashed.

If, after sentencing X, facts come to the attention of the magistrate which indicate that X did not commit the offence and the case has not yet been reviewed, the magistrate should ensure that the case is immediately reviewed by a judge and that the judge is appraised of these new facts. If it has already been reviewed and the proceedings have been confirmed, the new facts should immediately be brought to the attention of the High Court in order for the confirmation certificate to be withdrawn and the conviction to be quashed.

The special verdict

In terms of s 29 of the Mental Health Act, where a person is found to be mentally disordered at the time of the offence, but sane at time of trial, the judicial officer will return a verdict of "not guilty because of insanity" and court may order that:

- X be taken to institution or special institution for examination or treatment; or
- if the judicial officer is satisfied that X is no longer mentally disordered or intellectually handicapped or is otherwise fit to be discharged order his or her discharge and, where appropriate, his or her release from custody.

A petty case is one in which the judicial officer considers that the charge will not merit imprisonment without the option of a fine or a fine over level 3. In respect of such an offence, if the judicial officer finds that X was mentally disordered at time of offence but that he or she is sane at time of trial he or she must order

- that X submit himself to examination and/or treatment at a specified institution, or
- X's spouse, guardian or close relative to apply for a civil detention order;

and may give such orders as may be appropriate for X's release from custody or for the purpose of such examination or treatment.

Competent verdict

Where X is charged under common law and no alternative charge was preferred, it was held it is not competent to convict for statutory offence even where evidence showed that such an offence was committed: *Moyo* HH-43-03. The appellant was convicted of fraud. It was alleged that, with intent to defraud, she had misrepresented to the relevant vetting officers that she was a "war veteran", as defined in the War Veterans Act [*Chapter 11:15*] and had participated in the war of liberation in Mozambique. She had claimed a gratuity and pension for such participation. She left out several relevant parts of the form that had to be completed but in spite of this was accepted by the vetting officers as having been a war veteran. Held: she should not have been convicted of fraud. She did not make the misrepresentation alleged. She merely presented certain information upon which the vetting officers pronounced her a war veteran. If any misrepresentation was made, it was made by the vetting officers. Although she could have been charged with a contravention of s 24(b) of the Act, the State had chosen not to do so, and a verdict of contravening that section could not be substituted, even though her counsel agreed that would have been the right course.

Section 7

Sentencing

Reid-Rowland Chapter 25

General considerations

In *Ngulube* HH-48-02, the judge said that before assessing sentence, a magistrate must equip himself with sufficient information in any particular case to enable him or herto assess sentence humanely and meaningfully, and to reach a decision based on fairness and proportion. Where the accused is not represented, the magistrate has a duty to canvass all these aspects with the accused, if necessary postponing the trial to enable the information to be obtained.

In *Shariwa* HB-37-03, the court stressed that judicial officers must adopt a rational approach towards sentencing and must have adequate information before they pass sentences. It said that there is no room in our system for an "instinctive" approach to sentencing. Sentencing should be a rational process. The sentencing court must always strive to find a punishment which will fit both the crime and the offender. Whatever the gravity of the crime and the interests of society, the most important factors in determining the sentence are the person, and the character and circumstances of the crime. The determination of an equitable quantum of punishment must chiefly bear a relationship to the moral blameworthiness of the offender. However, there can be no injustice where in the weighing of offence, offender and the interests of society, more weight is attached to one or another of these, unless there is over-emphasis of one which leads to disregard of the other. The court should not be over-influenced by the seriousness of the type of the offence and fail to pay sufficient attention to other factors which are of no less importance in the actual case before the court. The over-emphasis of a wrongdoer's crimes and the under-estimation of his or her person constitute a misdirection which justifies the substitution of the sentence. Justice should also be tempered with mercy. The court should equip itself with sufficient and meaningful pre-sentencing information in order to come up with suitable punishment.

In *Manyevere* HB-38-03, the court stressed that the sentencing process is as distinct and vital a factual enquiry as the determination of the guilt of an offender. Punishment should as far as possible be individualised by conducting meaningful pre-sentencing investigations. Assessment of punishment should not be left to a haphazard guess based on no or inadequate information.

In *Ngulube* HH-48-02, the court stated that the needs of the individual and the interests of society should be balanced with care and understanding. Pre-sentencing information is very important. Whilst the age, marital and family status, employment, savings and assets are important aspects in the assessment of sentence, magistrates should always bear in mind that the reason why the accused committed the offence and the circumstances of the offence are of equal importance.

Proof of previous convictions

After conviction the prosecutor will state whether the person convicted has any previous convictions. If he or she has, the onus is on the State to prove them. It is the responsibility of the prosecutor to produce the record of any previous convictions. The prosecutor will read out these previous convictions to X. The court will then ask if X admits these previous convictions. If X denies any or all of the previous convictions the prosecutor has the right to request a remand so that he or she can bring evidence to prove them: s 327 CPEA.

In *McCormick* HB-56-90, X was not legally represented. Before sentence the prosecutor advised the court that X had previous convictions. The magistrate asked X, "Have you been convicted of the same offence before?" X replied in the affirmative.

The review court said it was wrong for the magistrate to proceed to sentence X on the basis of a general oral statement by the prosecutor that X had previous convictions and a general admission by X that he or she has a previous conviction for that offence. This was particularly the case because X was not legally represented.

The onus is on the State to prove X's previous convictions. The matter should have been postponed to enable the prosecutor to provide proof of X's previous convictions.

As regards the type of evidence which can be produced to establish previous convictions see ss 328-329 CPEA. A certified fingerprint record from a police officer, a prison officer or an immigration officer is admissible as *prima facie* evidence against X in relation to previous convictions: s 329 CPEA. The fingerprints of X will be submitted to the Central Criminal Bureau for a check to be done on whether he or she has any previous convictions.

If X admits the previous convictions contained in the ZRP Form 125 this form will become part of the record.

Imposing sentence for other offences

In terms of s 335 CPEA, the court convicting X of any offence, may, on application by X and with the prosecutor's consent, pass sentence upon X for other untried offences as if they had been separately charged, provided that the court is satisfied that X freely and voluntarily admits having committed those other offences. Although, under s 56 MCA, a magistrate does not normally have jurisdiction over offences committed outside his or her province or regional division, s 335(2) CPEA provides that a magistrates court may in this situation pass sentence on X, although no act, omission or event which is an element of the offence took place in the magistrate's province or regional division. The magistrate may impose sentence for each of the untried offences up to the limit of his or her sentencing jurisdiction.

The procedure which is followed when X makes application for other offences to be taken into account is set out in Chapter 34 of the *Prosecutors Handbook*. Basically when X makes such an application the magistrate must record the date, place and nature of the other offences and the sentence passed for each other offence. X is then deemed to have been convicted for the untried offences. The prosecutor should not consent to this procedure where he or she has no information about the additional offences admitted to. He or she should first consult with the police about these to ensure that the information given by X is correct.

John Reid Rowland notes that:

> " In practice, this procedure is invoked quite rarely. If X is willing to admit the [other] offences, he or she would usually be willing to plead guilty if they were charged separately. If the procedure is invoked, it usually happens when the police have arrested a habitual or professional thief who is charged with one or two offences. In order to close their records on the other crimes committed by X, the police prepare a list of untried offences and include it in the docket. If such a list is included in the docket, the prosecutor should establish before the trial that X is indeed willing for those offences to be dealt with under this procedure. X usually is willing because the sort of person involved is almost invariably an experienced criminal who knows that he or she will probably get a lighter sentence than if he or she were separately tried for those offences. After conviction, the prosecutor should advise the court that X wishes to request other offences to be dealt with under s 313. The magistrate will confirm with X that this is so; the prosecutor should then hand in the list of [other crimes]."

Evidence on sentence

Section 334(3) CPEA sets out the types of evidence and information which the court may receive for the purpose of informing itself as to the proper sentence to be passed. This includes evidence on oath from X and his or her witnesses or from State witnesses,

including hearsay evidence, an unsworn statement from X, written statements from the prosecutor, X or his or her legal representative, and affidavits and written reports tendered by the prosecutor, X or his or her legal representative. Hearsay evidence may only be tendered by one side if the other side consents. The court can decide to call the person who made any affidavit or written report submitted in evidence to give oral evidence.

Accused persons and witnesses who testify in relation to sentence are subject to cross-examination.

Mitigation

For a commentary on the factors which our courts have accepted may be mitigatory see Chapter 5: *A Guide to Sentencing in Zimbabwe* by G Feltoe. Depending on the circumstances these factors may serve to mitigate the sentence:

- various defences which do not amount to full defences in law in the circumstances, such as claim of right, compulsion and intimidation, protection of property, provocation, self-defence, ignorance or mistake of law, intoxication, diminished mental responsibility, emotional stress, trapping of the offender;
- good motive;
- non-payment of wages due where X has stolen from employer;
- poverty;
- temptation;
- assistance to police after crime committed [See *Buka* 1995 (2) ZLR 130 (S) and *Dube & Anor* 1995 (2) ZLR 321 (S) for the weight that will be attached to this factor];
- compensation and restitution [See, for instance, *Malume* 1998 (2) ZLR 508 (H)]
- delay in bringing the case to trial or hearing of appeal [See, for instance, *Corbett* 1990 (1) ZLR 205 (S); but is not necessarily a ground for reduction of sentence, *Gujral* 1990 (1) ZLR 320 (H)];
- X in employment and has dependants (See, for instance, *Katsaura* 1997 (2) ZLR 102 (H))
- good behaviour after conviction and before appeal;
- good character;
- grave physical injury to X at time of crime;
- ill-health;
- ill-treatment while in custody;

- imprisonment before trial [See, for instance, *Mutakwa & Anor* 2000 (1) ZLR 393 (H); *Aitken* 1995 (2) ZLR 395 (S) and *Dube & Anor* 1995 (2) ZLR 321 (S)];
- meritorious past conduct;
- pregnancy;
- remorse and guilty plea [See, for instance, *Dhliwayo* 1999 (1) ZLR 229 (H) and *Katsaura* 1997 (2) ZLR 102 (H) on weight to be given to guilty plea.] If there are multiple accused persons, the approach to be adopted where guilt is evenly apportioned, is to treat the accused persons the same: *Muleya & Ors*1988 (1) ZLR 359 (S), accordingly counsel ought to make submissions in that direction;
- failure of Government to explain and consult with traders concerning price controls: *Delta Consolidated (Pvt) Ltd & Ors* 1991 (2) ZLR 234 (S).

Note that in terms of s 12(4)(a) of the Supreme Court Act and s 38(4)(a) of the High Court Act the Supreme Court and the High Court, respectively, may have regard in criminal appeals to all the circumstances, including events which have occurred **after the date of conviction**. [See *Aitken* 1995 (2) ZLR 395 (S)]

The legal representative of X must be given the opportunity to lead mitigatory evidence and to address the court in mitigation of sentence. Without calling evidence, the legal representative may simply set out what he or she considers to be the salient mitigatory factors in the case: *Furisayi* 1981 ZLR 56 (A) at p 58. The prosecutor may either accept these facts or dispute them. However, as regards factors such as contrition, the court is likely to attach less weight to what a legal representative has said regarding his or her client's penitence than to a personal and credible expression of regret and repentance by X himself. The legal representative will often make submissions as to the appropriate sentence in the case, drawing the court's attention to salient case law.

There are some pleas in mitigation where the personal testimony of X will assist, such as where the crime was committed because of extreme hardship or destitution or because of a benevolent motive, such as to assist someone else. X should be called to testify in such circumstances, if his or her defence lawyer believes that he or she will give convincing testimony.

One factor which may be important is the attitude of the complainant. In *Kelly* HH-33-04 the court took the view that the attitude of the complainant in a criminal case is relevant to sentence. Where the complainant indicates that it is not his or her desire to have the accused incarcerated, a sentencing authority ought to attach weight to the expressions of the complainant, as such a factor has an impact on the form of sentence imposed.

Specifying extent to which mitigation has reduced sentence

In *Madembe & Anor* HH-17-03, the court stated that where a judicial officer has accepted any factor of mitigation he or she must clearly specify the amount by which he or she has reduced the sentence on account of that factor. In this way he or she will be able to avoid the criticism that he or she has not sufficiently taken into account any factor or factors of mitigation, and an the appellate court or a reviewing or scrutinizing judicial officer will be less inclined to decree, rather subjectively, that the other judicial officer erred. Where sentence is being assessed according to the value of the goods involved, and a comparison is being made with sentences approved in earlier cases, it is necessary to take into account the effect of inflation so a realistic comparison can be made.

Presentation of evidence in mitigation

X or his or her lawyer must be allowed the opportunity to present evidence and to address in mitigation of sentence.

Duty of prosecutor

The prosecutor is duty bound to dispute facts advanced in mitigation which he or she knows to be incorrect or if they are highly improbable or absurd. With the undefended accused the prosecutor is also expected to draw to the attention of the court any facts of which he or she is aware which are mitigatory, such as that X has paid compensation to his or her victim.

For a commentary on the factors which our courts have accepted may be mitigatory, see Chapter 5: of *A Guide to Sentencing in Zimbabwe* by G. Feltoe.

Undefended accused

X must always be afforded the opportunity to lead mitigatory evidence and to address the court in mitigation of sentence: *Million & Ors* HH-53-92. His or her address can contain both assertions of fact and an appeal to the judge for clemency. Additionally, the judge has the duty to ensure that the factors of mitigation are fully canvassed because X will often be unaware of the sort of things which are relevant when it comes to sentence. The court must thus offer guidance to X in this regard.

The court itself should also investigate what mitigatory features exist and take into account mitigatory factors which have emerged in evidence before conviction. This is particularly so when X is a juvenile: *W* HH-276-83.

The judge has a duty to make sure that he or she is in a position to arrive at a proper and just sentence. In order to arrive at such a sentence, he or she must have as much factual information about the circumstances as possible. Unless those facts have emerged from the evidence at the trial, if an unrepresented accused does not say anything in mitigation, then the judicial officer should put such questions to X as will elicit that information. He or she should endeavour to discover the necessary information by inquiry if X does not volunteer this information. This applies particularly where the unrepresented accused is unsophisticated and he or she has been convicted of a serious crime: *Mlilo* HB-27-88; *Mafu* HB-68-90.

In *Ngulube* HH-48-02, the judge said that before assessing sentence, a magistrate must equip himself with sufficient information in any particular case to enable him or her to assess sentence humanely and meaningfully, and to reach a decision based on fairness and proportion. The needs of the individual and the interests of society should be balanced with care and understanding. Pre-sentencing information is very important. Where the accused is not represented, the magistrate has a duty to canvass all these aspects with the accused, if necessary postponing the trial to enable the information to be obtained.

Defended accused

The legal representative of X must be given the opportunity to lead mitigatory evidence to and address the court in mitigation of sentence. Without calling evidence, the legal representative may simply set out what he or she considers to be the salient mitigatory factors in the case: *Fusirayi* 1981 ZLR 56 (A) at p 58. The prosecutor may either accept these facts or dispute them. However, as regards factors such as contrition, the court is likely to attach less weight to what a legal representative has said regarding his or her client's penitence than to a personal and credible expression of regret and repentance by X himself.

The legal representative will often make submissions as to the appropriate sentence in the case, drawing the court's attention to salient case law.

Onus of proof

In *Chinyani* 1969 (2) RLR 42 (A), the court stated that there were no rigid rules governing the burden of proof or the degree of proof in relation to evidence or statements in mitigation of sentence. It said that a high degree of flexibility must exist in considering the variety of factors which are relevant to sentence. It said that there need not always be proof of an assertion of fact before it is accepted for the purposes of sentence. If there is any doubt at the stage of sentence as to the existence of any relevant fact, the trial court must reach its own conclusions, as it thinks right, and is entitled to disregard any such fact for the purposes of sentence if it is not satisfied as to the existence thereof.

Aggravation

If the prosecutor wishes to do so, he or she must be allowed to address the court to draw attention to the aggravating features of the case and to make submissions as to the appropriate sentence in the case and to refer to any relevant case law in this regard.

For commentary on the factors which may aggravate sentence: see Chapter 7 of *A Guide to Sentencing in Zimbabwe* by G. Feltoe.

See also *Mangena & Ors* HB-22-05. These factors must be weighed against factors such as the age and personal circumstances of the accused. The sentencing court has a duty to enquire into the subjective elements in order to individualise the punishment.

As regards the factor of prevalence of a particular crime it was noted in *Sibanda* HB-102-06 that while the prevalence of an offence is a relevant factor in sentencing, it is not the overriding factor. It is not the function of the court to try to control crime by imprisoning people accused of crimes which the legislature, in its wisdom, considers trifling. While the courts should never be seen by the public to be trivialising serious offences, courts are equally enjoined not to make trivial cases serious. Either scenario is as much unjust as the other.

Particular aspects of sentencing

When difficult specific issues on sentencing arise reference should be made to *A Guide to Sentencing in Zimbabwe* by G. Feltoe published by the Legal Resources Foundation in 1990. This section will only deal with a few selected points of sentencing which have caused difficulty in the past.

The following things are legally impermissible:

- antedating a prison sentence: *Chahora* HH-349-84.
- imposing a prison sentence of less than four days: s 357 CPEA.
- imposing two sentences for one offence: *Chipxere* HH-314-83 (Magistrate wrongly imposing for one offence a prison term plus another prison term, wholly suspended on condition that X made restitution), *Sibanda* HB-36-86 (Magistrate wrongly imposing two separate prison sentences, subject to conditions, for same offence).
- making of fines run concurrently or a fine run concurrently with a prison sentence: *Kambuzuma* HH-60-86; *Gororo* HH-145-86.
- suspending a sentence of a fine where the fine is mandatory or giving the X time to pay such fine. In terms of s 356(2) as read with Sixth Schedule CPEA the court has no power to suspend any portion of a mandatory sentence of a fixed minimum fine. Nor may such a fine be postponed: *De Montille* 1979 RLR 105; *Kudavaranda* 1988 (2) ZLR 367 (H).
- suspending or postponing of a mandatory prison sentence. But where the legislature lays down that a mandatory prison sentence of a fixed term or of a length to be determined by the court must be imposed, the court may suspend all or a portion of the prison sentence: *Patel* S-63-87; *Muzambe* HH-

121-90. However, in *Horowitz* 1976 (1) RLR 238 at 241D it is stated that the court will not lightly suspend the whole of a mandatory prison sentence; it will only do so when the mitigatory circumstances clearly make such a course desirable.

It must be carefully noted that in terms of s 356(2) as read with paragraph 3 of the Sixth Schedule [s 337(1) as read with paragraph 3 of the Seventh Schedule] CPEA the court may not suspend or postpone the prison sentence where the statute in question not only prescribes a mandatory period of imprisonment for without the option of a fine but prescribes a minimum period of such imprisonment.

- imposing a standard sentence for the particular crime without considering the individual circumstances and the moral blameworthiness of X. As far as possible there is a need for individualised sentencing: *David & Anor* 1964 RLR 2 and *Mugwenhe & Anor* 1991 (2) ZLR 66 (S).

Deciding on sentence

Before passing sentence, the judge must give careful thought and consideration to what is the appropriate sentence in the circumstances and he or she should give full reasons for imposing the sentence which he or she has decided upon. Sentencing requires a rational process in which the court weighs all the relevant factors and decides what sentence is fair and appropriate. If the sentencer simply announces the sentence without giving reasons this may give the impression that sentencing is an arbitrary and unreasoned process.

The sentencing process should be a rational and objective process and magistrates should not allow their emotions to cloud their judgment as to what is a suitable sentence. If they allow themselves to get carried away by their emotions, they may end up exaggerating the seriousness of the offence and imposing a disproportionate penalty for the offence: *Harington* 1988 (2) ZLR 344 (S).

Whilst it is quite proper for the judge to express his or her disapproval of the criminal misconduct in formulating the sentence, the use of extravagant and overblown language should be avoided.

In *Mahati* 1988 (1) ZLR 190 (H), the trial magistrate said in his or her reasons for sentence:

> "... it is apparent that you were part of a well-organized ring of thieves that stole might-be millions of dollars worth of car-parts from the CMED. Your conduct is very treasonous ... you allow even the meagre cars and spares to be plundered most greedifully and most corruptly ... This seems to indicate that the ring was organized along mafia lines and vast government properties were lost to private capitalistic business people thus if anything at all the CMED is a hive buzzing with maladministration and corruption bleeding the people to death."

The review judge commented on this passage. He or she said at pp 2-3:

> " Extravagant and emotional language of this sort is not consistent with the dispassionate and objective approach expected of a judicial officer. Apart from anything else, there was no evidence to substantiate the factual content of this excerpt. X had accepted an offer of $100 to turn a 'blind' eye to the theft of a starter motor valued at $300. Whereas dishonesty may have been prevalent at this Government department, the facts actually proved at the trial were far removed from the suggestions conveyed in the passage cited."

The National Sentencing Committee has produced a questionnaire (to be completed in any case where the sentence is subject to review or sentencing) and an explanatory booklet about the matters to consider when assessing sentence. These are:

Accused's personal circumstances

Age

Very young and very old people are normally treated more leniently than mature people.

Young people (this term includes juveniles, but is not confined to juveniles) are more prone to making ill- considered and unwise decisions and cannot be expected to show the same stability, responsibility and self-restraint as a fully mature adult. A person in his or her early twenties may benefit from this. Note: there is no absolute dividing line as to when a person can be regarded as fully mature; even persons in their late twenties could be regarded as immature, but the nearer the person is to 30, the less weight will be attached to the factor of age.

Very old people seldom commit crimes. An elderly first offender, who probably has never been in prison before and whose health is not likely to be good, would suffer far more from imprisonment than a younger and more resilient person would. It would be undesirable than an elderly person should end his or her days in prison and so the very elderly should normally be exempted from imprisonment.

This does not mean that an elderly person should never be sent to prison. The offence may be such that there is no other option, or X may have a long criminal record.

Sex

Female first offenders are generally treated more leniently than males, for three reasons:

- males commit more offences;
- recidivism is commoner among males;
- women often have young children to care for.

In some cases, though, these factors may be absent or of lesser importance.

There may be circumstances where there is no reason to discriminate in favour of the woman, particularly where she is jointly convicted with a man and there is nothing to indicate that the man was the dominant partner. It should not be forgotten that women can often be just as dominating as men.

Where a female has a previous conviction for the same offence, she cannot expect the same leniency that is shown to female first offenders.

Marital status and dependents

If a person with a spouse and dependents is imprisoned, the family will suffer. If this can be avoided, it should, but sometimes it is unavoidable. It is often said that X should have thought of the consequences to his or her/her family before committing the crime, but this approach often overlooks human nature, the other circumstances of the case, and the actual effect on the family.

Employed/unemployed

Imprisonment is serious for any person, but it is more serious to imprison someone who is employed than someone who is not, because of the financial loss to X (and his or her dependents). Employment is also difficult to find and it may be hard to find another job.

The nature of the job and X's income are relevant to X's ability to pay a fine, whether immediately or in instalments.

The mere fact of conviction may result in X being dismissed, irrespective of the sentence imposed. This should not be overlooked.

Many people are not in formal employment, but have a steady or even substantial income from other sources in the informal sector. This should be investigated, particularly if a fine is being considered.

Likelihood of civil action

Many crimes may expose X to civil action by the complainant (if the action is not prescribed). The likelihood of such action and the possible consequences to X are relevant in determining the level of any financial penalty. If a civil action has already been brought, this should be established.

The crime itself

Effect on victim and victim's family

Financial effect

Evidence must establish the financial effect. The court cannot assume what the effect is.

Physical or psychological

This is not limited to crimes of violence. A housebreaking could severely affect a nervous person. But there must be some evidence, even if it is only that of the victim. The court should also be aware of the possibility of exaggeration by the victim.

Accused/victim relationship

This factor applies particularly to crimes of violence and sexual crimes, but is not confined to such crimes. Theft and other offences of dishonesty can be viewed in a more serious light if they involve a betrayal of trust, such as theft by a servant.

Marital or blood relationship

This is particularly important in cases of domestic violence and sexual crimes.

Master/servant, teacher/pupil

Again, this is important in sexual offences, where X's dominant position could result in coercion without physical violence.

Relative ages

This is particularly important in cases of "statutory rape". The closer the ages of the parties, the more likely it is that the incident was one of passion and not one of an adult taking advantage of an innocent child. It should be remembered that girls generally mature earlier than boys and that girls are just as capable of initiating sexual contacts. On the other hand, a great disparity in the ages of X and complainant is usually regarded as aggravating; and where there has in addition been a breach of trust, a prison sentence is regarded as the norm.

Victim's consent to acts

The rationale for creating the crime of "statutory rape" is the protection of young persons. The fact that the "complainant" consented or was even willing may be mitigating, depending on the relative ages and the relationship of the parties. Similarly, if the complainant has had previous sexual experience, this could be mitigating: some young persons lead promiscuous lives and it may be somewhat unrealistic to talk of protecting them.

Possibility of restitution, compensation, etc

It is highly desirable in crimes against property that X should make good the loss caused, whether by restoring stolen property or repairing or replacing damaged or destroyed property. X's willingness and ability to make restitution should be carefully investigated. But restitution will not necessarily mean a non-custodial sentence. It is mitigating, but its mitigatory nature must be weighed against the nature of the offence and any aggravating features.

Considerations specifically applicable to sexual offences

Relative ages of accused and complainant (see above);

- the relationship between the parties (see above);
- the complainant's age and previous sexual experience (note: the fact that a woman or girl has had previous sexual experience does not in any way mitigate rape. The complainant's lack of previous sexual experience could, however, be aggravating);
- the effect on victim (see above). In addition, it is relevant to consider whether HIV, AIDS or some other venereal disease was or could have been transmitted. In respect of such diseases, it is relevant to consider any knowledge on the part of X of his or her infection and the possibility of the disease being cured;
- the general circumstances of the offence, including such as whether:
    - the offence was an unprovoked attack by a stranger (statistics show that this is not the norm);
    - whether there had been persistent advances by X over a period (this could be aggravating);
    - whether there had been initial indications of willingness on the part of the complainant (this could be mitigating).

Other relevant factors

Plea of guilty

If there has been a plea of guilty, the plea must be indicative of penitence before weight can be attached to it. It may happen that X had little option but to plead guilty. On the other hand, it is NOT aggravating for X to plead not guilty. He or she is entitled to plead not guilty, though should offer either:

- an explanation of his or her attitude to the charge; or
- a statement indicating the basis of his or her defence.

If he or she fails to do so, he or she should be requested to make a statement outlining the nature of his or her defence and the material facts on which he or she relies. The consequences of failing to make such a statement must be explained.

Other indications of contrition

Assistance by X to the police, though not affecting his or her moral guilt, can be an indication of genuine repentance and if so is relevant to sentence. Voluntary recompense to the victim, without the court's intervention, would also be mitigating (see the comments under 2.3 above).

Previous convictions

Previous convictions must usually be taken into account, though the weight to be attached to them varies.

A previous conviction may be irrelevant, because the previous offence was trivial or occurred long ago or is totally unrelated to the current offence. For example, a conviction for a driving offence would generally not have bearing on what is an appropriate sentence for theft. But the commission of several offences different from that with which X is now charged may indicate a disrespect for the law.

A previous conviction may render X liable to a particular form of sentence or to a minimum sentence. It may render him or her liable to undergo a suspended sentence or to have a postponed sentence passed.

Other evidence of good character

There may be evidence of X's good character other than the mere lack of previous convictions. The nature of such evidence will vary from one person to another.

Aggravating circumstances (robbery)

A regional magistrate is given increased jurisdiction if robbery or armed robbery is committed in aggravating circumstances. These circumstances exist where it is proved that X or an accomplice (it does not matter which):

- possessed a firearm or dangerous weapon; or
- inflicted or threatened to inflict grievous bodily harm; or
- unlawfully killed a person

on the occasion that the offence was committed. The aggravating acts may have been committed before, during or after the commission of the substantive offence.

Other aggravating circumstances

There may be other aggravating circumstances which, though they do give an increased jurisdiction, indicate that a heavier sentence is appropriate. These should be listed specifically.

Entrapment

Entrapment may be mitigating if X was tempted to commit a crime which he or she otherwise would not have committed. If the trap did not constitute an inducement, then X should be treated as though there was no trap.

Motive

X's motive in committing an offence bears strongly on his or her moral guilt. An altruistic motive would be significantly mitigatory, such as where a person steals in order to feed his or her starving family. Conversely, where the motive for the crime is to enable to accused to commit another crime, his or her moral blameworthiness is higher. However, if X does commit another crime, and he or she is not charged with it, and if that other crime is more serious than the one with which he or she is charged, the fact that he or she committed that other crime should not be taken into account as an aggravating feature.

Prevalence of crime

The prevalence of a particular kind of offence and the difficulties of its detection are objective elements to which regard must always be had, but judicial officers should avoid the temptation to pass sentences of ever-increasing severity in an attempt to stem the tide of increasing lawlessness. The prevalence of an offence should not be taken too far as a factor.

The court should also bear in mind that a particular offence may be prevalent in one area and much less so elsewhere. The place of commission could thus be relevant.

The prevalence of the offence does not in itself make imprisonment appropriate where a fine would otherwise have sufficed; the case must be considered on its merits.

Where the offender knows that the courts have on numerous occasions issued warnings, aimed at deterring future offences, this could be taken into account, but in most cases it would be difficult to show that X had such knowledge. The man in the street is not likely to be aware of what individual judges and magistrates have said.

The prevalence of a particular kind of offence may be such that it is a matter of which a court could take judicial notice, but it might be necessary for statistical evidence to be led by the prosecutor or called by the court.

Other punishment or personal consequences

The fact that X has been assaulted by a member of the public as retribution for his or her offence or that he or she has been tortured or otherwise maltreated by the police before the trial will usually be mitigating. Similarly, dismissal from employment as a consequence of the offence will also be mitigating. The court should not seek to punish the person twice.

Accused's mental condition

X's mental state, if not sufficient to make him or her "not responsible according to law" for the act, may amount to "diminished responsibility" and thus be relevant to sentence. Clinical depression and post-traumatic stress could contribute to such a mitigating mental state. Evidence would have to be led.

Nature of punishment

General

The court must first decide what sort of punishment is appropriate and what the object of the sentence is. Is the object:

- to punish the offender?
- deter the offender?
- deter others?
- compensate the victim?
- rehabilitate the offender?
- protect the public?
- a combination of all or any of these objects?

Taking into account the object(s) of sentence in the case, and X's circumstances, fix a penalty appropriate for the offender and for his or her offence. Take into account ancillary matters, like whether X will lose as a result of forfeiture. Formulate reasons for your decision and explain them when passing sentence. Explain all aspects of the sentence which need to be explained to an undefended accused, such as time to pay a fine, the nature of the conditions attaching to a suspended sentence, and so on.

The worldwide trend is towards non-custodial sentencing. It should be recognised that it is highly desirable to keep anyone out of prison, particularly first offenders, if this can be avoided. Sometimes, though, the seriousness of the offence is such that imprisonment is the only sentence warranted. Short sentences of imprisonment are of highly questionable value. They have little reformative or rehabilitative effect; and they cause administrative problems that the prison authorities can do without.

Fine

General aspects

A fine must be a real option and not be excessive: *Kunesu & Ors* 1993 (2) ZLR 253 (H). The fine must be tailored to the means of X and, where necessary, X must be given time to pay or to pay in instalments: *Peti & Ors* 1966 RLR 591 at 593F; *Mamwere* 1978 RLR 374 (GD); *Mutandwa* HH-35-88; *Dlamini* HB-3-90.

In *Gumede* HB-40-03, the court stated that to impose a fine, alternatively imprisonment, when it is clear that accused is not in a position to pay a fine and will end up serving the prison sentence is wrong. If the court intends to keep an accused out of custody then the sentence should be clearly focused towards that goal and not depend on the hope of someone else coming to his or her rescue unless there is clear evidence that a third party has volunteered to do so. The courts should regard community service as their first port of call when it comes to sentencing.

The failure by the Minister to lay before Parliament a statutory instrument setting out levels of fines has the effect of rendering any imposition of fines incompetent under the circumstances: *Chandafira* HH-137-02.

Maximum fine

With a statutory offence, the judge should first take note of the maximum fine that may be imposed. The highest fine allowed must obviously be reserved for the most serious examples of the offence. The judge must assess the fine that is appropriate for the particular circumstances of the offence in question, taking into account the maximum fine that is allowed. The magistrate's jurisdiction may sometimes be less than the maximum fine provided.

Where provision for deposit fine

In respect of statutory offences, is the offence one for which a deposit fine is provided in the schedule of deposit fines? If so, is there any reason to depart from the deposit fine? The fact that X has elected to come to court rather than pay a deposit fine is *not* aggravating. There would have to be some aggravating circumstances before the court would be justified in imposing a fine above the deposit fine. On the other hand, do not hesitate to impose a lower fine, if the circumstances warrant it. There may well be mitigating circumstances.

Mandatory minimum fines

Some statutes provide for mandatory minimum fines. The normal criteria for assessment of fines would not apply in such a situation. Even so, the court usually has some discretion. For example, where an enactment provides for a minimum fine, the court usually has the power to impose a fine greater than the minimum. In that case, it should consider whether the minimum fine is adequate or whether there are grounds for imposing a higher fine. Where the amount of the fine is not in the discretion of the court and where it is far beyond the ability of X to pay the fine, the alternative sentence must not be excessive in relation to the fine. The extent of X's culpability is the factor by which to determine the length of imprisonment that should be imposed.

Accused's ability to pay

The object of imposing a fine is to keep X out of prison, and that object will be defeated if a fine is imposed which there is no reason to suppose that X can pay. The fine must be a *real* alternative to the sentence of imprisonment imposed in default of payment. It would not be a real alternative if X has no hope of paying. The fine does not, though, have to be within X's immediate means and resources. His or her financial prospects must also be taken into account. It may be necessary to give X time to pay. It should also be remembered that X's immediate ability to pay is not decisive. This might result in a fine being imposed that might create the impression that the court did not regard the offence in a sufficiently serious light. A very small fine, even though it might have the same proportionate effect on X as a heavier one would on a wealthier person, might have no deterrent effect at all. Before imposing a fine which is beyond the ability of X to pay, a proper enquiry should be held to determine whether other resources are available to X and the extent of them, such as his or her ability to sell assets or acquire a loan.

One way of avoiding a situation where X ends up in prison because he or she is unable to pay a fine is to impose a fine and, in the alternative, impose a term of community service if X does not pay the fine. Instead of this, if the court believes that X will not be able to pay any appropriate fine it may impose, the judge may simply impose a direct sentence of community service.

If a fine is imposed, and X does not have the funds immediately available, this does not mean that he or she should immediately go to prison. The court should make an effort to recover the fine and keep X out of prison. Methods of doing this include:

Giving X time to pay. Every effort should be made to afford X time to pay. The court may allow the fine to be paid as a lump sum, by a particular date, or in instalments, each instalment to be paid by a particular date. In considering whether X should be given time to pay, account should be taken of such factors as —

- whether he or she is employed
- his or her disposable income
- whether he or she is of fixed abode.

Making a **garnishee order** against his or her salary, if he or she is employed.

This should be used wherever possible, if X is employed.

Executing against his or her movable property

It should be noted that immovable property may not be attached in the first instance. The amount which may be levied must be sufficient to cover, not only the fine itself, but the costs and expenses of the warrant and of the attachment and sale. Where the proceeds of the sale are not sufficient to cover the amounts mentioned, the High Court may issue a warrant for the levy against X's immovable property of the amount unpaid. If the sentence was passed by the magistrates court, the High Court may authorise the magistrates court to issue such a warrant; the magistrates court may not issue one without such authorisation.

This procedure should be invoked where X is able to pay a fine but refuses to do so, for example where he or she is sentenced to a small fine but refuses to pay it and insists on going to prison to make a martyr of himself and a nuisance to the State. It also ought to be exercised in those cases where there is a fine plus outright imprisonment provided for the worst examples and the legislature intends that they be punished through the purse as well as through prison, particularly in those cases where X has made a profit out of his or her criminal activity.

Before the court invokes the power to issue a warrant, it should first satisfy itself that X is possessed of property capable of attachment and of sufficient value to pay the fine imposed, or at least a substantial portion of it.

Imprisonment

General

The first question must be: is imprisonment the only appropriate punishment? If so, why?

Imprisonment can confirm offenders as criminals rather than reform them. Imprisonment is also costly. But the offence may be such that nothing other than imprisonment is appropriate; or X might have such a bad record that a fine would be inappropriate for him, even if it would have been appropriate for a first offender. It may be argued that imprisonment might actually be beneficial for some offenders, such as alcoholics or drug users, as their access to alcohol or drugs should be much more restricted than when they are at liberty. The court should be careful of accepting this argument, unless it is clear that adequate medical back-up and counselling are available to deal with such persons, which is not usually the case.

The court should consider such factors as:

- the likelihood of reform: is X a person who is likely to reform himself? The chances of reform in prison must realistically be regarded as small;
- the deterrent value of the sentence;
- whether the sentence can be justified only in terms of retribution;
- whether the sentence can be justified on the basis of protecting society by keeping a hardened offender off the streets.

When deciding on the length of the sentence, there are several factors to consider:

- what is the maximum sentence provided (in the case of a statutory offence)? The maximum should be reserved for the most serious examples of the offence. If the desirable sentence is beyond the magistrate's jurisdiction, the magistrate should consider stopping the trial with a view to X being sentenced in the High Court;
- the minimum sentence of imprisonment permissible is four days: s 359 CPEA. Such a sentence can rarely be justified. It causes more trouble to the prison authorities than it is worth;
- precedents as laid down by the Supreme Court or High Court. Magistrates should make themselves familiar with the sentencing trends. If necessary, adjourn to research the matter. The prosecutor should also be in a position to advise the court;
- where a statute provides for a mandatory minimum sentence, the court may not pass a sentence less than the minimum, unless the statute allows such a course (usually where there are "special circumstances"). See the comments above, in relation to mandatory minimum fines.

Imprisonment is a severe punishment which must only be imposed as a last resort *Mpofu* (2)1985 (1) ZLR 285 (H). There is thus need to push for community service in appropriate cases: *Manyevere* HB-38-03; *Shariwa* HB-37-03.

It is the duty of the court to consider imposing community service where court decides that effective sentence of 24 months or less is appropriate, *Mabhena* 1996 (1) ZLR 134 (H) If the view is taken that the offence is not serious, consideration should be given to community service *Mutukura* HH-39-02.

Young offenders should be kept out of prison wherever possible: *Marachera* A-151-68; *Mantwana* S-20-82; *Mayberry* HH-248-86; *Ncube* HB-153-86; *Mudekwe & Anor* HH-7-86; *Munyariwa* HB-14-87; *Chadyamunda* HH-228-89; *Chitanda* HH-215-89; *Kanoyerera* HH-167-89; *Van Jaarsveld* HB-110-90; *Shariwa* HB-37-03. In *Munukwa* HH-35-02 the court said that offenders in the age group of 18 to 21 years are young offenders who, depending on the offence of which they are convicted and the circumstances thereof, must generally be treated differently from adult offenders. In this country, there are advanced, modern and appropriate provisions for the treatment of young offenders. Judicial officers are unfortunately behind in their treatment of young offenders and have not acclimatised to these alternative methods of treating youthful offenders. The routine imprisonment of such offenders should be avoided.

In *Shariwa* HB-37-03, the judge said that first offenders, especially young ones, should as far as possible be kept out of prison.

The court should consider suspending portion of prison sentence imposed on first offender, although there is no rule that must suspend portion: *Manaiwa & Anor* HB-72-90; *Mazowe* HB-36-91; *Gumba* S-50-91.

Female first offenders are generally treated more leniently than males, for three reasons:

- males commit more offences;
- recidivism is commoner among males;
- women often have young children to care for.

Harvey 1967 RLR 203 (A); *Malunga* 1990 (1) ZLR 124 (H)

However, in some cases, though, these factors may be absent or of lesser importance and there may be circumstances where there is no reason to discriminate in favour of the woman: *Malunga* 1991 (1) ZLR 124 (H); *Gwatidzo* HH-271-90. However, in *Malunga* 1990 (1) ZLR 124 (H) the court reiterated that a sharp distinction should be made between male and female offenders is still apposite and that the tendency in certain subsequent cases to innovate by adopting a more uniform approach between the sexes is premature.

The court should consider suspending portion of prison sentence imposed on first offender, although there is no rule that must suspend portion: *Manaiwa & Anor* HB-72-90; *Mazowe* HB-36-91; *Gumba* S-50-91.

Imprisonment in default of payment of a fine

Whenever a person is convicted of an offence punishable by a fine, the court *may*, in imposing a fine on X, impose a period of imprisonment as an alternative to the fine. The period may be up to the limits of the court's sentencing jurisdiction but, in respect of statutory offences, the period of imprisonment imposed as an alternative to the fine may not, either alone or together with any period of imprisonment imposed as a direct punishment, exceed the maximum period provided by the enactment for that offence.

The period of imprisonment in this situation is strictly secondary and alternative. It is an additional sanction intended to operate only should the primary one fail.

It is essential that judicial officers should observe a due proportion between the fine and the alternative period of imprisonment. The ratio of the fine to the period of imprisonment is very much within the discretion of the sentencing officer. While the period should be long enough to induce X to pay the fine, care should be taken to ensure that it is realistic in relation to the gravity of the offence and not excessive.

There must be some logical proportion between the fine and the alternative period of imprisonment. It would be illogical to impose a fine that is well below the maximum allowed, but provide an alternative period of imprisonment which is approaching or at the maximum.

The first stage of the enquiry is to assess the fine, then the alternative sentence of imprisonment, not the other way round. If X is to be given the option of a fine, the fine must bear some relation to his or her means (see above). If the fine must be related to X's means, the alternative period of imprisonment should equally be related to the fine, because if he or she cannot pay the fine he or she will suffer a disproportionate punishment. The period can be calculated, for lower income prisoners, by reference to the minimum wage. For higher income earners, it can be related to the time that it would have taken X to earn the equivalent of the fine.

Only if X simply has no means with which to pay a realistic fine should the judicial officer attempt at first to consider what period of imprisonment might reasonably be merited for the offence concerned.

It may happen that the court imposes a fine but does not impose an alternative period of imprisonment. If X does not pay the fine in full, or if it is not recovered in full by some other method, the court may have X arrested and brought to court. It may then sentence him or her to such period of imprisonment as it could have imposed on him or her as an alternative to the fine.

This power does, of course, not preclude the court from giving X further time to pay or taking other steps to recover the fine and it would be desirable that the court should take such steps rather than commit X to prison.

Periodical imprisonment

Where a person is convicted of an offence specified in the Sixth Schedule to the CP&EA, he or she may, instead of any other punishment, be sentenced to periodical imprisonment for a period of not less than 96 and not more than 2000 hours. It is a pre-requisite that the court should ascertain from the officer in charge of the appropriate prison that accommodation for the purpose is available. If it is not, then periodical imprisonment cannot be imposed.

The offences specified in the Sixth Schedule are:

- driving with a prohibited concentration of alcohol in the blood;
- driving while under the influence of alcohol or a drug;
- forging such documents as driving licences and insurance certificates or using such forged documents;
- refusing to supply a blood sample; and
- failing to pay maintenance.

Periodical imprisonment is not intended to meet the case of a person who is unable financially to pay a fine. If a fine is the appropriate sentence, then a fine should be imposed. Periodical imprisonment should be considered if imprisonment is the appropriate penalty for the offence and if, for example, it is desirable that the offender should be allowed to continue his or her work and support his or her family while serving his or her sentence. It is not intended for persons who are not in regular employment.

Community service

General aspects

Community Service provides an alternative to imprisonment and is particularly beneficial to first and youthful offenders. It gives the offender the opportunity to reflect on his or her wrongdoing. Most importantly, the offender is not only kept out of prison where he or she would otherwise get into contact with the worst elements in society but he or she is also made to pay reparation for his or her wrongs to society. It can be an exacting form of punishment and is not intended to be an easy way out for convicted persons. Community Service can have a positive effect on the ever-increasing prison population.

The regulations relating to the imposition of Community Service are included in Appendix to this Handbook.

Community Service may be imposed in respect of a non-serious offence case, that is a case in which the magistrate would have imposed an effective prison sentence of twelve months or less. Community Service can also be imposed as an alternative to the prison term imposed as an alternative to payment of a fine.

Community Service may not be imposed in cases of rape, armed robbery, robbery with violence, car theft, stock theft (of cattle). Special caution must be exercised in imposing Community Service for offences such as robbery, culpable homicide, infanticide, abortion etc. Only where the mitigatory circumstances are very compelling should Community Service be considered. The minimum number of hours of Community Service that may be imposed is thirty-five. There must be a proper enquiry before Community Service is imposed.

In terms of s 350A(1) CPEA, a court can now impose community service as a direct sentence rather than as an alternative to a fine or imprisonment. In terms of s 348A CPEA, the court can impose community service as an alternative to the payment of a fine. As regards the use of community service as a direct punishment and as an alternative to a fine: see Appendix 7 to this Handbook.

The magistrate must conduct a proper inquiry as to whether community service is an appropriate punishment for accused: *Chinzenze* 1998 (1) ZLR 470 (H) at 477E-F and *S* v *Gumbo* 1995 (1) ZLR 163 (H) at 168C-E.

The magistrate must apply his or her mind as to why wanted to impose direct community service and give reasons as to why he or she favoured such approach: *Chinzenze Ors* 1998 (1) ZLR 470 (H) at 477D-E.

There is a need for the court to specify the hours to work and times of starting and ending work. The court should take into account the fact that the convicted person is a full time student or is in full time employment: *Sithole & Anor* HH-101-03.

Where a person is in employment or is a full-time student, a court imposing a community service order must allow community service to be carried out over week-ends or after working hours, by arrangement with the institution concerned. The number of hours should be reduced from what it might otherwise have been. It is the duty of the trial magistrate to state the hours which the accused must work and the times when the service should be commenced and completed. Where the hours fixed by the court become inconvenient either to the institution or to the accused, then the court must be approached to vary the conditions imposed in the order. It is not for the institution to allow the accused time off.

If the court imposes a direct community service order in terms of s 360A, the question has arisen whether a magistrate can also impose a prison term in terms of s 358 suspended on condition that X makes restitution? There is conflicting case law on this point.

In Mugebe 2000 (1) ZLR 376 (H), Bartlett J and Garwe J ruled that this was impermissible to do this under s 360A. If the court imposes a direct community service order in terms of s 360A it can't then also impose prison sentence under s 358 suspended on condition that X makes restitution because under 360A(3) prison term may only be imposed as alternative to CS.

However in the cases of *Maramba & Anor* 2000 (2) ZLR 69 (H), Chatikobo J and *Mhlanga & Anor* 2000 (2) ZLR 73 (H) Chinhengo J the judges decided that the *Mugebe* decision is wrong. They ruled that it is competent for the court, in addition to imposing direct sentence in terms of to of s 360A, to impose in terms of s 358 a prison term, suspended on condition of restitution.

The higher courts have stressed that wherever a magistrate is considering imprisoning a person for less than 24 months, he or she should always consider whether to impose a sentence of community service instead of sending the person to prison. This applies particularly where the person concerned is a young offender or a first offender.

Community service is not appropriate for serious offences such as rape and robbery, but the option of community service should always be considered for other offences.

In *Manyevere* HB-38-03, the judge observed that imprisonment is a severe and rigorous form of punishment which should only be imposed only as a last, and not first, resort and where no other form of punishment will do. Failure to consider community service in appropriate cases is a misdirection. This was reiterated in *Shariwa* HB-37-03 where the judge went on to say that first offenders, especially young ones, should as far as possible be kept out of prison. Community service is one way of ensuring that this objective is achieved. The trial court should carry out a full enquiry, not only as to the accused's means, but also his or her general suitability for community service.

Community service may be imposed:

- as an alternative to a fine;
- as a condition of suspension of a sentence of imprisonment;
- directly, as a substantive sentence.

The court should be able to explain why, where it has imposed community service, it has done so in one way rather than another. Where community service is imposed as an alternative to a fine, it should only be imposed where the appropriate sentence is a fine and X is genuinely unable to pay the fine. Where X can pay the fine, steps should be taken to ensure that the fine is paid (see above under the heading fines). Community service could be imposed directly where the court does not wish X to go to prison or to pay a fine, for example, where the fine might be paid by someone else or where a fine would have little deterrent effect but imprisonment would be inappropriate.

Whichever way community service is imposed, the court should consider the following matters:

- It should be regarded as a fine on leisure time and is particularly appropriate for persons who exhibit anti-social behaviour, as it gives the opportunity for constructive activity as well as a possible change of outlook on the part of the offender. On the other hand, even if the offence is one for which community service is appropriate, the offender may not be: he or she may indicate unwillingness to carry out the service; he or she may fail to attend, requiring a warrant of arrest to be issued; or he or she may commit further offences. For these reasons, courts should err on the side of caution, for if inappropriate offenders are allowed the option of community service, or if it is imposed for inappropriate offences, public confidence in the system will be lost.

- is a suitable place available? If so, where? The court should make enquiries first, *before* imposing community service.
- is the work suitable as making reparation to the community? The work should not be such that it is demeaning and amounts to inhuman treatment, but on the other hand should not be so easy that it appears to be meaningless.
- if X is employed, can community service be arranged so as to enable him/her to continue in employment?

Rejection of recommendations of community service officers

In *Banda* HB-72-04, the judge pointed out that Community service officers are trained officers of the court whose main function is to assess the suitability of a candidate for community service. Their recommendations should not be disregarded without good cause. If a recommendation is not accepted, it is essential that the trial court show that it considered the recommendation and why it ignored it. Failure to do so is a misdirection.

The number of hours of community service should not be chosen arbitrarily; there must be a rational basis for the number of hours imposed.

The Community Service Guidelines provide detailed instruction in regard to the imposition of community service.

Concurrent/consecutive punishments

Where a person is convicted at one trial of two or more counts, the court may sentence him or herto particular punishments in respect of each offence.

Cumulative or consecutive?

When sentencing any person to multiple punishments, the court may direct the order in which the sentences will be served or that the sentences should run concurrently. Sentences of corporal punishment or of fines cannot be made to run concurrently. It is not possible, for example, to sentence a juvenile to 4 strokes on one count and 4 strokes on another and order that the sentences run concurrently. The proper procedure to adopt where a number of offences warranting corporal punishment or a fine are committed and the aggregate would be too severe, is to treat several counts as one for the purposes of sentence.

In fixing the length of each sentence, the court should take into account whether the sentence is going to be made consecutive to or concurrent with the other sentences. There is no requirement that the sentences on closely related counts should run concurrently with one another. The ultimate test is whether or not the aggregate sentence is reasonable in relation to the total culpability of X. An undue disparity in the sentences ordered to run concurrently may result in X getting an inappropriate overall sentence. **The overall sentence must always be borne in mind.** Even if the sentences on individual counts, taken separately, are appropriate, the total sentence may not be.

Where a person is convicted of several counts of varying degrees of gravity, it is wrong to assess an appropriate aggregate sentence and then divide it equally between the several counts. Inappropriate sentences should not be imposed on individual counts in order to arrive at an acceptable total. Each count should be treated separately on its own merits. There are two alternative correct methods. One is to impose a globular sentence (see below). The other is to impose an adequate and appropriate sentence on each count separately. If the total period is too high, the sentence, or part of it, on one count should be ordered to run concurrently with the sentence on another count; or a portion of the total may be suspended.

It may be appropriate to group related counts together and make the sentences on the counts within each group run concurrently. Where counts are grouped together, there should be some rational basis for doing so.

It is improper for the court to treat earlier counts on the same basis as previous convictions and increase the sentences passed on later counts.

Where counts are treated separately for the purposes of sentence (even if they are made to run concurrently), a judicial officer may impose any proper sentence in respect of each count which is within the limits of his or her punitive jurisdiction, even though the total sentence may be in excess of his or her jurisdiction.

Where X is sentenced separately on a number of counts, the court may aggregate the sentences on all counts and then order that a portion of the aggregate be suspended on conditions. The period of suspension need not be related to any particular count. If the court wishes the total period of suspension to begin to run after X has served his or her sentence on all counts, the way to express it is to set out the sentences for the individual counts, state whether and to what extent any of the sentences run concurrently with one another, and finally state:

> " Of the total sentence of Y years/months, X years/months will be suspended for ... on condition that ... "

Counts as one for sentence

Where X is convicted of two or more offences, it is preferable that he or she should be sentenced separately for each offence, especially where the offences are entirely different. In most cases, there is no practical advantage in imposing a globular sentence where all the counts are treated as one for sentence. An exception might arise where it is decided, in dealing with a juvenile, to place him or her in a training institute or impose a sentence of whipping. The imposition of a globular sentence often causes difficulties on appeal or review. Consequently, one globular sentence for two or more offences should only be considered where the offences are of the same or a similar nature and are closely linked in time. A common example would be charges of forgery and uttering.

Where counts are taken as one for sentence, a magistrate is limited to a globular sentence within his or her punitive jurisdiction.

In *Faku & Anor* 1997 (1) ZLR 389 (S), court held it was irregular for a magistrate to treat the counts as one for sentence, for the purpose of imposing corporal punishment, but treat them separately for the purpose of imposing a custodial sentence. The magistrate should either have treated each count individually for sentence or have treated them jointly for sentence. A hybrid approach was not permissible.

Where additional punishments – such as prohibition from driving or forfeiture of goods – are provided for in respect of one of the counts on which X was convicted, the fact that all the counts are treated as one for sentence does not take away the right of the court to impose the additional punishment for that one count. However, the court should make it clear that the subsidiary punishment relates only to a particular count.

Where there are numerous counts, it may be appropriate to group related counts together and impose globular sentences in respect of each group of counts.

Suspended sentence

Where a person is convicted of any offence other than an Eighth Schedule offence, the court may:

- postpone the passing of sentence for a period of up to five years and release the offender on such conditions as the court may specify; or
- pass sentence, but suspend the whole or part of it for up to five years on such conditions as the court may specify; or
- sentence X to a fine, and alternatively to a period of imprisonment, but give X time to pay.

The conditions that may be imposed are dealt with below.

Offences to which applicable

Passing of sentence may be conditionally postponed or a sentence conditionally suspended in respect of any offence other than an Eighth Schedule offence, that is, murder (other than the murder by a woman of her newly-born child), conspiracy or incitement to commit murder, or any offence for which a minimum sentence is imposed, or conspiracy, incitement or attempt to commit such an offence.

General considerations as to suspension or postponement

The purpose of a suspended sentence is rehabilitation and the court should be satisfied that a suspended portion of the sentence will have a rehabilitative effect.

There is no requirement that a first offender should receive a totally suspended sentence. Whether a totally suspended sentence is appropriate or not will depend on all the circumstances. In the case of a young first offender, for example, a suspended sentence is, more often than not, desirable and appropriate.

There is no general rule that before a court may impose a suspended sentence, whether total or partial, it must be satisfied that special or exceptional circumstances exist. But if the appropriate sentence is an effective term of imprisonment, special circumstances would have to be shown before the court would be justified in wholly suspending the sentence. Nor is there any rule that every first offender who is to be imprisoned is entitled to have a portion of the sentence suspended.

Conditions of suspension or postponement

The conditions must be appropriate to the crime and stated with such precision that X clearly understands the ambit of the condition. If there is any doubt as to how a condition should be interpreted, the doubt must be resolved in favour of X. Thus, if X is convicted of an offence involving assault, it would be appropriate to suspend the sentence or a part of it on a condition relating to physical violence. The use of the word "violence" alone may be vague and other wording may be needed to ensure that X knows exactly what he or she must do to avoid the suspend sentence being brought into operation. For example, "statutory rape" would probably not be an offence involving violence. Similarly, a condition that X does not commit any offence involving theft or dishonesty would not apply to housebreaking with intent unknown. It would only apply to offences akin to theft.

A condition of suspension must be reasonably capable of fulfilment; if the condition cannot be fulfilled, it should not be included.

It is improper for a court to attach more than one condition to the suspension of a portion of a sentence. Where X is convicted of theft and it is desired to suspend a portion of the sentence on conditions of both restitution and subsequent good behaviour, it would be better to suspend a portion on condition of restitution and suspend a further portion on condition of subsequent good behaviour. Any other course could lead to complications. Similarly, it would be improper to impose a single suspended sentence in respect of two unrelated offences.

Length of suspended sentence and period of suspension

In assessing sentence, a portion of which is to be suspended, the proper approach is to look primarily at the sentence which the offence should attract and, having determined that, consider what portion should be suspended. It is not correct to decide what effective sentence X should undergo and then add a suspended sentence.

The length of the effective sentence is also relevant. Where a very long sentence is imposed, there is no purpose in suspending portion of it on condition of good behaviour. If the long sentence just served does not deter X from future criminal activity, a suspended sentence will be unlikely to. On the other hand, there is no reason why portion of a lengthy sentence should not be suspended on the condition of restitution.

The period of suspension should also be considered judicially. The maximum period of suspension or postponement of sentence is five years and there is a tendency for the courts automatically to suspend or postpone sentences for the maximum period. The court should determine *in each case* whether the maximum period is warranted.

Some of the considerations are:

- the nature of the offence and the circumstances surrounding its commission – whether it was planned and premeditated or whether it was spontaneous;
- whether X has exhibited a tendency to commit the type of offence;
- the character of the offender: is he or she a person of advanced age who has up to now led a blameless life? Has he or she shown by genuine penitence or by the shock and disgrace of the trial that the chance of a similar transgression is unlikely?
- are the offences to which the suspension will relate the kind of offences that could be easily committed in circumstances of emotional distress or discomposure?
- is X being sentenced to a lengthy effective term of imprisonment? That itself should have the required rehabilitative effect without requiring a further long term of suspension.
- where the offence itself did not require an effective custodial sentence, it might be unfair if at some time within a period as long as five years X had to undergo the full sentence as well as the sentence for the later offence.

Other punishments

Prohibition from driving may be considered in respect of driving offences under the Road Traffic Act and in respect of common law offences (in particular, culpable homicide) involving the use of motor vehicle.

In respect of some offences, prohibition for a minimum period is mandatory. If the court is going to consider a period over the minimum, there must be some rational basis for selecting the longer period.

If prohibition is discretionary, the court should ask itself whether prohibition is necessary and, if so, why. For some people, a prohibition from driving can amount to a very severe punishment, because of the nature of their work, where they work, the lack of suitable public transport, the hours of work, and so on. A prohibition could also mean the loss of the person's job. Hiring a driver can be very costly and expecting other members of X's family to drive him or her could amount to a punishment on them too. Sometimes these results are unavoidable, but they should be considered.

There may be other statutory punishments or consequences of conviction, such as loss of licences. These may have severe financial consequences for X.

Sentencing by different judicial officer than one convicting accused

In *Ngwenya* HB-19-92, X had pleaded guilty to the charge and was found guilty after the magistrate had dealt with the case in terms of s 271(2)(b) CPEA. The case was then adjourned and later resumed before a different magistrate who proceeded to hear mitigation of sentence and then impose sentence.

On review, it was held that s 334(6) CPEA allows a magistrate other than the one who convicted X to impose sentence upon X. This can be done "in the absence of the magistrate who convicted" X. The words "in the absence of" should be given the widest possible meaning, namely that they apply whatever the reason for the convicting magistrate's absence. Thus, the absence may be due to retirement, leave, discharge from the service, death and so on. However, the second magistrate who sentences X must comply with the requirements of s 334(6), namely he or she must:

- note on the record the reasons for the absence of the trial magistrate;
- allow X the opportunity to address in mitigation; and
- consider the evidence recorded and on which the verdict is returned.

Reasons for Sentence

Reasons should be given for the penalty which is imposed. These reasons should be recorded in writing at the time sentence is pronounced. Full written reasons should be given even if the judge thinks that the reasons for the sentence are obvious. It is particularly important that the judge records his or her reasons for departing from any general policy which has been laid down by the higher courts in respect of sentence. The imposition of an inappropriate sentence is an injustice and the review or appeal court can only determine the appropriateness of a sentence if the reasons for the sentence are given: *Duri* HH-89-91; *Nyamupanda* HH-101-91.

In *Mkali & Ors* HB-23-93, the court said that reasons for any decision, including sentence, must be given to show that the judicial officer has heard and considered the evidence and arguments for each side and has not taken extraneous considerations into account. A fair trial requires not just a correct decision but that it can be seen to be based on reason.

In the Magistrates Court (Criminal) Rules, 1966 [RGN 871 of 1966], all that is laid down is that, where appropriate, the presiding magistrate must state shortly any special factors which he or she took into account in assessing sentenc e, and, where the sentence imposed exceeds twelve months imprisonment with hard labour, with or without the option of a fine, the judgment must be reduced to writing and it will become part of the record.

Public announcement of sentence

In terms of s 334(1) CPEA, all sentences in criminal proceedings against persons aged eighteen or above shall be pronounced in open court.

Referral to High Court for sentence

When a magistrate is of the opinion that the appropriate sentence which is warranted in the case he or she is trying is beyond his or her sentencing jurisdiction, he or she can refer the case to the High Court under s 54(2) MCA. He or she may feel that the crime itself is of such magnitude that he or she has inadequate sentencing jurisdiction or, once X's previous convictions have been disclosed, the magistrate may feel that he or she cannot impose an adequate sentence within the scope of his or her sentencing jurisdiction.

If the magistrate wishes to refer the matter to the High Court, the correct procedure to adopt is as follows:

- He or she must adjourn the proceeding and must submit a written report to the Attorney-General setting out why he or she is of the opinion that a sentence in excess of his or her jurisdiction is justified. The record of the proceedings must accompany the report.
- X is entitled to be informed on what basis the trial magistrate has decided to decline jurisdiction to sentence him or her and to proceed under s 54(2) MCA since X now faces the prospect of a higher sentence. X should thus be informed so that he or she has the opportunity to make proper submissions on sentence. He or she can only do this if the magistrate gives his or her reasons for opting to proceed under s 54(2) MCA.
- If the Attorney-General under s 225(b) CPEA directs that the case be transferred to the High Court for sentence, the magistrate must then comply

with s 226 CPEA causing X to appeal before him or her and by informing X of the Attorney-General's direction and then committing X to prison until he or she is sentenced by the High Court or is granted bail. He or she must also ensure that the record of the criminal proceedings, together with the reasons for conviction, are transmitted to the High Court. The record should include the report sent to the Attorney-General setting out why the magistrate was of the opinion that a sentence in excess of his or her sentencing jurisdiction was called for.

Dangarembizi & Anor 1987 (2) ZLR 196 (H); *Mandizha* HH-275-90; *Julieta* HH-74-98.

Difficult aspects of sentencing

When difficult specific issues on sentencing arise reference should be made to *A Guide to Sentencing in Zimbabwe* by G. Feltoe published by the Legal Resources Foundation in 1990. This section will only deal with a few selected points of sentencing which have caused difficulty in the past.

Legally impermissible sentences

The following things are legally impermissible:

- The antedating of a prison sentence: *Chahora* HH-349-84.
- The imposition of a prison sentence of less than four days: s 357 CPEA.
- The imposition of two sentences for one offence: *Chipxere* HH-314-83 (Magistrate wrongly imposing for one offence a prison term plus another prison term, wholly suspended on condition that X made restitution.); *Sibanda* HB-36-86 (Magistrate wrongly imposing two separate prison sentences subject to conditions for same offence.)
- Making fines run concurrently or a fine run concurrently with a prison sentence: *Kambuzuma* HH-60-86, *Gororo* HH-145-86.
- The suspending of a sentence of a fine where the fine is mandatory or giving X time to pay such fine: *De Montille* 1979 RLR 105, *Kudavaranda* 1988 (2) ZLR 367 (H).
- The suspending or postponing of a mandatory prison sentence without the option of a fine where there is a minimum period of such imprisonment prescribed: s 356(2) [337(1)] as read with para 3 of the Seventh Schedule to CPEA.

  But where the legislature lays down a mandatory prison sentence of a length to be determined by the court, the court may suspend all or a portion of the prison sentence. *Patel* S-63-87; *Muzambe* HH-121-90. However, in *Horowitz* 1976 (1) RLR 238 at 242D, it is stated that the court will not lightly suspend the whole of a mandatory prison sentence; it will only do so when the mitigatory circumstances clearly make such a course desirable.

- The imposition of globular sentences save in exceptional circumstances.

In *Chawasarira* HH-18-91, it was laid down that where an accused is convicted of two or more separate offences, separate punishments should, save in exceptional cases, be imposed for each separate charge. One globular sentence for two or more offences should be considered only where the offences are of the same or a similar nature and are closely linked in point of time. If these two requirements are not satisfied, then a separate sentence must be imposed in respect of each offence.

In cases of forgery and uttering it is usual, for the purposes of sentence, to treat the convictions for forgery and uttering as one since the offences are usually so interlinked that there is no impropriety in doing this. Likewise, where persons have been convicted of multiple counts of fraud or theft by conversion with the same *modus operandi*, offences that are closely related in point of time may be treated as one for the purposes of sentence. These cases, however, are the exception rather than the rule.

In this case, the court set aside a globular sentence imposed on X for assault with intent to commit grievous bodily harm and possession of dagga.

In *Chirai* HH-2-92, the review court ruled that a globular sentence imposed for a charge of attempted fraud and a charge of contravening s 3(1)(b) of the Prevention of Corruption Act, 1985 was inappropriate as the two offences were dissimilar.

There is no increased jurisdiction where several counts are taken as one for sentence; the overall sentence must still fall within the limits of the jurisdiction: *Chowdhry* HH-161-85.

Where there is insufficient sentencing capacity in such cases, the matter must be referred to the High Court for sentence.

Although it may be technically possible to exceed jurisdiction where X is sentenced to separate sentences on individual counts, there are serious doubts about a magistrate doing this. Again, a better course would be to refer the case to the High Court for sentence. *Makalima* HB-16-91.

- The imposition of a standard sentence for the particular crime without considering the individual circumstances and the moral blameworthiness of X. There is a need for individualised sentencing: *David & Anor* 1964 RLR 2; *Mugwenhe & Anor* 1991 (2) ZLR 66 (S).

- The imposition of a sentence of imprisonment on a company; only a fine may be imposed upon a company even if the statutory offence provides only for the imposition of imprisonment for the offence: s 372(3) CPEA.

Fines

General aspects

Fines are an important alternative to imprisonment. A fine can be an effective deterrent but it does not have the highly destructive consequences that incarceration often has. Fines are imposed when the offences are not serious enough to warrant imprisonment. However, the way in which fines are imposed can be highly discriminatory against the poor. As was pointed out in the case of *Munyakwe & Ors* HH-92-93, the failure to assess fines in accordance with means can result in grave injustice to poorer people.

Time and time again, the higher courts have stressed that there should be a proper investigation into the means of X to pay and that the fine should be tailored to his or her means. Unless judicial officers gather adequate information on the means of X, it will be impossible for them to tailor the fine to the means of X. In probing the means of X, it is vitally important that earnings from the informal sector be taken into account. This is because large numbers of the urban population now earn their livelihood in the informal sector.

If the process of adapting fines to means were to be taken seriously the end result would be a reduction in the numbers of persons in the prisons of Zimbabwe, as many who are fined cannot pay their fines and end up in prison. Frequently, however, in the past only lip service has been paid to these requirements. In the case of *Munyakwe & Ors* HH-92-93, the court stressed that magistrates must conduct more than a completely cursory inquiry into mitigation. In order to try to ensure that the trial court systematically and thoroughly matches the fine to X's means, it is recommended that the court should be obliged to fill in a form like the one set out in the Appendix to this address. This form obliges the judicial officer to extract all the salient financial information, to indicate what fine would normally be appropriate and how the fine has been tailored to X's means.

Fines and means

In *Mushangwe* HH-58-93, the court said that whenever a fine is appropriate, it must be made a real option, given with the intention of keeping a person out of prison, and therefore equated to his or her means (unless he or she is being made to disgorge illicit profits; or was engaged in some criminal enterprise where he or she must be prevented from thinking crime is profitable). If X has no apparent means, the fine should be based on the average income for someone of his or her station in life, as family or friends may help to keep him or her out of gaol. Here X had dependants and no employment; his or her means were obviously as limited as the magistrate's enquiry. In this case, X had been fined $700 (and a suspended prison term of four months) for hitting and kicking his or her ex-wife using moderate force, causing no permanent disability. This was a case of only common assault. The sentence was reduced to $150 (and 3 months' imprisonment suspended.)

In *Kunesu & Ors* HH-216-93, the court observed that the means of X is always the overriding factor. Any fear of making a serious offence seem trivial is not as important. Otherwise the courts do an injustice to the poor, and accommodation in prison is taken up unnecessarily by those who cannot pay their fines. Giving time to pay can enable the court to impose a more substantial fine, but this must not be taken too far or the poor will be punished more severely than the rich.

In the South African case of *Ntlele* 1993 (2) SACR 610 (W), the court pointed out that equality before the law means that the law must be even-handed; it must be fair, and a sentence must not be imposed which does not properly take account of the personal circumstances of X. When a sentence which is imposed for a particular offence can be paid by a rich offender out of one day's earnings but by a poor man only after he has toiled for 60 days, these requirements are manifestly not met. A sentence which does not take account of a poor man's inability to pay in circumstances where a fine is an appropriate sentence disregards one of the elementary criteria for punishment: the personal circumstances of X. For that reason alone, a court on review or appeal would be bound to conclude that the lower court's discretion was not properly exercised.

In *Mutandwa* HH-35-88, the court stated that if a court decides to impose a fine, the court must allow X a real option to pay it and must inquire into X's ability to pay, if necessary by instalments. A reasonable balance should be struck between the sum that X can pay and the sum that the gravity of the offence requires.

In *Dlamini* HB-3-90, the court stated that it is a misdirection for a judicial officer to hold that because he or she believes that X is incapable of paying the appropriate fine, he or she must therefore be sent to gaol. The proper approach was to consider first whether for the offence in question the appropriate punishment was a fine or imprisonment. If it was a fine, the amount of the fine should then have been set based upon the gravity of the offence and X's personal circumstances. If, on balance, it was necessary to impose a fine which was more than X can afford to pay, that is no reason to alter the sentence to one of imprisonment, X is still entitled to be given the option of paying a fine, even if in the end result he or she was unable to raise the finance to pay it. Similarly, in the case of *Ntlele* 1993 (2) SACR 610 (W), the court said that a fine beyond X's personal means is sometimes justified on the basis that he or she may be able to supplement his or her own resources by selling his or her assets or borrowing from family or friends. This approach should not be adopted on the mere supposition that these things may be done. Before a court is justified in imposing a fine clearly beyond X's ability to pay, a proper inquiry should be held to determine whether such other resources are available to X, and the extent of them.

Suspending fine on condition of Community Service

A new option is to impose a suitable fine suspended on condition X carries out a community service. This may be appropriate where there is an apparently unbridgeable gap between accused's available resources and the appropriate fine having regard to the gravity of the offence. See *Kunesu & Ors* HH-216-93.

In the case of *Mlambo* HH-117-95, a young married first offender stole goods worth $950 from his or her employer; it was all recovered. The magistrate imposed a fine of $1 000. The High Court pointed out that the trial magistrate had made the common mistake of equating the fine to the value stolen. As X made no ill-gotten gains, there was no justification for this: the fine must be related to the means of X or his or her ability to pay the fine. The fine was reduced to $500 (or 3 months) with the suspended prison sentence confirmed.

Giving time to pay

Nyirenda HH-116-88: Whenever a court sentences a person who is not legally represented to pay a fine, it should investigate the question whether or not he or she is to be given time to pay, even in the absence of an application by him or her for time to pay.

Motlaung 1993 (2) SACR 214 (NC): Where a judicial officer has decided to impose a fine on an accused and it is apparent that he or she will not be able to pay it in cash, the judicial officer must explain to him or her that there is provision for the fine to be paid in instalments. Only after explaining this and hearing X's representations will the judicial officer be in a position to assess a fine appropriately. The hearing granted to X person in these circumstances forms a cardinal and inherent part of the court's adjudication regarding the question of an appropriate sentence.

In the case of *Lekgwabe* 1992 (2) SACR 219 (T), the court said that where it is intended to impose a fine with the alternative of imprisonment upon an unrepresented accused, the court should bring to X's attention that the fine may be paid in instalments. If X indicates he or she wishes to pay the fine in instalments, the court must determine what kind of instalment would be within his or her reach.

Period of imprisonment in default of payment of fine

The alternative period of imprisonment should be related to the fine, and should generally be roughly the period X takes to earn the fine: see *Nyirenda* HH-116-88.

First offenders

First offenders should be kept out of prison wherever possible: *Mantwana* S-20-82; *Mayberry* HH-248-86; *Munyariwa* HB-14-87; *Chadyamunda* HH-228-89; *Chitanda* HH-215-89; *Kanoyerera* HH-167-89; *van Jaarsveld* HB-110-90.

Young first offenders, particularly, should be kept out of prison wherever possible: *Marechera* A-151-68; *Mudekwe & Anor* HH-7-86; *Ncube* HB-153-86.

Normally, female first offenders are treated more leniently than their male counterparts: *Harvey* 1967 RLR 203 at 205D; *Malunga* 1990 (1) ZLR 124 (H); *Gwatidzo* HH-271-90.

The court should consider suspending a portion of prison sentence imposed on a first offender although there is no rule that it must suspend a portion: *Manaiwa & Anor* HB-72-90; *Mazowe* HB-36-91; *Gumba* S-50-91.

Juveniles

Under s 351(2) CPEA, instead of sentencing a person under the age of 19 to a fine, imprisonment or to corporal punishment, the court convicting him or her can order that he or she be referred to a juvenile court to be dealt with in terms of the Children's Act.

The juvenile court can call for a probation report on the offender and can, amongst other things, order him or her to be placed in the custody of a suitable person or be returned to the custody of his or her parents or guardian. A juvenile can also be ordered to be placed in a training institute for a specified period: s 351(2)(b) and 351(3) CPEA.

Where there is insufficient evidence of an offender's age, the magistrate may estimate his or her age based on his or her appearance and on any information, including hearsay evidence, which may be available: s 387 CPEA.

Special reasons/circumstances for not imposing mandatory minimum sentence

General aspects

Sometimes, the legislature sees fit to prescribe minimum sentences for particular offences. It does so for serious crimes which are prevalent and are causing grave economic or social harm. The legislature prescribes such sentences where it believes that stern deterrent punishments are required and feels it is not enough simply to lay down high maximum sentences and to exhort the courts to impose stiff sentences for these offences as a deterrent. By prescribing mandatory minimum sentences, the legislature is interfering with the normal sentencing discretion of judicial officers to decide upon an appropriate level of sentence based upon the particular circumstances of the offence and the offender and the various mitigating and aggravating factors in the case. With mandatory sentences the sentence is no longer individualised. At least the mandatory minimum sentence must be imposed. Research has shown that where a minimum term of imprisonment is made mandatory, sentences are considerably longer than would normally be imposed for the crime in question.

To temper the potential harshness that would follow if the mandatory sentence had to be imposed in all cases, the legislature has added the rider that the minimum sentence does not have to be imposed if there are special reasons for not imposing the sentence or special circumstances which justify the imposition of a sentence less than the minimum. This is a legislative device whereby rigours of a particularly severe prescribed sentence may be avoided **in exceptional cases**; it is a sort of a safety valve.

The Supreme Court has held that such mandatory sentences are constitutional where the court is allowed to find special circumstances and impose a lesser sentence: *Arab* 1990 (1) ZLR 253 (S) and *Chichera* v *A-G* S-98-04.

Circumstances and reasons the same

It has been judicially recognized that there is no difference between "reasons" and "circumstances" in this context: *Chisiwa* 1981 ZLR 666 (H) at 670C. If the legislature simply says that the mandatory sentence must be imposed unless there are special reasons for not doing so or unless there are special circumstances justifying it not doing so, then the court is entitled to take into account both the circumstances surrounding the commission of the offence and circumstances, facts and conditions affecting and peculiar to the offender. However, sometimes the legislature defines special circumstances more narrowly, as in s 49 of the Road Traffic Act [*Chapter13:11*]. Here, special circumstances are defined so as to include only circumstances surrounding the commission of the offence and to exclude circumstances peculiar to the offender.

"Special" means "extraordinary"

Special reasons or special circumstances are reasons or circumstances which are **out of the ordinary**, either in their nature or extent: *Moyo* 1988 (2) ZLR 1 (S). Not all factors which would be mitigatory in ordinary criminal cases will be "special" in this sense. Deciding which factors are special in this sense involves a value judgment and is a matter of degree. In *Mbewe & Ors* 1988 (1) ZLR 7 (H), it was stated that mitigating factors, such as good character or particular hardship stemming from the sentence, cannot be taken as special circumstances, nor can contrition or co-operation on the part of the offender. In *Siziba* 1990 (2) ZLR 87 (H), the court stated that special circumstances must mean more than the natural consequences which flow from the imposition of the punishment prescribed. On the facts of *Siziba*, the court held that any hardship that would be suffered by the woman and her family if she were unable to pay the fine and had to serve the alternative prison sentence would be no more or less than that which always occurred when a wage earner and supporter of a family is sent to gaol. This factor did not therefore constitute special circumstances.

But where, for example, X was *bona fide* ignorant of the statutory provision concerned or was, as a result of a trap, tempted into committing a crime which he or she would not otherwise have committed or was compelled by circumstances to commit the offence, these factors may constitute not only mitigatory factors but also special circumstances (see cases below).

Combination of factors

The cumulative effect of a number of factors can constitute special reasons or special circumstances. Again, this involves the making of a value judgment: *Gumbo* HB-48-89; *Chidembo* S-118-89.

Attempts, conspiracies and incitements

The mandatory sentence does not apply to attempts, conspiracies and incitements: *Mutengwa* HH-116-90; *Takavarasha* HH-18-92.

Torture

Torture and ill-treatment at the hands of the authorities can constitute "special circumstances" for not imposing mandatory minimum sentence also includes torture and other ill-treatment at the hands of authorities: *Blanchard & Ors* 1999 (2) ZLR 168 (H).

Lengthy delay in bringing to trial

This can amount to a special circumstance: *Moyo* 1988 (2) ZLR 79 (H).

Finding of special circumstances

If magistrate finds special circumstances, he or she is obliged to record the special circumstances of the case which justify the imposition of the lesser penalty.

Suspension of mandatory sentence impermissible

Where the court decides that the mandatory **minimum** term of imprisonment or fine prescribed by the legislature has to be imposed, it may not suspend all or even a portion of the mandatory minimum prison sentence or fine. See s 337(1) as read with paragraph 3 of the Sixth Schedule CPEA, as read with *De Montille* 1979 RLR 105; *Kudavaranda* 1988 (2) ZLR 367 (H).

On the other hand, where the legislature lays down that it is mandatory for the court to impose imprisonment for a particular type of offence but that the term of imprisonment is to be determined by the court, the court may suspend all or a part of the prison term: *Patel* S-63-87. However, in *Horowitz* 1976 (1) RLR 238 at 241D, it was stated that the court will not lightly suspend the whole of the sentence where imprisonment has been made mandatory for an offence.
Undefended accused

Where an unrepresented accused is charged with an offence carrying a mandatory minimum sentence in the absence of special circumstances, the court must explain to X what special circumstances are: *Chaerera* 1988 (2) ZLR 226 (S) and *Maharangwe* S-5-90. Before the court imposes the mandatory prison sentence, it must explain in some detail what is meant by special reasons and the consequences of a failure to give special reasons: *Kaja* S-129-89.

Where an undefended accused admits possession of a prohibited item, the court must establish just what X is admitting as possession is a difficult legal concept: *Dube & Anor* 1988 (2) ZLR 385 (S).

The court should consider whether the case is a complex one. It should take into account factors such as:

- whether the ascertainment of facts includes difficult legal concepts such as "possession" "consent" or "knowledge";
- whether the facts themselves are complex or difficult;
- whether there is a need to prove "special reasons" or "special circumstances to avoid a minimum sentence;
- whether a long prison sentence is likely to follow on conviction.

In such cases, the court should consider to enter a plea of not guilty even if X has pleaded guilty and proceed in terms of s 272 CPEA.

It should also consider whether it would be fair and appropriate to advise X of the complexities of the matter and ask him or her if he or she has considered obtaining legal representation. If the court is satisfied that X should have legal representation but cannot afford it, the court should certify that legal representation be provided under the Legal Aid Act.

X should have been told that the offence involved a minimum mandatory sentence, unless they established special circumstances, and that these circumstances can be peculiar to the offender or to the commission of the offence. It is a procedural irregularity not sufficiently to explain or explore special circumstances: *Takawira* HH-155-91

The record must show that magistrate advised an unrepresented accused either during trial or during the sentencing procedure that he or she was in jeopardy of having a heavy minimum sentence imposed and could avoid this by showing special reasons: *Makawa & Anor* S-46-91

Suspension of mandatory sentence impermissible

Where the court decides that the mandatory **minimum** term of imprisonment or fine prescribed by the legislature has to be imposed, it may not suspend all or a portion of the mandatory minimum prison sentence or fine. See s 337(1) as read with paragraph 3 of the Sixth Schedule of the Criminal Procedure and Evidence Act. See *De Montille* 1979 RLR 105; *Kudavaranda* 1988 (2) ZLR 367 (H).

On the other hand, where the legislature lays down that it is mandatory for the court to impose imprisonment for a particular type of offence **but that the term of imprisonment is to be determined by the court**, the court may suspend all or a part of the prison term: *Patel* S-63-87. However, in *Horowitz* 1976 (1) RLR 238 (A) at 241D it was stated that the court will not lightly suspend the whole of the sentence where imprisonment has been made mandatory for an offence.

Cases in which special reasons/ circumstances existed

In most of the cases which follow the trial court or appeal court found that special circumstances or reasons existed for not imposing the mandatory sentence. A few cases are mentioned which point out factors which do **not** amount to special reasons or circumstances.

Exchange Control Act

Impossibility

In *Telecel Zimbabwe (Pvt) Ltd* HH-55-06, the appellant company was charged with a number of offences under the exchange control regulations. It had bought foreign currency on the unofficial, "parallel", market in order to service its debts outside the country, to pay for capital equipment and make other payments essential to keep the company in business. The *court a quo* found no special reasons in the particular case which would result in the imposition of a fine of not less than the value of the currency involved. It was held save in those situations where the legislation in question contains a definition of "special reasons" or "special circumstances" and that definition specifically confines the determination of such reasons or circumstances to the commission of the offence to the exclusion of the offender, the broad approach is preferable, which allows the court to consider the triad of the offender, the offence and the interests of society, the factors which any sentencer must always bear in mind, to arrive at an appropriate sentence. The appellant had two choices: either it had to behave in an ethical manner and search for foreign currency on the official market, where it was unavailable, and thereby commit corporate suicide or it had to enter the parallel market and survive. It chose life instead of death. It was necessary for its survival to purchase foreign currency from unauthorised dealers without Exchange Control authority at parallel market rates. Special reasons therefore existed not to impose the minimum sentence.

Remorse and righting of wrong:

Holmes 1982 (2) ZLR 267 (H): X intended to export from Zimbabwe two cheques expressed in foreign currency which he had bought. He changed his mind and deposited the cheques instead at a local bank. The genuine remorse and early and voluntary determination to right the wrong he had committed were special reasons.

Foolish action not causing prejudice:

McGregor HB-26-91: for reasons which were not investigated X took about Z$7500 out of country concealed in his car but he then brought this money back the next day. No one was prejudiced and his actions were foolish rather than wicked. The offences were of rather technical nature. Special reasons were found to exist.

On the other hand, the absence of prejudice to the country was held not to amount to special reasons in *Patel* S-63-87 because "it was no thanks to the appellant that the foreign currency did not leave the country."

Ignorance of law

Ndekete 1978 RLR 377: an unemployed tribesman had received a request for assistance from a sick relative in South Africa. He had sent Zimbabwean currency through the post to him, but the letter containing this currency had been intercepted by the authorities. He was probably unaware that what he was doing was unlawful. The court found that there were special reasons, in that this was an unconscious contravention and moral guilt was virtually absent.

Chisiwa 1981 ZLR 666 (H): the court stated that in appropriate circumstances a *bona fide* mistake of law would amount to special reasons.

See also *Musa* HH-144-89; *Mutengwa* HH-116-90; *Smith* S-182-90; *Trinder* HB-52-91.

Firearms Act

Purpose of possession

Mhiripiri HH-163-88: X had a .22 rifle for purpose of protecting crops and wild animals. Although his possession of the weapon was illegal, the court held that the purpose for which he possessed it amounted to special reasons.

Age of X and purpose of possession

Mutowo HH-458-88: X was 18 year old in form I who found an automatic pistol while visiting Moçambique and intended to use it for shooting birds. The age of X and the purpose of possession constituted special reasons.

Negligent possession of dismantled rifle

Robertson S-75-88: X possessed a dismantled FN rifle. He had kept it hidden for ten years at business premises where he worked. He had no intention to use for political purpose or to commit a crime. It was found when he left his or her employment. This was a case not so much of defiance of law but of considerable negligence. The combination of these factors constituted special reasons.

Finding unloaded and non-functional weapon

Chidembo S-118-89: a farm manager found an unloaded and non-functional revolver lying on ground. The fact that he found the weapon by chance and that it was unloaded and non-functional constituted in combination special reasons.

Purpose of possession and attempts to renew firearms certificates

Rudolph 1990 (1) ZLR 45 (S): X had three weapons to shoot vermin. He or she had firearms certificates for the weapons. He had applied for renewal of these certificates but had received no response despite giving a reminder. The fact that he had not kept these weapons for a sinister purpose and that the firearms authority was partly to blame because of its failure to respond to his or her application constituted special reasons.

See also *Rusike* HH-31-89 (unlawful possession of firearm); *Kaja* S-129-89 (unlawful possession of firearm).

Parks and Wildlife Act

Single, isolated act of possession

In *Mbewe & Ors* 1988 (1) ZLR 7 (H), the court pointed out that a single isolated act of unlawful possession of unregistered raw ivory or horn, whether or not the possession is for the purposes of trade, can make an offender liable to mandatory minimum sentence in absence of special circumstances.

Killing of animal and possession of its horns

Kudavaranda HH-450-88: X killed a rhino and was in possession of the horns taken from this animal. He was sentenced to a mandatory minimum fine on each count. Because the two offences were completely interlinked, the killing of the animal being in consequence of X's desire to possess its horns, there were special circumstances in relation to X's possession of the horns, justifying the court in not imposing the mandatory minimum sentence for that offence.

Technical breach of the law

Hill HB-106-89: the appellant had bought a rhino horn and two elephant tusks in 1957 and had kept them ever since as ornaments. He was ignorant that his possession had become unlawful in 1975. The court found that this was a technical breach of the law and the trial court should have found that there were special circumstances.

Disparity in sentence

Ncube & Anor HB-143-91: the second accused was an unsophisticated communal dweller who found the bit of ivory in the bush and picked it up simply to give it to a witchdoctor. The first accused was a city dweller who persuaded his co-accused to sell the piece of ivory and took it for that purpose. Both accused were sentence by the trial court to the mandatory 5 year jail term.

The review court found that there were special circumstances in respect of the second X and reduced his or her sentence to 6 months' imprisonment. The court found that although the mandatory minimum sentence is aimed at poachers and dealers, there were no special circumstances for the first X other than the disparity in sentence between him and his co-accused, which was not justified by the difference in their moral blameworthiness. This unjustified disparity was itself a special circumstance in the case. It therefore altered the sentence imposed on the first accused.

See also *Chaerera* 1988(2) ZLR 226 (S); *Siziba* HB-61-88; *Botha* HH-183-88; *Dube & Ors* 1988 (2) ZLR 385 (S); *Mangando & Anor* HH-277-90.

Precious Stones Trade Act

Stones of minimal value

Mugangavari 1984 (1) ZLR 80 (S): the fact that the stones are of minimal value does not *per se* constitute a special reason for non-imposition of the mandatory sentence.

Woman holding stones for husband

Anand 1988 (2) ZLR 414 (S): a woman was convicted of possessing uncut emeralds worth $150 which had been hidden in her bedroom. She accepted sole blame because her husband was a sick man. The court held that the fact that she probably possessed emeralds on behalf of husband and that she had decided to sacrifice his or her wife by shifting responsibility on her constituted special reasons for not imposing the mandatory minimum penalty.

Delay in bringing to trial

Moyo 1988 (2) ZLR 79 (H): through no fault of his or her, X was not brought to trial for nearly 4 years after possessing precious emeralds, and in the mean time he had nearly completed a prison sentence imposed on him for a subsequent offence. It was held that the delay in bringing to trial amounted to a special reason for not imposing the mandatory sentence.

Police trap

Kamtande 1983 (1) ZLR 302 (HB): where X is trapped into committing the offence by the police, the fact that the police trap had promoted the commission of the offence by someone who would not otherwise have committed it may be regarded as special reason.

Negligible value

Gumbo HB-48-89: X was in possession of an uncut emerald worth $3. He was a hotelier who had been given the stone as a keepsake by a guest many years ago. The cumulative effect of the following factors constituted special reasons: the negligible value of the stone, that it was acquired as a gift before the Act provided for the minimum penalty, that it had been kept for ten years and that there was no question of financial gain for X.

Woman keeping stones of no commercial value

Moyo HB-6-90: the court found that there were special reasons because of the cumulative effect of these factors: the emeralds had no commercial value, the woman possessing them was keeping them for another, she was a first offender and she had two sick children.

See also *Takavarasha* HH-18-92.

Road Traffic Act

Mandatory prison sentences:

Under s 40 the Road Traffic Act a person must be imprisoned up to the specified maximum term for driving whilst prohibited from doing so unless there are special circumstances justifying the imposition of the lesser sentence of a fine. Special circumstances are not restrictively defined and thus include special circumstances relating to the crime and to the offender.

Mandatory prohibition from driving:

It is mandatory for the court to prohibit a person from driving when he or she has been found guilty of certain offences unless there are special circumstances surrounding the commission of the offence (not circumstances peculiar to the offender). The offences in this category are:

s 53 reckless driving;

s 54 driving with prohibited concentration of alcohol in blood (but the prohibition is mandatory only if there is a previous conviction for a similar offence or if the vehicle being driven was a bus);

s 55 driving under the influence of alcohol;

s 78 (read with s 77(6)) refusal to undergo breath test.

Garwe HH-249-89: mandatory prohibition for drunken driving.
Erasmus S-84-91: special reasons for not imposing mandatory prohibition from driving in a hit and run case.

Criminal Law (Codification and Reform) Act

The Criminal Law Code also provides for a number of mandatory sentences.

- s 80 provides for a mandatory prison sentence of at least 10 years to be imposed upon a person who was infected with HIV when he or she commits certain sexual crimes. The crimes concerned are rape; aggravated indecent assault; indecent assault; sexual intercourse with a young person; and an indecent act with a young person involving penetration of the body which involves a risk of transmission of HIV.
- s 114(2)(e) provides for a minimum mandatory sentence of 9 years for stock theft involving any bovine or equine animal stolen in circumstances were there are no special circumstances to be found in the accused person's favour.
- s 156(1)(e)(i) provides a mandatory sentence of imprisonment of 15 years in relation to the crime of unlawful dealing in dangerous drugs, where special circumstances cannot be found.

What happens where minimum mandatory sentence is introduced for a crime but X committed the crime before the mandatory sentence came into operation but he or she was convicted after the mandatory sentence came into operation? This question arose and was answered in *Mzanywa & Ors* HB-9-06. The court held that the mandatory penalty may not be imposed for that crime because s 18(5) of the Constitution provides that "no penalty shall be imposed for any criminal offence that is severer in degree or description than the maximum penalty that might have been imposed for that offence *at the time when it was committed*". See also *Ndlovu & Anor* HH-70-06.

Summary

Not all mitigatory factors amount singly or in combination to special circumstances or reasons. Special circumstances or reasons are mitigatory factors which are out of the run of the mill considered singly or in combination.

Onus of proof

Where there is an onus on X to prove special circumstances, it is not possible to discharge the onus through address alone. There must be some factual basis established by evidence or agreed facts: *Dube & Anor* HB-30-92.

Undefended accused

Where an unrepresented accused is charged with an offence carrying a mandatory minimum sentence in the absence of special circumstances, the court must explain to X what special circumstances are: *Chaerera* 1988 (2) ZLR 226 (S) and *Maharangwe* S-5-90. Before the court imposes the mandatory prison sentence, it must explain in some detail what is meant by special reasons and the consequences of a failure to give special reasons: *Kaja* S-129-89.

Where an undefended accused admits possession of a prohibited item, the court must establish just what X is admitting as possession is a difficult legal concept: *Dube & Anor* 1988 (2) ZLR 385 (S).

The court should consider whether the case is a complex one. It should take into account factors such as:

- whether the ascertainment of facts includes difficult legal concepts such as "possession" "consent" or "knowledge";
- whether the facts themselves are complex or difficult;
- whether there is a need to prove "special reasons" or "special circumstances to avoid a minimum sentence;
- whether a long prison sentence is likely to follow on conviction.

In such cases, the court should consider to enter a plea of not guilty even if X has pleaded guilty and proceed in terms of s 272 CPEA.

It should also consider whether it would be fair and appropriate to advise X of the complexities of the matter and ask him or her if he or she has considered obtaining legal representation. If the court is satisfied that X should have legal representation but cannot afford it, the court should certify that legal representation be provided under the Legal Aid Act.

X should have been told that the offence involved a minimum mandatory sentence, unless they established special circumstances, and that these circumstances can be peculiar to the offender or to the commission of the offence. It is a procedural irregularity not sufficiently to explain or explore special circumstances: *Takawira* HH-155-91

The record must show that magistrate advised an unrepresented accused either during trial or during the sentencing procedure that he or she was in jeopardy of having a heavy minimum sentence imposed and could avoid this by showing special reasons: *Makawa & Anor* S-46-91

Suspension of mandatory sentence impermissible

Where the court decides that the mandatory **minimum** term of imprisonment or fine prescribed by the legislature has to be imposed, it may not suspend all or a portion of the mandatory minimum prison sentence or fine. See s 337(1) as read with paragraph 3 of the Sixth Schedule of the Criminal Procedure and Evidence Act. See *De Montille* 1979 RLR 105; *Kudavaranda* 1988 (2) ZLR 367 (H).

On the other hand, where the legislature lays down that it is mandatory for the court to impose imprisonment for a particular type of offence **but that the term of imprisonment is to be determined by the court**, the court may suspend all or a part of the prison term: *Patel* S-63-87. However, in *Horowitz* 1976 (1) RLR 238 (A) at 241D it was stated that the court will not lightly suspend the whole of the sentence where imprisonment has been made mandatory for an offence.

Delay in bringing to trial

See 1996 Vol. 8 No. 1 *Legal Forum* 35.

See *Kumusana* S-110-89; *Makoni* S-9-90; *Dube & Anor* 1989 (3) ZLR 245 (S); *Ruzario* 1990 (1) ZLR 359 (S); *Kundishora* 1990 (2) ZLR 30 (S); *Mlambo* S-221-91.

In the case of *Sibanda* HH-78-94, there was a delay of almost 7 years before bringing X to trial: his or her lawyer asked the magistrate for a permanent stay of prosecution; this was refused; he or she asked for the decision to be reviewed by a Judge of the High Court before the trial proceeded on the grounds:

- that the magistrate had no jurisdiction to decide the issue; or
- that he or she should have found that X's constitutional rights had been violated.

It was held that the High Court will only review criminal proceedings before they are completed in exceptional circumstances, which must be set out. The matter was therefore, not properly before it.

A magistrates court can decide on an application for a stay of prosecution itself unless either party asks it to refer the matter to the Supreme Court or if it considers the request for referral frivolous or vexatious. As it had not been asked to refer this case, its decision was competent.

The lawyer could have asked the magistrates court to grant a stay of prosecution or alternatively to refer the matter to the Supreme Court.

It was still open to him or her at the resumed hearing in the magistrates court to request that the matter be referred; as the case involved such a long delay, it could hardly be said to be frivolous or vexatious - the court would be obliged to refer it.

Crime victim compensation

Part XIX (ss 361-375 CPEA) lays down the procedures for awarding compensation to victims at the end of criminal trials. As a result of amendments effected in 1992 (Part XIX of Act 1 of 1992), all criminal courts now have very extensive powers to order the payment of compensation by convicted persons to persons who have been physically injured or suffered loss or damage to their property as a result of commission of the crimes in question.

Previously, the courts could award compensation at the end of a criminal trial only for property damage. Now they can also award compensation for physical injury. These provisions are intended to enhance the prospects for compensation being paid. Often victims are unaware of their rights to claim compensation in separate civil actions or lack the means to mount such separate civil actions. The extended capacity to award compensation at the conclusion of criminal cases is aimed at ensuring that as many victims of crime as possible are compensated. However, if the convicted persons, as is often the case, have no financial means or property which can be used to pay compensation, the victims will not be able to recover compensation under this system.

At the end of the criminal trial, a court may award compensation for personal injury and for damage or loss to property. Even if it is a magistrates court it is not limited in the amount it may award.

But a magistrate may not award compensation for loss or injury resulting from motor accidents or in personal injury cases, if the:

- amount of compensation is not readily qualifiable;
- extent of liability of the wrongdoer is not readily ascertainable.

However, it may only award such compensation if the injured party, or the prosecutor acting on the instructions of the injured party applies for such an award. It may not make such an award in traffic accident cases or where the amount of the compensation, or the convicted person's legal liability to pay compensation, is not readily ascertainable.

The court is under an obligation to ensure, wherever possible, that the injured person is acquainted with his or her right to apply for this award of compensation. The prosecutor should also draw the attention of the injured party of his or her right to claim compensation at the end of the criminal trial and, if requested to do so, must make the application on behalf of the injured party.

Forfeiture of items

In terms of s 62 CPEA, the court is given the discretion to order the forfeiture of certain items which have been used in connection with criminal activity. This discretion lies with the court and its exercise does not depend on prior application for forfeiture by the prosecution.

In summary, a court can order forfeiture:

- in respect of any crimes — weapons, instruments and articles used in the commission of crimes can be declared forfeit to the State;

- in respect of theft related crimes — vehicles used to transport stolen goods;
- in respect of statutory offences relating to possession, conveyance or supply of habit-forming drugs or harmful liquids, possession or dealing in precious metals or stones, theft under common law or statute and housebreaking with intent to commit a common law or statutory offence — vehicles, containers and articles used in the commission of these offences.

The factors which should be taken into account when deciding whether to order forfeiture are set out in the case of *Ndhlovu* (1) 1980 ZLR 96 (GD). These are:

- the nature of the article;
- what its role was in the commission of the offence;
- what possibility there is of the article being used again to commit similar offences;
- the effect of the forfeiture on the person or persons affected by it;
- whether, in the light of the value of the article, its forfeiture will lead to the imposition of a penalty which is disproportionate to the gravity of the offence committed;
- where the article is of considerable value, such as a motor-vehicle, whether that article has previously been used for a similar criminal purpose.

Forfeiture is part of the punishment and the value of the goods which may be declared to be forfeit must be taken into account. Especially, where these may be of substantial value, the courts should make some inquiry to determine their value: *Poswell & Anor* 1969 (4) SA 194 (R); *Barclay* 1969 (4) SA 195 (RA); *Pretorius & Anor* 1969 (4) SA 198 (R); *Kurimwi* 1985 (2) ZLR 63 (S) (forfeiture of motor vehicle inappropriate where used for smuggling only small amount of goods).

There are also specific forfeiture provisions in a number of other pieces of legislation. Some of the more important of these are:

- Section 188 of the Customs and Excise Act [*Chapter 20:02*] pertaining to forfeiture of smuggled items and things used in the commission of smuggling such as cars, ships and aircraft: *Mahomed* 1977 (2) RLR 207 (GD);
- Section 7 of the Exchange Control Act [*Chapter 22:05*] laying down that when the court convicts of certain offences under this Act involving gold, currency, goods or other property it may order forfeiture of these items unless the convicted person satisfies the court that there are special reasons for not ordering forfeiture.
- Section 106 of the Parks and Wildlife Act [*Chapter 20:14*] empowering the court to order forfeiture of the spoils of offences under this Act such as

trophies and animal carcasses and of items used in connection with offences under this Act such as weapons, explosives, tents vehicles and aircraft.

- Section 62 CPEA – forfeiture of ungraded meat illegally offered for sale: *Mutasa* 1988 (2) ZLR 4 (S).
- Section 31 of the Firearms Act [*Chapter 10:09*] empowering the court convicting of offences under this Act to order forfeiture of items such as firearms and ammunition.

Bringing into effect suspended sentence

Where the prosecutor applies for a suspended sentence to be brought into operation after X has been convicted of the current offence, the judge must examine the following things:

- whether the new offence was committed before the period of suspension expired; and
- if the period of suspension has not expired, whether the present crime amounts to a breach of the conditions of suspension.

Deciding whether period of suspension has expired

A sentence may be suspended for up to five years. The period of suspension normally commences on the date that X was sentenced. If, however, only a portion of a prison sentence has been suspended and X has had to serve a term of imprisonment, the period of suspension only begins to run after X is released from prison after serving that term with or without remission of sentence. Evidence from the prison service of the date of release should be elicited where necessary.

Sentences are usually suspended on condition that X does not **commit** a particular type of offence during the period of suspension. In this case, the vital question is whether he or she committed the offence during the period of suspension. If he or she did so, the fact that he or she is only tried for the offence after the suspended sentence expired does not prevent the suspended sentence from being brought into operation: *Deuss* 1972 (1) RLR 121 (GD).

Sometimes sentences are suspended on condition that X is not **convicted of** a particular type of offence during the period of the suspension. Here the vital question will be whether or not the period of suspension had expired at the date when X was convicted of the current offence.

Deciding whether accused had breached conditions of suspension

The criminal action of X must constitute a breach of the conditions laid down for suspension of the previous sentence. If the condition was that he or she does not commit a crime of dishonesty during the period of suspension, the commission of the crime of negligent driving or assault will not amount to a breach of this condition.

Suspended sentence imposed by High Court

A magistrate cannot bring into effect a suspended sentence imposed by the High Court: s 358(5) CPEA; *Chitengu* 1980 ZLR 84 (GD). After sentencing X for his or her current offence, the magistrate must proceed in terms of s 54(2) of the MCA and refer the case to the High Court so that the High Court can bring into effect the suspended sentence if it considers that it is appropriate to do so.

A suspended sentence does not have to be brought into operation by the judicial officer who originally imposed it. A judicial officer other than the judicial officer who originally imposed it can bring into effect a suspended sentence. If a different judicial officer is dealing with the current case, the second judicial officer should have before him or her the record of the original trial.

Where passing of sentence has been postponed

Most of what is stated above relating to suspended sentences applies to situations where it emerges that previously the passing of sentence on X was conditionally postponed. The judge convicting and sentencing X for the current offence must also decide whether X must also now be sentenced for the previous offence because he or she has breached the conditions of the postponement within the period for which sentence was postponed. However, it must be noted that the period of postponement begins on the date of conviction. As with suspension, a magistrate cannot pass sentence if the High Court postponed the passing of sentence. Again the case must be referred to the High Court.

Subsequent amendment of sentence

In terms of s 201(2) CPEA, when a wrong sentence is mistakenly handed down it may be amended before or **immediately after** it has been recorded.

It is not every mistake which can be corrected under this provision. The mistake must be a genuine one. In handing down sentence the judicial officer must have said something different from what he or she had intended to say or must have pronounced what he or she realises afterwards was an incompetent sentence. For example, if the judicial officer intended to impose a sentence of six weeks' imprisonment and he or she discovers immediately afterwards that he or she erroneously recorded a sentence of six months" imprisonment, he or she may correct the record accordingly: *Sikumbuzo* 1967 (4) SA 602 (RA). In both the following cases, the review court decided that the magistrate had been wrong in using this section to try to alter the sentence as, in both, the magistrate had imposed competent sentences and then merely had second thoughts afterwards. The provision could not be used in these sorts of circumstances as the magistrate was *functus officio*.

In *Chikumbirike* HH-307-84, the magistrate imposed a jail sentence on a juvenile and then some time later called X back to court and said he or she had decided that, being a juvenile, he or she should not be in prison. He or she then purported to substitute a corporal punishment sentence for the sentence of imprisonment.

In *Nyamufarira* HH-335-83, the magistrate imposed a fine for cycle theft. Later on the same day, he or she had X brought back to court and announced to the prisoner that, on reflection, the sentence he or she had imposed was too lenient and proceeded to substitute a prison sentence for the fine!

Where the error is only discovered some time after the sentence was recorded, the matter should be referred to a judge for amendment.

Thus in *Ncube & Ors* HB-150-88, the magistrate purported to alter a sentence imposed upon X a month previously because it had come to light subsequently that they were juveniles. It was held that it was too late to have relied on s 201(2) and the matter should instead have been referred to a High Court judge.

The judicial officer can only amend the sentence if the mistake was his or her own. He or she cannot amend the sentence if the mistake was that of the prosecutor.

In *Mamwere* 1978 RLR 374 (GD), X was sentenced to a fine. Later the same day the public prosecutor informed the magistrate that he or she had just discovered that X had a previous conviction for the same type of offence and that he or she had therefore been wrongly treated as a first offender. X was recalled and he or she admitted the previous conviction. The magistrate set aside the sentence and substituted a prison sentence. The review court said that s 201(2) did not apply as the mistake was that of the prosecutor, not the magistrate.

Passing of sentence by judicial officer other than judicial officer who convicted

In *Manga* HH-122-06, the judge pointed out that under s 334(7) CPEA, sentence may, "in the absence of" the magistrate who convicted the offender, be passed by any magistrate of that court. In order to use this provision, the sentencing magistrate must, firstly, note on the record the absence of the trial magistrate and the reasons for such absence. Secondly, the accused must be given the opportunity of addressing in mitigation. Finally, it is incumbent on the second magistrate to consider the evidence recorded and upon which the verdict is returned. The words "in the absence of the magistrate who convicted" are unqualified by the statute and should be given the widest possible meaning, which is that the magistrate in question could be absent for whatever reason, e.g. retirement, leave, discharge from service, death, or lengthy absence abroad for whatever reason. While these are normal forms of absence, there can be no doubt that any absence for an appreciable length of time would bring into play the provisions of the section, especially if prejudice were to be caused if the convicted person made to await the return of the magistrate to the courthouse. Similarly, the fact that the trial magistrate is an appreciable distance away from the court would allow the provision to be invoked. The phrase must thus be measured in terms of the triad of time, space and circumstances.

Change of plea after verdict and sentence

When a person has been convicted on a guilty plea and sentenced, and the required procedure has been followed, the trial court is *functus officio*. *Mudambi* S-156-95.

If a person has been convicted and sentenced and then wishes to change his or her plea on the basis that he or she had been unduly influenced by the police to plead guilty, he or she should make such application on appeal rather than in an application under s 41 of the High Court Act, 1981.

In *Muchamba* S-27-92, on appeal against a conviction for smuggling, counsel for appellant argued that the appellant's guilty plea in the trial court had not been made voluntarily, advisedly and understandingly, and that there had therefore been a miscarriage of justice. He submitted that the sentence imposed should be set aside and the case should be remitted to the trial court so that an application could be made to change the plea to one of not guilty. It was held that as the trial court had already convicted and sentenced the appellant it was *functus officio* and that the court could not therefore entertain an application for change of plea.

See also *Kaiwona & Ors* S-182-93.

Section 8

Judicial Officer's duties in regard to undefended accused

General

Remember that if X is not legally represented he or she is normally at a severe disadvantage by comparison with the person who has a lawyer to represent him. X is usually completely unfamiliar with the law and with the rules of evidence and procedure. The formal legal environment will often be completely alien to him or her and he or she may be totally overawed by the atmosphere.

As he or she is facing criminal charges he or she will be anxious and apprehensive and may not be able to compose himself or herself and put forward a proper defence. He or she will often not know what he or she must do to defend himself or herself and what is relevant in relation to the charges he or she is facing. This will particularly be the case when the charges are complex and involve technical elements. Whereas X may be out of his or her depth entirely, the State is represented by a trained prosecutor who is schooled in the law.

Bearing all this in mind, the judicial officer is under an obligation to ensure that X receives a fair trial. The judicial officer must assist X to the extent that is necessary to ensure that justice is done. This is not to say that the judicial officer must assume the role of being X's defence lawyer. He or she or does not have to conduct the defence. He or she does, however, have to try as far as possible to ensure that points which are pertinent to the defence case do emerge.

What follows is a summary of the main obligations which judicial officers have at different stages of criminal proceedings to safeguard X's interests.

In *Musindo* 1997 (1) ZLR 395 (H), during the trial the magistrate wrongly delegated his or her responsibilities of explaining X's rights and other aspects of the trial to the court interpreter. The interpreter's explanation was not recorded. The High Court pointed out that X's right to maintain his or her silence had been severely eroded by legislation. This inroad into X's age-old privilege can be justified only where there is the strictest of explanations to him or herof the extent of his or her rights and by the clearest of cautioning to him or her of the consequences of failure to give an explanation where an innocent person may be expected to do so. The only person who can ensure that X understands the choices open to him or her and the consequences of the choice he or she makes is the presiding officer. Where he or she abrogates his or her responsibility and leaves the function of explanation to an interpreter, a court on review cannot repose any confidence in that magistrate.

Duties during pre-trial period

At confirmation of statement proceedings:

- Explain that if X admits he or she made the statement freely and voluntarily, the statement is admissible on production at his or her trial;
- If X says it was not freely and voluntarily made, find out on what basis he or she is saying this and explain that if he or she fails to mention relevant facts pertaining thereto this may lead to adverse inferences being drawn later.

At remand:

- Whether or not X raised this, check that there is information which leads to a reasonable suspicion that he or she committed a crime and thus that there is a proper basis for a remand;
- Ensure that X is not kept on remand for unreasonably long periods;
- Where the State asks for a remand in custody, carefully probe the reasons for opposing bail in order to check that they have substance. (Do not automatically disallow bail whenever the State opposes bail.)

Duties during trial

In trial proceedings:

- Ensure that the charge is properly and clearly formulated.
- Be extremely careful in checking a guilty plea before accepting it.
- If the case is complex and serious, consider whether X will only be able to receive a fair trial if he or she is legally represented. If this is the situation and X does not have the money to employ his or her own lawyer, certify that it is desirable in the interests of justice that he or she be assigned a lawyer paid for by the State.

- Carefully explain that failure to mention salient features of defence at the outset may lead to adverse inferences being drawn. Explain that this is because usually an innocent person would disclose these features right at the start to establish his or her innocence.
- Inform him or her of right to cross-examine State witnesses, explaining to him or herwhat cross-examination is for and the necessity for him or her to ensure that where he or she disagrees with their evidence his or her version must be put to them so that they can comment thereon. Make sure he or she understands that if he or she disagrees with any evidence they have given, he or she must challenge it in cross-examination. Failure to do so might be held against him.
- Where accused does not do so, ask pertinent questions of State witnesses so that lines of defence raised by X in his or her outline are explored with the State witnesses.
- At the close of State case, examine whether State made out *prima facie* case such as to require accused to be put to his or her defence. (Do this even where there is no application for discharge).
- Where X is put to his or her defence, explain to him or her that he or she has a right to call witnesses and to testify himself. (If he or she wishes to call witnesses and they are not present, adjourn so that they can be called).
- If X calls witnesses assist him or her in extracting relevant information from those witnesses and prevent prosecutor from exceeding the bounds of proper cross-examination.
- If X testifies but then refuses to answer questions carefully explain that adverse inferences may be drawn from refusal to answer questions which an innocent person would be expected to respond to.
- If X does not testify but questions are put to him or her which he or she refuses to answer, carefully explain to him or her that adverse inferences may be drawn as an innocent person would not refuse to answer such questions.
- X must be told of his or her right to sum up his or her case at the end of the trial.

In *Musindo* 1997 (1) ZLR 395 (H), the court criticized a magistrate who had made little inquiry into why there had been a delay of almost 7 years in bringing the matter to trial. It said that while X had not raised this issue, as he or she was undefended he or she was entitled to look to the magistrate to ensure that his or her rights were not infringed by the machinery of the State. In this case, the magistrate's inquiry and the prosecutor's explanation were brief and inadequate. A prima facie breach of X's constitutional rights was left unexplained and constituted an irregularity.

Explaining rights regarding mitigation of sentence

If X is found guilty, inform him or her of his or her right to call evidence in mitigation of sentence and to address in mitigation. If he or she does not know what sorts of factors are salient in regard to sentence, tell him or her what sort of things may constitute mitigation.

Suggested ways of explaining matters to accused

The duties of the judicial officer to safeguard the rights of undefended accused are set out above. It is the duty of the judicial officer to explain in a simple and understandable way what rights the undefended accused has at the different stages of a criminal case. What follows are some suggestions as to how these explanations can be formulated so as to ensure that X understands what it is that he or she must do during criminal proceedings.

Confirmation of warned and cautioned statements

The judicial officer must first read out the brief allegations against him. These will be found in the preamble to the warned and cautioned statement.

Regarding the statement itself the judicial officer should say these things to X:

- If you admit that you made this statement freely and voluntarily, the statement will be confirmed by me and it can be produced in evidence at your trial.
- You now have a chance to tell me about how this statement came to be made. You must tell me if you made this statement and if you made it freely and voluntarily. You must tell me if the police did or said anything to you to force, pressure, induce or trick you into making the statement? If you fail to mention relevant details about how you were forced or induced to make this statement and you only tell the court about these things when you are on trial, the court may end up disbelieving these details.

If accused says the statement was not made by him or her but was concocted by the police and he or she was then forced to sign it:

> You have told me that the police forced, tricked or induced you to sign a statement which was concocted by the police and not made by you. What exactly did the police do to force or induce you to sign this statement? Who did these things to you and when were they done? Do you know the names and ranks of the police officers concerned or can you describe them to me if you do not know their names?

If accused says he or she made the statement but it was not made freely and voluntarily:

> You have told me that you did not make this statement freely and voluntarily. You must tell me why you are saying this. You must tell me exactly what happened

> which caused you to make a statement when you did not want to do so. Who did these things to you and when were these things done? Do you know the names and ranks of the police officers concerned or can you describe them to me if you do not know their names?

If X alleges that he or she was assaulted:

> What injuries did you sustain as a result of these alleged assaults? Do you still have any injuries or marks on your body which show that these assaults were in fact committed? If yes, please show me these injuries.

If the judicial officer intends to have a medical examination carried out on X, the judicial officer should tell X what is going to happen and why.

Questioning on guilty plea

When X pleads guilty:

> You have pleaded guilty to the charge. I will now ask you a series of questions so that I can satisfy myself that you are properly admitting to this charge.

The judicial officer must then ask a series of questions to satisfy himself or herself that X is admitting to all the essential elements of the crime and to the material facts upon which the charge is based and that he or she has no defence to this charge. In particular, questions must be asked to clarify points such as the intent in cases of assault with intent to do grievous bodily harm and the nature of possession in rhino horns and ivory cases. The question "Why did you do it?" will often reveal a defence such as provocation, intoxication or self-defence.

Explaining to accused that he or she must give an outline of his or her defence

- You have pleaded not guilty to the charge. You have heard the summary of the State case against you. You now have the opportunity to outline your defence and state the basis upon which you deny these allegations. When you make this statement you must refer to every important fact upon which you rely for your defence. If you fail to mention an important fact, the court may hold this failure against you.
- What I need from you at this stage is only a summary of your defence. You should tell me what your defence is to the charge/charges (why you say you are not guilty) and the main facts upon which this defence is based. Later in the proceedings after the State has produced its evidence against you will be able to present your own evidence in detail.

Note. Although X is supposed only to outline his or her defence at this stage, if X wants to give full details of his or her defence rather than simply a summary, he or she should be allowed by the judicial officer to do so. He or she may not be able to understand the difference between a summary and a full presentation of his or her defence at the outset. If he or she wishes to describe his or her defence in detail it is in the interests of justice that he or she be allowed to do so.

Production of extra-curial statement by State

Before any extra-curial statement allegedly made by X to the police or to anyone in authority over him, such as his or her employer, is produced in evidence, the judicial officer must ask X:

> Did you make this statement and did you make it freely and voluntarily and without undue influence being used?

If he or she says "No" a further enquiry and possibly a trial within a trial will have to follow.

Explaining right to call witnesses

You have a right to call witnesses to testify on your behalf. Do you have any witnesses whom you want to call?

In *Musindo* 1997 (1) ZLR 395 (H) the court criticized a magistrate who, when the accused indicated that he wanted to call a person who at been summoned as a State witness but not called by the State, the magistrate acted in so hectoring and minatory a fashion as to result in the accused failing to call the witness.

Explaining right to cross-examine State witnesses

- Listen carefully to the evidence of the State witnesses. After the prosecutor has asked them questions, you will be given the opportunity to ask them questions. If a witness says anything which you think is untrue or with which you disagree you must ask the witness questions about these things. If you do not ask questions about the things which you disagree with the court may assume that you do not disagree with these things.
- If you think that the witness knows things favourable to your defence but which he or she has not told the court about, you should also ask him or her questions to draw out these things. [It sometimes helps to offer X a pen and paper to make notes on the points he or she wants to challenge.]

After X has finished cross-examining the witness, the judicial officer should draw X's attention to "damaging" aspects which have not been canvassed by him or her and invite him or her to ask questions on those aspects.

The judicial officer should also put to State witnesses any points contained in X's initial outline of his or her defence which he or she has not raised during cross-examination.

Defence case

Right to produce evidence:

> You have heard the evidence against you from the State witnesses. You now have the opportunity to produce evidence in your defence. You yourself may give evidence. If you wish to testify yourself, you must take the oath and swear that that you will tell the truth. If you testify the prosecutor will be able to ask you questions about what you have said. If you decide not to give evidence on oath yourself, the prosecutor and the court may still put questions to you. If you refuse to answer these questions the court may hold this failure against you. You may also call any witnesses whom you think will support your defence and help to disprove the State case.

If X wishes to give evidence himself as well as calling witnesses the judicial officer should state:

> You should give your own evidence first before you call your witnesses. If you have any reason for wanting your witnesses to give evidence before you testify, you should tell me what those reasons are and if I think that they are good reasons I will permit you to call your witnesses first before you testify. [In terms of the proviso to s 188(5) CPEA X must normally give his or her testimony before he or she calls his or her witnesses.]

Accused persons should normally give evidence from the witness box and not from the dock. Sometimes, however, accused persons do not want to give evidence from the witness box, possibly because they think that this is "the enemy camp". In such cases magistrates should not insist that they take the witness stand. They can give sworn evidence from the dock.

In a proper case, X should be allowed to sit while giving evidence.

When first defence witness is called tell X:

> You can put questions to your defence witnesses to draw out their evidence but you must not put questions to them which suggest the answers they are to give. You must let them tell their own stories and you must not put words in their mouths.

Re-examination of defence witnesses:

> You can now ask the witness further questions but you may only now ask him or herquestions on new matters which have come up in response to the questioning of the witness by the prosecutor. You must not question him or her about things which

you questioned him or herabout previously unless new matters have come up on these points in response to questions from the prosecutor.

Questioning of accused who elect to remain silent

You have refused to answer the questions which have been put to you. I must tell you that this refusal may lead the court to form an unfavourable impression and to hold this refusal against you because the allegations made by the State against you, through the its witnesses, will then be uncontradicted and unexplained by you.

Summing up

You now have the right to sum up your case. You should highlight the important points in your defence case and point out what you consider to be the weaknesses of the State case and any serious contradictions in the evidence of the State witnesses.

Evidence in mitigation

I have already found you guilty of the crime of ... Before I impose sentence upon you, you have a chance to give evidence in mitigation of sentence. You must tell me anything about this case which you think serves to lessen your moral blameworthiness. You should also tell me anything about your personal circumstances at present which you think may persuade me to impose a more lenient sentence.

Guilty plea: Where X has pleaded guilty, the court must investigate the motive of X in the commission of the crime to find out whether the motive was something like dire economic need which would amount to a mitigating factor.

Not guilty plea: Where X had pleaded not guilty, any factors of a mitigatory nature which have emerged during the trial must be taken into account by the court even if X does not raise them at the time of mitigation.

Personal circumstances:

- Are you married? How many children do you have and how old are they?
- What do you pay each month for food, accommodation and travel and what other expenses do you have?

Where the judicial officer is contemplating imposing a fine, he or she should ask these sorts of question:

- Are you employed and what is your take-home pay?
- You have told me that you are not in regular employment. Do you have any

source of income at all? [i.e. does he or she work in the informal sector?] What is the amount of your average weekly earnings?

- Do you have any savings? How much? [This question should be asked whether or not X is employed.]
- You have told me you are unemployed and have no savings, Do you have any possessions which you could sell to raise money? Do you have any friends or relatives who would be prepared to lend you money to pay a fine which I might impose?
- Do you have money on your person to pay a fine?
- Can you pay a fine in weekly or monthly instalments and what amount of instalment can you pay? (I cannot give you more than 12 months to pay the full amount of the fine I impose.)

Where X's actions have caused damage or pecuniary loss:

The judicial officer should ask X these sorts of questions:

- (If this has not been canvassed in evidence:) Do you agree that X suffered damage or loss?
- It is in your interests that you make good the loss caused by the offence which you committed. If you make restitution or pay compensation the court may take this into account in your favour when it imposes sentence upon you.
- Do you wish to make good the damage or the loss?
- How will you do this and when?

In cases of malicious injury to property involving the destruction of a hut:

- Are you willing to rebuild the hut and, if you are, over what period of time will you do this?

Section 9

Record of Proceedings

Reid-Rowland 16-39 – 16-44

Full record

Where there is no mechanical recorder for recording the evidence, the trial judge must keep a full handwritten record of the proceedings. He or she must make full, clear and accurate written notes of everything that is said and everything that happens during the hearing of the case which is of any relevance in relation to the outcome of the case and the sentence.

All applications made to court must be recorded, together with the reasons why these were made: *Maniko & Ors* HH-44-91. Evidence-in-chief can normally be paraphrased by the recording judge except for important aspects which must be fully recorded. All cross-examination must be taken down in question-and-answer form.

The keeping of a proper record is vitally important. Where there are substantial and material deficiencies in the transcript this will constitute a gross irregularity necessitating the quashing of the conviction as the absence of a proper record makes it impossible for a review or appeal court properly to assess the correctness or validity of the proceedings.

In *Moyo & Ors* HB-15-93, the court said that a record must be clear and intelligible. The handwriting should not be illegible and the judicial officer must not use obscure abbreviations. There is no excuse for not recording the questions and answers with sufficient clarity.

Records forwarded for review or scrutiny must be full and accurate. The blame for sending incomplete records for review or scrutiny lies entirely with the trial judge, not the clerk of court, because it is the former who certify that the records are complete. Before so certifying, it is incumbent on the trial judge to check that all documents used in the proceedings are included in the records.

See *Davy* 1988 (1) ZLR 386 (S); *Ndebele* 1988 (2) ZLR 249 (H); *Ndlovu* HB-98-89; *Nyedziwa* HB-33-90; *Maniko & Anor* HH-44-91.

The evidence must be recorded in such a way that the appeal or review court can understand it. When the witness says: "He or she then turned in this direction" and indicates the direction or "He or she was this height" and indicates the height, the judge must put a note in brackets "(Indicates left)" or "(Indicates a height of approximately two metres)".

Arrangement of record

The record should be arranged in this sequence:

1. The judgment (verdict and sentence and reasons therefor) or, if there has been a guilty plea which was accepted, the reasons for the sentence.
2. Charge sheet or summons.
3. Details of prosecution allegation or agreed statement of facts.
4. Recorded evidence (numbered and in correct numerical sequence and stapled together).
5. Documentary exhibits, including the State and defence outlines or statement of facts.
6. Any document recording previous convictions or certifying the absence of previous convictions.
7. The warrant committing X to prison, if any.

All these papers must be secured together and placed in a case cover.

Lost record

Although all possible care must be taken to ensure that records of cases do not go missing, from time to time records do get lost. The record may go missing prior to or subsequent to the reaching of verdict and the imposing of the sentence.

If the record goes missing whilst the trial is still taking place (i.e. before all the evidence has been heard and the judicial officer has arrived at his or her verdict), then X is entitled to have the case proceed from the point at which it left off. Thus with part-heard cases, the clerk of court under the direction and supervision of the presiding judicial officer, must reconstruct the record from the best secondary evidence. Affidavits should be taken from witnesses and those present.

Where X had pleaded guilty the case can then proceed on the basis of the restored record, provided there is no prejudice to X. If, however, he or she has pleaded not guilty the witnesses who have previously given evidence must be recalled in order to ascertain whether they agree that the version of their testimony in the reconstructed record is correct. X and the State should be permitted to cross-examine the witnesses relating to the correctness of the reconstructed record: *Sibanda* HH-80-91.

If the trial has been completed, the trial judge is *functus officio* (has finished dealing with the matter) and the clerk of court must, by affidavit, state that the record has been lost and proceed to reconstruct the record by obtaining affidavits from the judge, witnesses and others present as to the contents of the record. Both parties must be given an opportunity to peruse the reconstructed record and to give their versions. Thereafter the record will be sent for review or appeal: *Sibanda* HH-80-91.

Tampering with record

Liver HH-196-92: When a magistrate was advised that she had passed an incompetent sentence, she tore up the original sheet and substituted a competent sentence. The trial court has no power to "correct" its decision like that; such tampering with a record as a criminal offence; the case could only be referred to the High Court for correction there. The amended sentence was set aside and a permissible sentence substituted.

Section 10

Appeals

Reid-Rowland Chapter 27

Appeal on merits

An appeal in a criminal case is a rehearing of the case on the merits and the appeal is usually heard on the basis of the evidence on which the decision appealed against was given. Only in very limited circumstances can new evidence be introduced in such an appeal.

Appeals from the magistrates court to the High Court

Nature of appeal

A person convicted in the High Court can appeal to the High Court

- against conviction for any offence,
- conviction and sentence,
- sentence; or
- any order of the court following the sentence.

[s 60(1)(a) MCA]

Leave to appeal

There is no requirement that an accused must obtain leave to appeal from the magistrate who convicted him or her before he or she can proceed to take the case on appeal.

If the Attorney-General is dissatisfied with a decision to discharge the accused at the end of the prosecution case, he may, with the leave of a judge of the Supreme Court, appeal to the Supreme Court against the ruling. [s 198(4)(a) CPEA] See *AG v Mzizi* 1991 (2) ZLR 321 (S).

The Attorney-General may, with the leave of the Supreme Court, appeal against a judgment of the High Court if he is dissatisfied with that judgment:

- on a point of law; or
- because the High Court acquitted or quashed the conviction of the accused on a view of the facts that could not reasonably be entertained. (For this to be satisfied the verdict of innocence must be an unreasonable and perverse inference on the basis of the primary facts.) See *AG v Paweni Trade Corporation (Pvt) Ltd* 1990 (1) ZLR 24 (S)
  [s 61 MCA]

The Attorney-General may, with the leave of a judge of the Supreme Court, appeal against a sentence imposed by the High Court, if he considers that the sentence was inadequate either:

- in the light of the findings of the court and the nature of the charge; or
- because the sentence was based on findings of fact for which there was no evidence or on a view of the facts which could not reasonably be entertained.

[s 62(1)(b) MCA]

Magistrate's response to noting of appeal

Within seven days of the noting of an appeal by a legally represented person the trial magistrate must, insofar as this may be necessary having regard to the judgment already filed, deliver to the clerk of court a written statement setting out the facts he or she found to be proved and his or her reasons for judgment and sentence and dealing with the grounds on which the appeal is based: Rule 23 of Supreme Court (Magistrates Court) (Criminal Appeals) Rules, 1979 [SI 504 of 1979].

Within four days of the noting of an appeal by a person who is not legally represented, the magistrate may deliver to the clerk of court a statement containing any comments which he or she may wish to make on the grounds of Appeal: Rule 28 of the Supreme Court (Magistrates Court) (Criminal Appeals) Rules, 1979.

The magistrate's response to the noting of the appeal enables the appellant to amend his grounds of appeal if he wishes to do so.

Where a notice of appeal contains allegations about the conduct of a case, the magistrate has a duty to comment on the allegations. This is why the notice of appeal is served on the magistrate: *Chikafa* S-162-88.

In *Chari* 1989 (1) ZLR 231 (S), a magistrate had failed to comment on a notice of appeal which correctly alleged that he or she had misdirected himself by declaring a witness to be hostile without following the correct procedure. Held that the magistrate had a duty to assist the appeal court by commenting on the allegation concerning his or her misdirection and he or she had failed in this duty.

In *Gujral* HH-73-90, a regional magistrate had delayed commenting on the appellant's notice of appeal until after the record had been transcribed, which was done eight months after the notice had been lodged. The judge pointed out that it was the magistrate's duty to ensure that his or her reply to the notice was given expeditiously. He or she said that arrangements must be made for magistrates to give their responses to notices as soon as possible after the notices are filed and not many months later when records are transcribed.

In a number of cases in the Supreme Court, it has been stressed that if the certified record is inadequate, because, for instance, it does not indicate what facts were found by the trial court or no reasons for the decision are given, the appeal court may have to set aside the conviction because it will not be possible for the court to be satisfied that the conviction was warranted: *Makawa & Anor* S-46-91; *Marevesa* S-108-91.

Where the appeal to the High Court involves a question of law only, a judge of the High Court may request the magistrate to state the question of law, together with all the circumstances under which the question arose. In this instance, a full copy of the record does not have to be prepared. All that is necessary are the particulars of the trial, the notice of the appeal, the stated case and such other documents as the judge directs. [s 37 HCA]

Bail pending appeal

Reid-Rowland 6-17 – 6-20

Third Schedule offences

Where a person has been convicted of a Third Schedule offence, a magistrate may only admit a person to bail or alter his or her bail conditions if the Attorney-General has given his or her consent: proviso (iii) to s 123(1) CPEA. The specified offences are:

The specified offences in Part 1 of the Third Schedule are:

- murder where it was committed in certain specified circumstances such as where it was premeditated;
- rape or aggravated indecent assault where it was committed in certain specified circumstances such as multiple rape of a victim;
- robbery where it was committed in certain specified circumstances such as where firearms were used;
- assault or indecent assault of a child under 16 involving the infliction of grievous bodily harm;

- kidnapping or unlawful detention involving the infliction of grievous bodily harm;
- contravening the following sections of CLCA: 20 (treason); 21 (concealing treason); 22 (subverting constitutional government); 23 (insurgency, banditry, sabotage or terrorism); 24 (recruiting or training insurgents, bandits, saboteurs or terrorists); 25 (training as insurgent, bandit, saboteur or terrorist); 26 (supplying weapons to insurgents, bandits, saboteurs or terrorists); 27 (possessing weapons for insurgency, banditry, sabotage or terrorism) or 29 (harbouring, concealing or failing to report insurgent, bandit, saboteur or terrorist);
- An offence in Part II of the Third Schedule where the accused has previously been convicted of any offence specified in the Third Schedule or has allegedly committed such offence whilst on bail in respect of an offence in the Third Schedule.

The offences specified in Part II to the Third Schedule are:

- treason;
- murder in circumstances other than those specified in Part I;
- attempted murder involving the infliction of grievous bodily harm;
- malicious damage to property involving arson or conspiracy, incitement or attempt to commit this offence;
- theft of a motor vehicle or conspiracy, incitement or attempt to commit this offence;
- any offence relating to dealing in or smuggling of ammunition, firearms, explosives or armaments or the possession of an automatic or semi-automatic firearm, explosives or armaments or conspiracy, incitement or attempt to commit this offence;
- any offence where the Attorney-General has notified the magistrate of his or her intention to indict the case direct to the High Court.

Other offences

Where a person who has been convicted of an offence, other than one of the specified ones, applies for bail, the magistrate who has convicted him or her has the discretion to grant bail pending the appeal. The criteria to be taken into account in making this decision have been explored in a number of cases. The main factors to weigh in the balance are the interrelated factors of the prospects on appeal and whether the granting of bail will jeopardise the interests of the administration of justice.

In *Kilpin* 1978 RLR 282 (A), the appeal court pointed out that the principles governing the granting of bail after conviction were different to those governing the granting of bail before conviction. Where the person has not yet been convicted he or she is still presumed innocent and the courts will lean in favour of granting him or her liberty before he or she is tried. On the other hand, where he or she has already been convicted, the presumption of innocence falls away. There are certain cases where bail pending appeal should not be granted such as where the person has been convicted of an offence which almost invariably attracts a lengthy prison term and there are no reasonable prospects of an appeal against the lengthy prison term succeeding to a material degree. The trial magistrate had thus been wrong to automatically extend bail granted before trial to the post-trial stage where the person had pleaded guilty to such an offence.

Where the evidence of guilt is overwhelming there are no reasonable prospects of a successful appeal against conviction, but if there is room for a difference of opinion regarding conviction there would be a reasonable prospect on appeal.

However in *Williams* 1980 ZLR 466 (A), the appeal court said that even after conviction the court should lean in favour of liberty if this would not endanger the interests of the administration of justice. The prospects of success on appeal must be balanced against the interests of the administration of justice. The less chance of success on appeal the greater the chance there was of the convicted person absconding. But it was putting it too highly to say that bail should only be granted where there was a reasonable prospect of the appeal succeeding. On the other hand, in serious cases even where there was a reasonable prospect of success on appeal, bail should sometimes be refused, notwithstanding that there is little danger of the convicted person absconding. See also *Benatar* 1985 (2) ZLR 205 (H).

In deciding whether the administration of justice will be prejudiced if bail is granted, the court should take into account the seriousness of the offence, the seriousness of the penalty imposed, whether the appeal is against conviction or only against sentence and the prospects of success on appeal. With a serious offence which normally attracts a substantial prison sentence there will be a pronounced risk that the convicted person will flee from justice if released, especially if he or she has no reasonable chance of successfully appealing against conviction. There will be a very great risk of flight if X is only appealing against sentence and the most he or she can hope for is that the prison sentence will be subject to some minor adjustment. Even where there is a reasonable prospect of success on appeal against such a conviction, the convicted person may not be inclined to take the chance of the appeal succeeding, but may take flight instead if he or she is released pending appeal. With less serious offences not attracting drastic penalties the position will be radically different.

In assessing the prospects of success on appeal, the magistrate is obviously placed in a somewhat difficult position as, to a certain extent, he or she is being asked to come to a decision on the reliability of his or her conviction and/or sentence. He or she must try to assess this as objectively as possible.

Appeals from High Court to Supreme Court

See Reid Rowland Chapter 27.

Nature of appeal

There are several types of appeal:

- a person convicted in the High Court can appeal to the Supreme Court against conviction, conviction and sentence, or sentence;
- a person convicted in the magistrates court who has appealed unsuccessfully to the High Court against conviction, sentence or conviction and sentence can appeal further to the Supreme Court;
- a person dissatisfied with the judgment of the High Court on review (other than a review in terms of s 57 MCA) can appeal against the judgment to the Supreme Court.

Appeal as of right

There is an unrestricted right of appeal if the appeal:

- is on a point of law only [s 44(2)(a) HCA];
- is against conviction if a sentence of death has been imposed [s 44(2)(c) MCA];
- is against sentence if a sentence of death has been imposed [s 44(2)(c) MCA];
- if the sentence was fixed by law and the appeal is on the ground that the sentence passed was not the sentence fixed by law. [s 44(2)(d) MCA]. This allows for an appeal against an incompetent sentence e.g. where a sentence of imprisonment is imposed where only a fine was allowed or where the sentence is in excess of the court's jurisdiction or above the maximum provided.

Appeal with leave of court

Leave to appeal is necessary for any appeal to the Supreme Court:

- where the ground of appeal involves a question of fact only or a question of mixed law and fact. The ground of appeal is that there was no evidence, or insufficient evidence, to justify the conviction will be treated as an appeal involving a question of fact alone [s 44(3) HCA].
- where the appeal against sentence involves grounds other than those referred to above in respect of which no leave to appeal is required [s 44(2)(e) HCA].

- where the appeal is against an interlocutory order or given an interlocutory judgment in relation to criminal proceedings in the High Court. (An interlocutory order or judgment is one where the decision does not finally decide any issue between the parties, such as a ruling on jurisdiction, or on the admissibility of evidence.) [s 44(5) HCA]

When application for leave to be made

The application for leave to appeal should be made orally to the trial judge immediately after sentence has been passed. The applicant's grounds for appeal should be recorded as part of the record.

If an oral application is not made immediately, a written application may, in special circumstances, be filed with the registrar within twelve days of the date of the sentence. The application must state why an oral application was not made, the proposed grounds of appeal and the grounds on which it is contended that leave to appeal should be granted. [r 263 High Court Rules.] One situation where special circumstances would be present is there the judgment was very lengthy and complex and counsel could not have been expected immediately to have dealt with the many issues raised in the judgment. In such an instance counsel should intimate to the court that a written application of appeal with be submitted later.

A copy of the written application must be served on the Attorney-General immediately after it is filed with the registrar. Within two days of service on him, the Attorney-General may file written submissions with the registrar. The registrar will then place before the presiding judge the application together with any submissions from the Attorney-General. The judge may require oral argument on any particular point or points raised. The judge may hear such argument in chambers or in open court. The judge may grant or refuse the application.

If a High Court judge refuses to grant leave, an application can be made to a judge of the Supreme Court for leave to appeal. This application must be made within ten days of the date when leave to appeal was refused, or within fifteen days of conviction, whichever is the later date. [r 3 &19 Supreme Court Rules.]

Basis for decision on whether to grant leave

The decision as to whether or not to grant leave to appeal depends on the prospects of the appeal succeeding. There must be a reasonable prospect of success. It is not enough that the case is merely an arguable one.

An application for leave to appeal against sentence should be dealt with more liberally as sentencing is a difficult task and there is usually room for a difference of opinion on the appropriate sentence, particularly where the circumstances are unusual and without precedent: see *McGown* 1995 (2) ZLR 81 (S)

Appeals by Attorney-General

If the Attorney-General is dissatisfied with a decision to discharge the accused at the end of the prosecution case, he may, with the leave of a judge of the Supreme Court, appeal to the Supreme Court against the ruling. [s 198(4)(a) CPEA]. See *AG v Mzizi* 1991 (2) ZLR 321 (S).

The Attorney-General may, with the leave of the Supreme Court, appeal against a judgment of the High Court if he is dissatisfied with that judgment:

- on a point of law; or
- because the High Court acquitted or quashed the conviction of the accused on a view of the facts that could not reasonably be entertained. (For this to be satisfied the the verdict of innocence must be an unreasonable and perverse inference on the basis of the primary facts.) See *AG v Paweni Trade Corporation (Pvt) Ltd* 1990 (1) ZLR 24 (S)
  [s 44(6) HCA]

The Attorney-General may, with the leave of a judge of the Supreme Court, appeal against a sentence imposed by the High Court, if he considers that the sentence was inadequate either:

- in the light of the findings of the court and the nature of the charge; or
- because the sentence was based on findings of fact for which there was no evidence or on a view of the facts which could not reasonably be entertained.
  [s 44(7)(b) HCA].

Requirement for clear and specific grounds of appeal

Appeal against conviction

Weight of evidence argument

The appellant cannot simply make a general statement that the conviction is against the weight of evidence or the evidence does not support the conviction. The appellant must set out in more detail the basis for this assertion. He must say whether the attack is based on the quality or quantity of prosecution evidence or both.

Errors of law

Again it is not enough to make a general statement that the conviction is wrong in law, or the trial court made a mistake of law. The appellant must set out what error of law was made.

Mistake on the facts

The appellant must set out what mistake was made such as that the court erred in accepting the evidence of a particular person or in regarding that evidence as sufficient to prove that offence. If, for instance the ground is that the court erred in accepting the complainant's evidence, the appellant would have to say why the court erred. For example, the evidence should not have been accepted because of improbabilities or contradictions in the evidence or its incompatibility with the evidence of other witnesses

Appeal against sentence

The appellant must say what specifically he is alleging that court did wrong such as what error of law it made or that it took into account a wrong factor or failed to take into account a salient factor.

However, the appellant may simply allege that the sentence was manifestly excessive although it would be best for the legal practitioner to spell out on what basis this contention is made.

Power of appeal court to call for evidence or remit for further evidence

When the High Court and Supreme Court hears criminal appeals, they have to power to call evidence or remit the cases to the trial court for futher evidence. See s 41 HCA and s 17 SCA. However, the appeal court will exercise this power sparingly. They will only do so where the circumstances are exceptional and such that a grave miscarriage of justice might result if this power is not used.

The powers of an appeal court to call evidence are these:

- it may order the production of any document, exhibit or other thing connected with the proceedings;
- it may order any witness who would have been compellable at the trial (whether or not he or she was called at the trial) to give evidence before it. Alternatively, it may order that the witness be examined before any judge, or any other officer of the court, a justice of the peace or any other person. [The procedure for this is set out in Order 46 of the High Court Rules];
- it may receive evidence, if tendered, of any witness, including the appellant and, on special application, the appellant's spouse, if such an application would have been necessary at the trial;
- having set aside the conviction, the court may remit the case to the trial court for the leading of further evidence.

Where one of the parties requests that the court to call evidence or remit the matter for further evidence, the party must indicate the nature of the evidence proposed to be led and must state the reasons for the failure to lead the evidence at the proper time: *Ngombo* 1964 RLR 232 (A) The party must show that the evidence could not have been produced at the trial: *Ndlovu* 1983 (2) ZLR 263 (S) and give a reasonable explanation for the failure to lead it: *Bira* 1971 (1) RLR 263 (A)

Section 11

Automatic Review and Scrutiny

Reid-Rowland 26-3 – 26-13

Automatic review

The system of review is there to ensure "that every accused person who obtains a sentence of some severity automatically enjoys an independent investigation of his or her conviction and sentence by a senior judicial officer who is enjoined to satisfy himself that the proceedings meet the requirement of being in accordance with substantial justice ...": taken from an address to the Magistrates Forum by Chief Justice Gubbay. The Chief Justice went on to say in this address:

" In a society such as ours where the overwhelming majority of persons standing trial in the magistrates courts are members of the less favoured section of the community, and on the whole unrepresented, it is imperative to ensure that the review system, which is aimed at providing a curb upon any misdirected or arbitrary exercise of power, is administered efficiently and speedily."

He or she then pointed out that the magistrate:

> " should not live in fear of the reviewing judge and constantly be looking over his or her shoulder, but should rather regard the reviewing judge as the second member of a two-man team. The reviewing judge is not there to criticize, to nit-pick or to show off his or her knowledge and experience; he or she is there to assist as far as he or she is able in the administration of justice; and to ensure that X receives fair treatment."

The High Court automatically reviews all criminal cases decided in the magistrates courts where accused have been sentenced to terms of more than 12 months imprisonment or fines exceeding level 6. See s 57(1) of MCA.

Where the sentence for the offence for which X has been convicted is below the reviewable limit, but a suspended sentence has to be brought into operation, then the total of the two sentences will determine whether the proceedings are subject to automatic review.

Where an accused is charged and convicted under separate summonses relating to different charges and where the aggregate sentence imposed falls within reviewable range, all such summonses should be sent for review in the same way as if the convictions had appeared as separate counts on a single summons. This also applies to separate admission of guilt forms.

If the case is being taken on appeal then it will not be subject to review. The case of a person who was legally represented at his or her trial will only go on review if, within three days of the magistrate's determination, his or her lawyer requests the clerk of court to forward the case on review. With a case involving a company, again the matter will only go on review if, within three days of the magistrate's determination, a representative of the company requests the clerk of court to forward the matter on review.

In *Nyathi* HB-90-03, the judge decided that, other than in exceptional cases, the accused is not allowed to use the review procedure to attack the conviction. Normally the accused must lodge an appeal if he or she is arguing that the conviction was wrong. In the present case X had been convicted and sentenced to a term of imprisonment. The proceedings had been confirmed on review. His or her legal practitioner sought to bring the matter on review again. He or she attacked the conviction and, in addition, submitted that the proceedings were defective. He or she alleged that the magistrate had not allowed the accused to secure legal representation. The accused had wished to secure the services of a particular practitioner, but the practitioner died before the trial began. It was also alleged that the magistrate had not granted a postponement to enable a defence witness to be called. The court held that the legal practitioner should have taken the matter on appeal.

The requests to forward the matter on review must be in writing and must be accompanied by a brief statement of the reasons for the request. The magistrate who decided the case is entitled, if he or she so wishes, to append his or her remarks to the record which is being forwarded on review. The Registrar of the High Court must ensure that these cases are submitted as soon as possible to a judge in chambers.

The clerk of court at the magistrates court must forward to the Registrar of the High Court the records of all cases which are subject to automatic review: (With cases which have been mechanically recorded, the magistrate's handwritten notes must be forwarded.) [s 57(1) MCA]

In the case of Musa 1997 (2) ZLR 149 (H), the record was sent for review some three months later, and two months after the accused had been committed to prison. The magistrate blamed the clerk of court for the delay. The court held that the responsibility for forwarding the record was the magistrate's, not the clerk of court's, and the magistrate's excuse was a lame one. The magistrate was required to submit the record without delay; this he or she did not do, with the result that the accused would have served his or her sentence before the record reached the High Court.

If the judge decides that the proceedings before the magistrate were not in accordance with real and substantial justice, he or she will certify accordingly and the main powers of the judge are to:

- alter or quash the conviction;
- reduce or set aside the sentence or order of the trial court to substitute a different sentence from that imposed by the trial court but it may not substitute imprisonment for a fine unless the enactment under which the person was convicted does not permit the imposition of a fine;
- impose a more severe sentence than that originally imposed except in relation to a legally represented person or a company where the lawyer or company requested the matter to be forwarded on review;
- set aside or correct the proceedings or give such judgment or impose such order as the trial court ought to have given, imposed or made;
- remit the case back to the trial court to hear further evidence;
- convict X of some other offence than that of which he or she was convicted.

s 29(2) HCA.

Scrutiny by regional court

The regional magistrates court will scrutinise all decisions in the magistrates courts, except those handed down by regional magistrates, where accused have been sentenced to more than 3 months but not more than 12 months' imprisonment or to a fine exceeding level 4 but not exceeding level 6: s 58 MCA. The clerk of court must forward all such cases to the regional magistrates court within a week of the determination in the case. However, cases going on appeal will not be forwarded. If X was legally represented or was a company, the matter will only be forwarded if, within three days of the determination, the lawyer or company representative respectively requests in writing that the case be forwarded.

Regional magistrates must then scrutinise such cases as soon as possible after receiving them. If satisfied that the proceedings were in accordance with real and substantial justice, the regional magistrate will so endorse it. However, if he or she doubts that they were in accordance with real and substantial justice, he or she must forward the case to the registrar of the High Court who will lay it before a judge: s 58(3)(b)A of MCA.

White letters

The reviewing judge or scrutinising magistrate may seek clarification or comment on aspects of judgments from the magistrates who tried the cases. These queries are contained in what are known as "white letters".

Each point raised by the reviewer or scrutiniser must be dealt with in the reply from the trial magistrate and responses should be sent promptly.

Failure by trial magistrates to comply with time limits

It is essential that magistrates strictly comply with the time limits which are laid down for sending cases for review and for scrutiny. These limits are prescribed so that mistakes can be corrected as soon as possible. The review judge may decide to set aside the conviction and the sentence imposed. Yet if there have been long delays in submitting it for review, the whole of the sentence may already have been served. This is obviously grossly unfair. Or the review, the judge may substantially reduce a period of imprisonment but because the referral for review process has been badly delayed, X has already served a far longer period of imprisonment than the review court decided was appropriate. Only by strict compliance with the prescribed time limits can such gross injustices be avoided.

In *Manyami* HB-36-90, the High Court emphasised that magistrates must send cases on review within the prescribed periods. This was particularly important when queries have been raised about cases by scrutinising magistrates.

In *White* HH-1-92, the court said it is imperative that records are submitted for scrutiny or review within one week as required by law. Magistrates who are dilatory and fail to comply with this requirement are failing in their duty. By the time this case reached the High Court, X had already served a prison sentence imposed by the magistrate. X was a 20-year-old first offender and the High Court decided that he or she should have been fined and not imprisoned. The delay in submission of the case for review had therefore led to X serving a prison term when he or she should not have gone to prison at all.

In a recent review case the judge went so far as to order that an inquiry be held to ascertain the reasons for non-compliance with the time limits and serious delays in referring the case for review. The judge recommended that the official responsible should be charged with misconduct unless he or she has a reasonable excuse.

Submission for review of non-reviewable cases

In terms of s 64(4) of MCA, a magistrate who entertains doubt as to the propriety of his or her conviction of X in a case which is not subject to automatic review may submit the case for review to the High Court.

Accused's statement regarding sentence

Whether or not a case is subject to automatic review, there is a procedure provided for in s 59 MCA whereunder a person convicted by a magistrate may question the severity of the sentence imposed by submitting a statement to the High Court setting out why he or she considers his or her sentence to be unduly severe. The magistrate who imposed the sentence should send a full reply to this statement to the reviewing judge. Under this procedure, X may only make representations about the sentence; he or she may not challenge his or her conviction. If he or she wishes to challenge the conviction he or she must appeal: *Stokie* 1980 ZLR 280 (GD).

Section 12

Miscellaneous Matters

Contempt of court

Reid-Rowland 28-5

If contempt of court is committed during the proceedings in court (in the face of the court), the court may summarily convict and punish the offender: 71(1) MCA. This type of contempt is committed if, for instance, X swears at the judge or makes rude gestures at him, or if X tries to assault the judge or to tear up court documents, or if someone in the courtroom continues to shout and disrupt the proceedings after he or she has been warned to remain quiet, or if a lawyer or a witness arrives in the courtroom in a completely drunken condition.

By accused person

In the case of *Musa* 1997 (2) ZLR 149 (H), X was arraigned before a magistrate on a charge of housebreaking. After the allegations had been read to him, he said in Shona that he did not want to be tried by the magistrate. Warned that he was being insolent and contemptuous, he repeated the remark, whereupon he was committed to 30 days' imprisonment for each utterance. The magistrate said that he had convicted the accused, not in terms of the Magistrates Court Act, but under his or her common law power. The court held that the magistrate had no common law power to commit for contempt. His powers were derived from the Act. It held further that when X expressed a disinclination to be tried by the magistrate, he was in effect asking the magistrate to recuse himself, something he was quite entitled to do. The Act requires that any insult of the court must be wilful, which means that *mens rea* is required. The court did not ask the accused to explain himself, so there was nothing which would enable the court to determine the accused's state of mind. The magistrate's failure to ask the accused to explain himself was a misdirection. When the accused said that he did not wish to be tried by the magistrate, the magistrate should have first warned him or her that he or she proposed to consider whether he or she should be convicted of contempt. This would have opened the doors for the accused to proffer his or her explanation or defence. It would only be in exceptional circumstances that the *audi alteram partem* principle would not apply to a case where an offender is tried summarily for contempt. One such case might be where the alleged conduct had the effect of disrupting the proceedings, which was not the situation here. The magistrate had not conducted the proceedings fairly. The magistrate's finding that X's utterances were intended to belittle the magistrate could not be upheld. The power to commit for contempt is not to be used to vindicate the magistrate as a person. The magistrate appeared confused about whether the alleged contempt was *ex facie curiae* or *in facie curiae*. The contempt in this case was *in facie curiae*. The punishment was not such as would enhance the dignity of the presiding magistrate. It was wrong to treat X's actions as two counts; they were part of the same transaction. The punishment was also disproportionate to the offence and grossly excessive. A fine would have been appropriate. It was doubtful whether the court's dignity could be protected by punishing a fool for his indiscretion. It would have been wiser for the court to take time for reflection; this might also have given the accused time to reflect. A magistrate is bound to subordinate his or her personal dignity to the overall decorum of the court over which he or she presides. This does not mean that he or she should not exercise firm control; but keeping firm control is a far cry from saying that the slightest affront to the court's dignity should be visited with summary committal for contempt.

By legal practitioner

In the case of *In re Muskwe* 1992 (1) ZLR 44 (H): a magistrate at the resumed hearing of a criminal case in which a legal practitioner was representing X, fined the legal practitioner for contempt of court in contravention of s 79(1) of the MCA [now s 71(1) of MCA]. At the previous hearing there had been an altercation between the magistrate and the legal practitioner over the legal practitioner's line of questioning of a witness. The legal practitioner had told the magistrate that if he was not allowed to conduct the questioning as he saw fit, he would not be able to continue with the case. After an exchange between the magistrate and the legal practitioner in which the magistrate seemingly gave her permission for the legal practitioner to renounce his agency and depart, the legal practitioner left the courtroom. The magistrate decided he was guilty of contempt in that he or she had done an act calculated to bring the dignity of the court into disrepute. The court decided that the conviction must be set aside because the magistrate had failed to give adequate reasons for his decision and, in particular, had failed to examine whether the vital element of intention was present and whether, if there had been a contempt, it had been purged by the subsequent apology by the legal practitioner.

In *Mushonga* 1994 (1) ZLR 296 (S), the court commented upon whether disobedience by a legal practitioner to an invalid order of court could constitute contempt of court. It ruled that disobedience to such an order can still constitute contempt of court. In order to ensure the proper administration of justice, a person must normally obey a supposedly invalid order and thereafter seek redress by way of appeal or review. However, in exceptional circumstances a person can disobey an invalid order without committing contempt of court. This would be so where, for example, blind compliance with an obviously invalid order would itself tend to weaken respect for the administration of justice. It went on to point out that the crime of contempt is only committed if the accused had actual or legal intention to bring the administration of justice into contempt. Intention is absent if the seemingly insulting behaviour is the result of forgetfulness, ignorance or inadvertence. It may also be absent where the accused disobeys an order under a genuine belief that the order is invalid. It pointed out that non-appearance of a lawyer in a case may go beyond mere discourtesy and amount to a criminal contempt of court, provided that there was intention to interfere with the process of the court and the administration of justice. However, in the present case, X had genuinely believed that the presence in his or her stead of his or her professional assistant would be acceptable and had thus had no intention to violate the dignity or authority of the court. Finally, it said that in most cases of alleged contempts by legal practitioners the matter should simply be referred to the Law Society for investigation and possible disciplinary action. Only in an exceptional case, such as where the legal practitioner has used scurrilous language *in facie curiae*, should the court invoke its criminal jurisdiction to deal with the matter.

Where a magistrate proceeds in terms of s 71(1) MCA in dealing with a contempt he or she must certify the statement of the proceedings relating to the contempt as correct and X must be furnished with a copy of such a certified statement: *Bango* HH-356-84; *Sibanda* HH-9-86.

This power to punish summarily for contempt is essential for the court to uphold its dignity and authority. However, this power is a drastic one which should not be resorted to lightly but only with circumspection. Trivial contempts are best ignored. Even with more serious contempts, the dignity of the court can often be upheld by allowing the offending party the chance to apologise.

Where the power is exercised, the judicial officer must not act in the heat of the moment in anger. The atmosphere will be emotionally charged so he or she must recover his or her temper and act objectively. He or she must remind himself that in this sort of case he or she is acting as prosecutor, witness and judge in the same cause. He or she must be particularly careful in respect of situations where defence lawyers have had altercations with him or her during the course of the presentation of the defence case. A lawyer may sometimes direct insulting remarks towards the bench when he or she believes that the adjudicator has acted unfairly towards his or her client. The usual response to such a case should be to warn the defence counsel about his or her behaviour and to allow him or her to retract his or her remarks and apologise.

In the case of *In re: Chinamasa* 2000 (2) ZLR 322 (S) the Supreme Court ruled that the species of contempt known as scandalizing the court was constitutional. Although under the right to freedom of expression there is a right to criticize the court judgments, the right to freedom of expression did not permit the making of comments imputing corrupt or improper motives to the judicial officers as this would create a real or substantial risk of impairing public confidence in the administration of justice. In this case the Attorney-General had severely criticized the sentence imposed by a judge.

Altercations between judicial officer and defence counsel

In *Nkala* HB-64-93, the trial magistrate adjourned a case in mid-trial at X's request and sent it on review to be set aside and remitted afresh before a new magistrate. In altercations with the magistrate before withdrawing from the case, defence counsel's conduct bordered on contempt; he or she was possibly trying to create a situation in which he or she could avoid continuing with the case, but as the resultant atmosphere was not conducive to the proper administration of justice, the proceedings were set aside and remitted as requested.

Binding over orders

Reid-Rowland 28-3

A binding over order to keep the peace in terms of s 388 CPEA is a protective mechanism. It is not meant to punish the person upon whom it is imposed; it is aimed at preventing and deterring future misconduct by that person against the person who has sought the order.

Prescription period for criminal offences

Reid-Rowland 3-9

All the criminal offences which are within the jurisdiction of the magistrates courts become prescribed if prosecutions are not brought against the offender within twenty years from the time that the crime was committed. In other words, the offenders can no longer be prosecuted for these offences after twenty years: s 23 CPEA.

Inquests

See Reid-Rowland 2-8

List of cases

Adams en Andere 1993 (1) SACR 611 (C)
Aitken & Anor v *Attorney-General* 1992 (1) ZLR 249 (S)
Aitken (2) 1992 (2) ZLR 463 (S).
Anand 1988 (2) ZLR 414 (S)
Ananias 1963 R&N 938 (SR)
Anock 1973 RLR 154 (A)
Attorney-General v *Blumears & Anor* 1991 (1) ZLR 118 (S)
Attorney-General v *Bvuma* 1987 (2) ZLR 96 (S)
Attorney-General v *Fundira* S-33-04
Attorney-General v *Jakubec* 1979 RLR 267 (A)
Attorney-General v *Phiri* 1987 (2) ZLR 33 (H)
Attorney-General v *Ruturi* HH-26-03
Attorney-General v *Slatter & Ors* 1984 (1) ZLR 306 (S)
Austin & Anor v *Minister of State (Security) & Anor; Bull* v *Minister of State (Security) & Anor* 1986 (2) ZLR 28 (S)

Banana 2000 (1) ZLR 607 (S)
Banda HB-72-04
Bango HH-356-84
Barclay 1969 (4) SA 195 (RA)
Barros & Ors 2002 (2) ZLR 17 (H)
BC & Anor HH-255-84
Beahan 1991 (2) ZLR 98 (S)
Benatar 1985 (2) ZLR 205 (H)
Bennett 1976 (3) SA 652 (C)
Betserai S-65-95
Bhanke & Ors HH-123-02
Bhebhe & Ors 2002 (1) ZLR 137 (H)
Bira 1971 (1) RLR 263 (A)
Biti 2002 (1) ZLR 115 (H)
Biti 2002 (2) ZLR 209 (S)
Bizwick 1987 (2) ZLR 83 (S)
Blanchard & Ors 1999 (2) ZLR 168 (H)
Botha HH-183-88

Botha v *Zvada & Anor* 1997 (1) ZLR 415 (S)
Buitendag 1976 (1) RLR 345 (A)
Bull v *Minister of Home Affairs* 1986 (1) ZLR 202 (S)
Bvunda HH-278-90

C (a juvenile) 1997 (2) ZLR 395 (H)
Capital Radio (Pvt) Ltd v *Min of Information & Ors (2)* 2000 (2) ZLR 265 (H)
Chadyamunda HH-228-89
Chaerera 1988 (2) ZLR 226 (S)
Chaerera 1988 (2) ZLR 367 (H)
Chahora HH-349-84
Chakwinya 1997 (1) ZLR 109 (H)
Chamba & Ors A-43-79
Chamukwanda HB-17-90
Chamurandi HH-182-86
Chandafira HH-137-02.
Chari 1989 (1) ZLR 231 (S)
Chatanga HH-19-90
Chatyoka S-75-92
Chawasarira HH-18-91
Chiadzwa 1988 (2) ZLR 19 (S)
Chibi v *Minister of Internal Affairs* 1970 (1) RLR 88 (GD)
Chichera v *A-G* S-98-04.
Chidembo S-118-89
Chidodo & Anor 1988 (1) ZLR 299 (H)
Chidota 1966 RLR 178 (A)
Chigova 1992 (2) ZLR 206 (S)
Chikafa S-162-88
Chikasha S-94-94
Chikukutu 1996 (1) ZLR 702 (S)
Chikumbirike HH-307-84
Chimukuche 1997 (1) ZLR 533 (H)
Chinemo 1985 (1) ZLR 32 (H)
Chinamasa, In re: 2000 (2) ZLR 322 (S)
Chinyani 1969 (2) RLR 42 (A)
Chinzenze Ors 1998 (1) ZLR 470 (H)
Chipxere HH-314-83
Chirai HH-2-92
Chirimuuta S-3-95
Chirodzero HH-14-88
Chisiwa 1981 ZLR 666 (H)
Chisiwa 1981 ZLR 666 (S)
Chitanda HH-215-89
Chitate 1966 RLR 251 (A); 1966 (2) SA 690 (RA).

Chitiyo 1989 (2) ZLR 144 (H)
Chitongo HH-53-95
Chiunye HH-153-94
Chiweshe S-38-93
Chiyangwa v *A-G & Ors* S-1-04
Choma 1990 (2) ZLR 33 (H)
Chowdhry HH-161-85
Cloete 1994 (1) SACR 420 (A)
Collett 1978 RLR 288 (GD)
Corbett 1990 (1) ZLR 205 (S)

Dangarembizi & Anor 1987 (2) ZLR 196 (H)
David & Anor 1964 RLR 2
David HH-204-94
Davy 1988 (1) ZLR 386 (S)
De Montille 1979 RLR 105
Dedza v *Ekblad* S-196-91
Deka & Anor S-199-88
Delta Consolidated (Pvt) Ltd & Ors 1991 (2) ZLR 234 (S)
Demba HH-133-89
Denhere & Anor S-39-91
Denhere & Ors GS-235-80
Deuss 1972 (1) RLR 121 (GD)
Dhliwayo 1987 (1) ZLR 1 (H)
Dietrichson v *Resident Provincial Magistrate Hwange & Anor* HB-35-95
Dlamini HB-3-90
Donaldson & Anor S-5-95
Donga & Anor S-169-93
Dube & Anor 1988 (2) ZLR 385 (S)
Dube & Anor 1989 (3) ZLR 245 (S)
Dube & Anor HB-30-92
Dube & Anor S-126-89
Dube & Anor 1995 (2) ZLR 321 (S)
Dube & Ors 1988 (2) ZLR 385 (S)
Dube 1965 RLR 177 (A)
Dube HB-65-93
Dube S-139-95
Dube S-216-93
Dube S-25-92
Dube S-53-95
Duri HH-89-91

Edward 1966 (2) SA 359 (R)
Edwards 1949 SR 30

Elliott v *Commissioner of ZRP* 1986 (1) ZLR 228 (H)
Elsworth S-55-95
Erasmus S-84-91
Eva 1967 (1) RLR 113 (GD)

F 1988 (1) ZLR 327 (H)
Faku & Anor 1997 (1) ZLR 389 (S)
Feldman v *Minister of Home Affairs* S-210-92
Fikilini v *Attorney-General* 1990 (1) ZLR 105 (S)
Fourie 1973 (1) SA 100 (D)
Frank 1968 (1) RLR 257 (A)
Fusirayi 1981 ZLR 56 (A)

Garande HH-46-02
Garwe HH-249-89
Gomo HH-21-93
Gore 1999 (1) ZLR 177 (H).
Gororo HH-145-86
Gous v *Minister of Home Affairs & Ors* 1992 (2) ZLR 142 (H)
Gquma & Ors (2) 1994 (2) SACR 182 (C)
Gujral HH-73-90
Gumba S-50-91
Gumbo HB-48-89
Gumbo 1995 (1) ZLR 163 (H)
Gumede HB-40-03
Gwatidzo HH-271-90
Gwatiringa HH-128-88
Gwenyure v *Minister of Home Affairs* HH-702-87

Hackwell 1965 RLR 1 (A)
Hammer & Ors 1994 (2) SACR 496 (C)
Harington 1988 (2) ZLR
Hartlebury & Anor 1985 (1) ZLR 1 (H)
Harvey 1967 RLR 203
Hativagone & Anor, In re S-67-04
Hill HB-106-89
Hlongwa 1979 (4) SA 112
Hlupe 1964 RLR 333 (GD)
Holmes 1982 (2) ZLR 267 (H)
Honde & Ors HB-27-91
Horowitz 1976 (1) RLR 238 (A)
Hove S-20-92
Hove S-64-88
Hudson 1980 (4) SA 145

Hunzvi 2000 (1) ZLR 540 (S)
Hussey 1991 (2) ZLR 187 (S)

Ismail S-52-94
Isolano 1985 (1) ZLR 62 (S)

J 1958 (3) SA 689 (SR)
Jackson HH-201-02
Jambani 1982 (2) ZLR 213 (H)
Jana S-172-88
Janyure 1988 (2) ZLR 470 (S)
Jesse v *Attorney-General & Ors* HH-213-94
Jesse v *Pratt & Anor* 2001 (1) ZLR 48 (H)
Jongwe 2002 (2) ZLR 209 (S)
Julieta HH-74-98
Juwaki & Anor 1964 RLR 604 (A)

Kachipare 1998 (2) ZLR 271 (S)
Kaiwona & Ors S-182-93
Kaiwona S-192-93
Kaja S-129-89
Kajokoto HH-32-05
Kamanga HH-134-91
Kambuzuma HH-60-86
Kamodzi S-60-88
Kamtande 1983 (1) ZLR 302 (H)
Kanoyerera HH-167-89
Kapurira S-110-92
Karimazondo & Anor v *Minister of Home Affairs* 2001 (2) ZLR 363 (H)
Kaseke 1996 (1) ZLR 51 (S)
Katerere S-55-91
Katsaura 1997 (2) ZLR 102 (H)
Kelly HH-33-04
Kendai HH-269-82
Khupe & Anor HB 30-83
Kilpin 1978 RLR 282 (A)
Knight NO v *van Tonder & Anor* 1962 R&N 405 (SR)
Knight NO v *van Tonder* 1962 R&N 405 (SR)
Kondile & Anor 1995 (1) SACR 394 (SEC)
Kudavaranda 1988 (2) ZLR 367 (H)
Kumusana S-110-89;
Kundishora 1990 (2) ZLR 30 (S)
Kunesu & Ors HH-216-93
Kurimwi 1985 (2) ZLR 63 (S)

Kuruneri HH-111-04

Lamont 1977 (1) RLR 112 (A)
Lawrence & Anor 1989 (1) ZLR 29 (S)
Lekgwabe 1992 (2) SACR 219 (T)
Liver HH-196-92
Lotriet & Anor 2001 (2) ZLR 225 (H)
Lupepe v *A-G & Anor* HB-130-93

M & Ors 1995 (1) SACR 667 (BA)
Mabhena 1996 (1) ZLR 134 (H)
Machakaire S-30-92
Machakata S-106-89
Machokoto 1996 (2) ZLR 190 (H)
Machona & Ors 1982 (1) ZLR 87 (S)
Madembe & Anor HH-17-03
Madziwa S-191-90
Mafu HB-68-90
Magoge 1988 (1) ZLR 163 (S)
Mahango HH-132-87.
Maharaj 1976 (3) SA 205 (D)
Maharangwe S-5-90
Mahata v *Chigumira NO & Anor* HH-24-04
Mahati 1988 (1) ZLR 190 (H)
Mahomed 1977 (2) RLR 207 (GD)
Makalima HB-16-91
Makamba S-30-04
Makanyanga 1996 (2) ZLR 231 (H)
Makawa & Anor 1991 (1) ZLR 142
Makhado 1999 (1) ZLR 467 (H)
Maki & Ors (1) 1994 (2) SACR 630 (E)
Makombe & Ors HH-120-86
Makoni & Ors S-67-89
Makoni S-9-90
Makore HH-75-89
Makuni HH-75-84
Malume 1998 (2) ZLR 508 (H)
Malumjwa HB-34-03
Malunga 1990 (1) ZLR 124 (H)
Mambo 1992 (1) ZLR 245 (H)
Mamwere 1978 RLR 374 (GD)
Manaiwa & Anor HB-72-90
Mandizha HH-275-90
Mandwe S-142-93

Manera 1989 (2) ZLR 92 (S)
Manga HH-122-06
Mangando & Anor HH-277-90
Mangena & Ors HB-22-05.
Maniko & Anor HH-44-91
Mantwana S-20-82
Manyami HB-36-90
Manyevere HB-38-03
Mapfumo & Ors 1983 (1) ZLR 250 (S)
Maradu 1994 (2) SACR 410 (W)
Maramba & Anor 2000 (2) ZLR 69 (H)
Maratera S-93-91
Marechera A-151-68
Marevesa S-108-91.
Martin v *A-G & Ors* S-53-93
Masango 1990 (1) ZLR 176 (S)
Masawi & Anor HH-111-94
Masedza 1998 (1) ZLR 36 (H)
Maseko 1986 (2) ZLR 52 (S)
Masundulwane HB-22-06
Masendeke, In re 1992 (2) ZLR 5 (S)
Matare 1993 (2) ZLR 88 (S)
Matekukamizora HH-192-94
Matimba 1989 (3) ZLR 173 (S)
Matongo HH-132-87
Mavingere 1988 (2) ZLR 318 (S)
Mavingere 1988 (2) ZLR 318 (S)
Mavunga 1982 (1) ZLR 63 (S)
Mayahle 1968 (1) RLR 133 (A)
Mayberry HH-248-86
Mazanyane HB-102-95
Mazono & Anor 2000 (1) ZLR 347 (H)
Mazowe HB-36-91
Mbewe & Ors 1988 (1) ZLR 7 (H)
Mbizi S-184-84
Mboma S-28-92
McCormick HB-56-90
McGregor HB-26-91
Melrose 1984 (2) ZLR 217 (S)
Menzou HH-90-93
Mfungelwa 1967 RLR 308
Mhandu 1985 (1) ZLR 228 (S)
Mharapara 1985 (2) ZLR 211 (S)
Mhiripiri HH-163-88

Mhlanga & Anor 2000 (2) ZLR 73 (H)
Mhona & Anor HB-56-05
Michael & Anor 1962 R&N 374
Micklethwait 2003 (1) ZLR 26 (H)
Millar 1971 RLR 159 (A)
Miller 1973 (2) RLR 387
Million & Ors HH-53-92
Mkali & Ors HB-23-93
Mlambo HB-72-03
Mlambo HH-117-95
Mlambo S-221-91
Mlauzi v *Attorney-General of Zimbabwe* S-48-92
Mlilo HB-27-88
Mokoena 1956 (3) SA 81 (A)
Moll v *Commissioner of Police & Ors* 1973 (1) ZLR 234 (H)
Montille 1979 RLR 105;
Motlaung 1993 (2) SACR 214 (NC)
Moyo & Anor S-12-93
Moyo & Ors HB-15-93
Moyo & Ors HB-211-87
Moyo (2) 1978 RLR 469 (GD)
Moyo 1988 (2) ZLR 79 (H)
Moyo 1989 (3) ZLR 250 (S)
Moyo HB-18-84
Moyo HB-6-90
Moyo 1994 (2) ZLR 24 (H)
Moyo HH-43-03
Mpofu & Anor S-150-89
Mpofu (2) 1985 (1) ZLR 285 (H)
Mpofu S-192-90
Mposi S-22-94
Msindo HH-63-97
Mtandwa HH-233-87
Mteiswa 1976 (1) RLR 314 (GD)
Mthombeni S-80-90
Mubaiwa 1980 ZLR 477 (A)
Mubaya S-5-93
Muchamba S-27-92
Muchindu & Ors 1994 (2) SACR 179 (C)
Mudambi S-156-95
Mudekwe & Anor HH-7-86
Muendawoga HH-10-04
Mugangavari 1984 (1) ZLR 80 (S)
Mugebe 2000 (1) ZLR 376 (H)

Mugwenhe & Anor 1991 (2) ZLR 66 (S)
Muhlaba & Ors 1973 (1) RLR 178 (GD)
Mujuru 1976 (2) SA 900 (RA)
Mukonda HH-15-87
Mukuze & Anor v A-G (2) HH-17-05
Muleya 1992 (1) ZLR 68(4),
Munukwa & Ors 1982 (1) ZLR 30 (S)
Munyakwe & Ors HH-92-93,
Munyaradzi S-74-89
Munyariwa HB-14-87
Mupah 1989 (1) ZLR 299 (S)
Mupanedungu S-197-94
Mupatsi 1998 (1) ZLR 224 (H)
Mupfudza 1982 (1) ZLR 271 (S)
Murambiwa 1952 SR 271 (SR)
Murambiwa S-62-92
Musa 1997 (2) ZLR 149 (H)
Musa HH-144-89
Musakwa S-1-95
Musariri HB-41-95
Musekiwa & Ors 1965 RLR 225 (A)
Mushangwe HH-58-93
Mushayandebvu 1992 (2) ZLR 62 (S)
Mushonga 1994 (1) ZLR 296 (S)
Musindo 1997 (1) ZLR 395 (H)
Muskwe, In re 1992 (1) ZLR 44 (H)
Mutakwa & Anor 2000 (1) ZLR 393 (H)
Mutambara & Ors v *Minister of Home Affairs* 1989 (3) ZLR 96 (H)
Mutandwa HH-35-88,
Mutengwa HH-116-90
Mutowo HH-458-88
Mutizwa HB-4-06
Mutsinziri 1997 (1) ZLR 6 (H)
Mutters & Anor S-66-89
Mutukura HH-39-02
Mutumbila HH-139-89;
Muzambe HH-121-90
Muzabazi v *Jambawu & Ors* 1992 (2) ZLR 314 (H)
Muzonda v *Minister of Home Affairs & Anor* S-17-93
Muzonza & Ors S-217-88,
Muzuza & Ors S-105-89
Mvambo 1995 (1) SACR 180 (W)
Mvurume HH-198-02

Ncube & Anor 1975 (2) RLR 150 (A)
Ncube & Anor 2002 (2) ZLR 524 (H)
Ncube & Anor HB-143-91
Ncube & Ors HB-150-88
Ncube & Ors S-56-93
Ncube & Ors HB-61-03
Ncube HB-153-86
Ncube HH-174-83
Ncube (2) 1989 (2) ZLR 232 (H).
Ncube 2001 (2) ZLR 556 (S)
Ndebele 1988 (2) ZLR 249 (H)
Ndekete 1978 RLR 377 (GD)
Ndhlovu (1) 1980 ZLR 96 (GD)
Ndhlovu 1981 ZLR 618 (S)
Ndhlovu 1992 (2) ZLR 231 (S)
Ndhlovu 2001 (2) ZLR 261 (H)
Ndiweni S-149-89
Ndlovu & Anor HB-30-02
Ndlovu 1983 (4) SA 507 (ZS)
Ndlovu 1988 (2) ZLR 465 (S)
Ndlovu HB-98-89
Ndlovu S-3-88
Ndlovu 1997 (2) ZLR 540 (S)
Ndlovu 1983 (2) ZLR 263 (S)
Ndou & Ors 1971 (1) SA 668 (A)
Nduna & Anor HB-48-03
Nemachera S-89-86
Ngara 1987 (1) ZLR 91 (S)
Ngombo 1964 RLR 232 (A)
Ngulube HH-48-02
Ngwenya HB-17-95
Ngwenya HB-19-92
Njiva S-120-89
Nkala HB-64-93
Nkomo & Anor 1989 (2) ZLR 117 (S)
Nkomo & Anor 1993 (2) ZLR 131 (S)
Nkosana S-143-95
Nsimango S-205-94
Ntlele 1993 (2) SACR 610 (W)
Nyabvure S-23-88
Nyajena 1991 (1) ZLR 175 (S)
Nyamaro 1987 (2) ZLR 222 (S).
Nyamayaro 1987 (2) ZLR 318 (S)
Nyamhoko & Ors v *OC ZRP Manicaland Province & Ors* HH-37-06

Nyamufarira HH-335-83
Nyamupanda HH-101-91
Nyatanga v *Mlambo NO* 2003 (1) ZLR 503 (H)
Nyathi & Anor 1988 (1) ZLR 221 (H)
Nyathi & Ors S-52-95
Nyathi HB-90-03
Nyedziwa HB-33-90
Nyekete HH-46-92
Nyirenda HH-116-88
Nyoni S-118-90
Nzimande 1993 (2) SACR 218 (N)

P & Ors 1976 (1) RLR 142 (GD)
Pandehuni 1982 (2) ZLR 133 (S)
Patel 1970 (3) SA 565 (W)
Patel S-63-87
Peterson & Ors 1970 RLR 49
Phiri HB-62-93
Ponder 1989 (1) ZLR 235 (S)
Pongolani S-48-89
Poswell & Anor 1969 (4) SA 194 (R)
Pretorius & Anor 1969 (4) SA 198 (R)
Prinsloo & Anor v *Newman* 1975 (1) SA 481 (A)
Prior HH-163-02
Purcell-Gilpin 1971 (1) RLR 241

Ramalope 1995 (1) SACR 616 (A)
Rautenbach 1982
Rembani S-141-95
Robertson S-75-88
Rudolph 1990 (1) ZLR 45 (S)
Rumboid & Anor HB-170-88
Rusero HH-151-86
Rusike HH-31-89
Ruzani HB-63-84
Ruzario 1990 (1) ZLR 359 (S);

S C Shaw (Pvt) Ltd v *Minister of Lands* S-32-05
Sabawu & Anor 1999 (2) ZLR 314 (H)
Samakomva HH-8-05
Sambo S-22-90
Sauls & Ors 1981 (3) SA 172 (A)
Schaube-Kuffler 1969 (1) RLR 78 (A)
Shand 1994 (2) ZLR 99 (S)

Shariwa HB-37-03
Shaw HH-122-88
Shezi 1994 (1) SACR 575 (A)
Shingadia S- 56-91
Shuma & Anor 1994 (4) SA 583 (E)
Sibanda (1) 1980 ZLR 413 (GD)
Sibanda (2) 1963 R&N 601 (SR)
Sibanda 1989 (2) ZLR 329 (S)
Sibanda 1993 (1) SACR 691 (ZS)
Sibanda A-10-72
Sibanda HB-102-06
Sibanda HB-36-86
Sibanda HB-102-06
Sibanda HH-78-94
Sibanda HH-80-91
Sibanda HH-9-86
Sibanda S-55-94
Sikumbuzo 1967 (4) SA 602 (RA)
Sikurlite 1964 (3) SA 151 (SR)
Simakonda 1956 R&N 463 (SR)
Simon 1980 ZLR 162 (GD)
Siphambili 1995 (2) ZLR 337 (S)
Sithole & Anor HH-101-03
Sivako v *A-G* 1999 (2) ZLR 271 (S)
Siziba 1990 (2) ZLR 87 (H)
Siziba HB-61-88
Slatter & Ors 1983 ZLR 144 (H)
Smith S-182-90
Smyth v *Ushewokunze & Anor* 1997 (2) ZLR 544 (S)
Stambolie v *Commissioner of Police* 1989 (3) ZLR 287 (S).
Standard Chartered Finance Zimbabwe Ltd v *Georgias & Anor* 1998 (2) ZLR 547 (H)
Stokie 1980 ZLR 280 (GD)

Takavarasha HH-18-92
Takawira HH-155-91
Tamba S-81-91
Tao HH-182-96
Tashu HH-172-94
Tebie & Anor 1965 RLR 198 (GD)
Telecel Zimbabwe (Pvt) Ltd HH-55-06
Tirivanhu S-170-91
Toms S-200-93
Trinder HB-52-91
Tshumba & Anor S-137

Tsorayi 1985 (1) ZLR 138 (H)
Tsvangirai & Ors 2003 (1) ZLR 618 (H)
Tswangira S-184-95
Tugwete HH-672-87
Tuhwe S-97-94

V v *A* 1984 (2) ZLR 139 (S)
Valacia 1945 AD 826
Van Jaarsveld HB-110-90
Vengesayi S-26-93
Vhere HH-211-86

W HH-276-83
Watson S-17-06
Weinberg HH-29-93
White HH-1-92
Williams 1980 ZLR 466 (A)
Williams 1987 (1) ZLR 184 (H)
Woods & Ors 1993 (2) ZLR 258 (S)
Woods & Ors S-60-93
Worswick S-27-88
Wright S-183-89

Yusuf 1997 (1) ZLR 102 (H)

Zacharia 2002 (1) ZLR 48 (H)
Zakeyu 1963 SR 434 (FS)
Zaranyika & Ors HH-41-95
Zata S-64-91
Zimbowora S-7-92
Zvakurumbira S-7-90
Zvinyenge & Ors 1987 (2) ZLR 42 (S)

www.ingramcontent.com/pod-product-compliance
Lightning Source LLC
Chambersburg PA
CBHW020851150926
51501CB00041B/740
9780797450707